VALUING LIFE

STUDIES IN MORAL, POLITICAL,
AND LEGAL PHILOSOPHY

General Editor: Marshall Cohen

A list of titles in the series
appears at the back of the book

VALUING LIFE

John Kleinig

PRINCETON UNIVERSITY PRESS
PRINCETON, NEW JERSEY

Library of Congress Cataloging-in-Publication Data

Kleinig, John, 1942–
Valuing life / John Kleinig.
p.   cm. — (Studies in moral, political, and legal philosophy)
Includes bibliographical references and index.
ISBN 0-691-07388-0
1. Life.   2. Life (Biology)   I. Title.   II. Series.
BD431.K59   1991
179'.1—dc20   90-24965

This book has been composed in Adobe Palatino

Princeton University Press books are printed
on acid-free paper, and meet the guidelines
for permanence and durability of the Committee
on Production Guidelines for Book Longevity
of the Council on Library Resources

Printed in the United States of America by
Princeton University Press, Princeton, New Jersey

1   3   5   7   9   10   8   6   4   2

For my mother

CONTENTS

CONTENTS

ACKNOWLEDGMENTS

The material for this book first began to see the light of day in the Spring Semester of 1985, when I conducted a doctoral seminar on "Respect for Persons and the Value of Life" at the Graduate Center, City University of New York. That I was able to do so owed much to the generosity of the Council for International Exchange of Scholars (Fulbright Scheme) and to John Jay College of Criminal Justice. The first of several substantial revisions commenced when I returned to Macquarie University in Australia for the latter part of 1985. During this period I was fortunate enough to have Ted Sadler as my research assistant. His interest in European philosophy was a great boon to me as I attempted to come to terms with the writings of Wilhelm Dilthey, Albert Schweitzer, and Hans Jonas. At this time, others also provided me with feedback on my early drafts. Raoul Mortley looked over the classical material. William Heffernan and Tziporah Kasachkoff read through large slabs of dense gropings, and then later tackled a complete draft. Work on the manuscript slowed down considerably during the arduous process of permanent removal to the United States. But Sandy Thatcher kept nudging me—as he did so many others—and a draft eventually emerged. Besides Heffernan and Kasachkoff, several others were inveigled into reading part or all of the script. W. Rogers Brubaker, Stephen Buckle, Daniel Callahan, and Andrew von Hirsch allowed their friendship to be exploited, and the late Michael Bayles and James Rachels were Princeton's encouraging and helpful readers. Bayles in particular made numerous searching criticisms of my arguments, and my occasional failure to respond probably says more about my own stubbornness than any weakness on his part. Most of all, however, I must thank Gerald Gaus, whose twenty pages of judicious criticism and "innocent" questioning were invaluable to my final revisions. His professional stimulus was matched at a personal level by Tziporah Kasachkoff, who would impishly remark to others—with some justification— that I was too busy writing about the value of life to do many of the things that give life its value. It is now time to do them.

INTRODUCTION

In November 1975, Justice Robert Muir, Jr., of the Superior Court of New Jersey, refused an application for the withdrawal of mechanical life support from Karen Quinlan, several months after she had lapsed into what was generally acknowledged to be an irreversible coma. It was, he claimed, the Court's task to protect and aid the best interests, "in a temporal sense," of those suffering under disabilities, and, he opined, the termination of life support would not be in Karen Quinlan's best interests: "The single most important temporal quality Karen Quinlan has is life. This Court will not authorize that life to be taken from her."[1] His judgment was later overruled, and Karen Quinlan was taken off the respirator which it was believed had sustained her. As it turned out, she did not immediately die, but remained in a comatose state for a further ten years.

The case of Karen Quinlan is just one of many that have led to a serious rethinking of what in some respects has been the most taken-for-granted of all values, the value of life. For in Justice Muir's view, this is what was at stake—Karen Quinlan's "most important temporal quality": her life. But was it? To her? In what was its importance supposed to reside? Its intrinsic character as life? What it had previously brought forth, or, more improbably, might yet bring forth? Was his claim simply that, of the qualities remaining to Karen Quinlan, the most important was life? Justice Muir did not address these questions. Perhaps he thought them unnecessary. As Edward Shils once expressed the point, "to persons who are not murderers, concentration camp administrators, or dreamers of sadistic fantasies, the inviolability of human life seems to be so self-evident that it might appear pointless to inquire into it."[2] But the life remaining to Karen Quinlan was not uncontroversially of the self-evidently inviolable kind. Perhaps, as Shils goes on to say, the reluctance to make such an inquiry also reflected embarrassment because, "once raised, the question seems to commit us to beliefs we do not wish to espouse and to confront us with contradictions which seem to deny what is self-evident."

Whether self-evident or not, Justice Muir's assertion particularizes a widespread and deeply held commitment—a commitment that is sometimes accorded foundational significance. Such, it would appear, is the understanding of the Reverend James V. Schall, speaking in a slightly different, though related, context: "The essence of civilization, of morality, of dignity is this: All life, Down's syndrome or whatever, is worth living."[3] But despite such imposing claims, and, perhaps, our growing appreciation of the real capabilities of Down syndrome children, the questions won't go away. There are still the anencephalics and the Karen Quinlans. By virtue of what is "all life"—here, presumably, human—worth living? To whom is it worth living? Must it be worth living to the person whose life it is? Or may a life be worthwhile without being worth one's while? And may a life have worth, but not enough to make it worth living?

Schall's loose reference to "all life" raises an even more general question for those whose valuing of life seems characterizable as a valuing of vital processes. Do plants and animals, by virtue of their livingness, have an irreducible value that possesses some moral—whether or not enforceable claim on us? Muir and Schall would probably demur. Yet vitalism has not been without its supporters. Albert Schweitzer, an inspiration for much recent environmentalist thinking, saw in a universal "reverence for life" the very essence of morality:

> A man is truly ethical only when he obeys the compulsion to help all life which he is able to assist, and shrinks from injuring anything that lives. He does not ask how far this or that life deserves one's sympathy as being valuable, nor, beyond that, whether and to what degree it is capable of feeling. Life as such is sacred to him. He tears no leaf from a tree, plucks no flower, and takes care to crush no insect. If in summer he is working by lamplight, he prefers to keep the window shut and breathe a stuffy atmosphere than see one insect after another fall with singed wings upon his table.[4]

Are these merely the words of a noble eccentric, or do they reveal a moral depth that has been obscured by a perverse anthropocentrism? If so, wherein resides life's sacredness—in its nature, its origins, or in something else? And is obedience to "the compulsion to help all life" to be understood as a moral requirement or a moral ideal? When choices between lives must be made, as Schweitzer's medical role demanded, on what basis may they be acceptably made?

To ask such questions is not obviously corrupt or pointless. Indeed, they seem to be demanded. Yet their resolution is far from simple, for we are dealing not with matters of detail but of fundamental orientation, with the way in which we see ourselves and other living things, individually, socially, and cosmically.

It has become popular, in recent years, to approach these questions in an essentially negative fashion—that is, to consider the conditions under which "life" may be terminated or permitted to expire. It is less common to consider what may be said on its behalf. It is the positive question, in its various ramifications, that I attempt to address in this essay. Strictly speaking, of course, the negative issue cannot be separated from the positive one. For it is only on the assumption of a certain "valuing" of "life" that an inquiry into the conditions under which it may be terminated is necessitated, and any justification of those conditions will need to take into account what may be said on its behalf. Nevertheless, there is a difference of emphasis that gives the present project a distinctive character.

In the last paragraph I scarequoted "valuing" and "life." I did so to draw attention to the ambiguity of these terms, and, at least in the case of "valuing," to the large variety of positive characterizations that "life" attracts. Some writers are content to speak generally of "life's" (intrinsic? instrumental?) *value*. Others talk instead or as well of its *sacredness, sanctity, worth, dignity, inviolability,* or *sacrosanctity*. Still others call us to have *respect* or *reverence* for it, or remind us of our *right* or *entitlement* to it. Sometimes these characterizations are used loosely and almost interchangeably; at other times they are strongly distinguished. Unfortunately, there seems to be little consistency in the use of such terminology. I shall endeavor to provide some. Without being rigidly analytic, I shall seek to preserve those terminological distinctions that carry some normative importance.

But it is not only the valuational and normative terminology that causes difficulties. There is frequently an ambiguity in "life," when appeals are made to life's value, that context does little to remove. Is all life—animal and vegetable—in view, or is the appeal more particularly to human life? And if the latter, is it to individual human life or human species life (or something broader or narrower)? The possibilities begin to multiply as soon as the question is carefully considered. What is more, a reading of the literature indicates that many of those who consider life so valuable have not given much thought to these distinctions.

Part of my task in this essay will be the clarification of appeals to "the value of life" as they are made in human and nonhuman contexts. I will attempt to display their variety, and the kinds of justificatory structures appropriate to them. But my task will not end there. My purposes are substantive, and ultimately practical, and the bulk of my discussion will be given to an exploration of cases that might be made for the varied valuings of life.

It is to this latter end that chapters 3–6 critically survey arguments that have been used to establish, in order, some value for life-in-general, then plant, animal, and human life. Though several of these arguments can be mounted in more than one context I have generally introduced them in the context of their widest plausible application. The ordering of these chapters presented an interesting logistical problem. Although there is a certain logical "progression" evident in the movement from life-in-general through plant, animal, and human life, much of the normative argument moves in the opposite direction: the "value" of human life is taken as self-evident or paradigmatic, and the "value" of animal and plant life and life-in-general are then assessed by reference to human life. In the end I considered it heuristically preferable to adopt the present order of chapters.

Even so, there is a somewhat bewildering array of arguments and strategies for the valuing of plant, animal, and human life. I could wish that these arguments showed some congruence or at least connectedness. Alas, that is not so. Chapters 3–6 provide no clear theory of the valuing of life, only a tangle of threads, knots, and loose ends. In chapter 7, however, I seek to disentangle these threads and weave them into something approaching a coherent morality of life. No doubt that theory stands in need of more elaboration than I have provided, but I am hopeful that the lines of argument I have traced will be sufficiently clear and worthwhile to encourage others to develop them further.

One way in which a theory can be elaborated and tested is by seeing how it works in the context of concrete problems. The final chapter takes a few, albeit small, steps in that direction by exploring the role played by appeals to life's value in a number of the contentious areas in which it is often heard: vegetarianism, the beginning and end of human life, capital punishment, and genetic engineering. Although this cycle of topics raises many more issues than those relating to life's value, it is, nevertheless, to some such value (or lack thereof) that much weight is given in the debates that they engender.

This project, like most I have undertaken, began in puzzlement, and was an attempt to resolve that puzzlement. I do not think that I have finally succeeded in this—even to my own satisfaction. For what we ultimately confront here is not simply prejudice or dogma—though there is plenty of each—but diverse and competing visions of the world and of life, choice between which is as much a matter of sensibility as of argument.[5] We might just as soon resolve the fundamental questions of epistemology and ethics.

VALUING LIFE

O N E

VALUING LIFE

The sense of the world must lie outside the world. In the world everything is as it is, and everything happens as it does happen: *in* it no value exists—and if it did exist, it would have no value.   —Ludwig Wittgenstein[1]

Invocations of "the value of life" are common. Discussions of abortion, euthanasia, and capital punishment are replete with them. But they are also heard in debates over war, pacifism, and genocide; genetic engineering and fetal experimentation; environmental and animal rights; risk-taking, rescue and compensation. In some of these contexts, it is not unusual for appeals to "life's value" to be accorded the status of a moral "bottom line," an argumentative *terminus a quo*, moral rationality's final appeal. Those who would gainsay "life's infinite value" are suspected of being morally reprobate, or at least morally untrustworthy. Yet the issue is not as clear as the confidence of such appeals would sometimes suggest. Not only is their precise character left vague and undefined, but their cogency is, if not doubtful, at least disputable.

What kind of value is life claimed to have, and what kind of life is claimed to have value? It requires only a little reflection to realize that these questions are more complex than is intimated by a simple invocation of "life's value." Assertions of value, or at least action-guiding attributions, take a variety of forms, often possessing distinctive nuances and presupposing specialized ideological or normative contexts. In the moral debates to which I have referred, it is not only the *value* of life that is appealed to, but also its *sanctity*, *sacredness*, *worth*, *dignity*, and/or *inviolability*. Or life is appealed to as something for which *respect* or *reverence* is due, or something to which there is a special *right* or *entitlement*. What is true of "value" is equally true of "life." Is it human life that is in view, or life in some general sense, equally shared by plants and animals? Or life of a kind unequally shared with plants and animals, such as sen-

3

tient or conscious life? And if, as it frequently is, it is human life, then is it human life generally, or human life that has reached a certain stage of development or retains certain powers of expression? We need to clarify some of these questions before we become too involved in an examination of the cogency of appeals to the value of life, lest we find our subject shifting awkwardly beneath us, and we lose ourselves in a quicksand that leaves the discussion to those who can shout loudest or act toughest. Such clarification as I can provide will be the focus of this and the next chapter.

It would be wrong to assume that the varied appeals to "value," "sanctity," "dignity," etc. all come to the same thing, that they are merely literary embellishments of a single shared moral conviction. These characterizations, though sometimes used with a degree of looseness and interchangeability, frequently possess different moral colorations, and sometimes reflect distinctive moral backgrounds. For that matter, we cannot even assume that all appeals to life's "value" will come to the same thing. "Value," along with the other rubrics under which life is sometimes set apart, may be understood in a number of ways. And in addition we need to be clear about the qualifications that are often implicit in appeals to life's value (subjective/objective; intrinsic/instrumental; finite/infinite; absolute/relative; and so on).

In this chapter, my primary task will be to clarify some of the valuational terminology most commonly involved in appeals to "life," and in so doing to indicate a few of the wider contextual considerations that will need to be taken into account when the question of justification is raised. Just because this mapping of the valuational landscape requires us to traverse, or at least to skirt, some of the most treacherous and inaccessible philosophical terrain, my sketch will necessarily be rough and unfinished. Nevertheless, I hope to make clear the variety of practical purposes for which we have evolved the language of value, and also to display a richness to our conceptualization that will stand us in good stead when confronted by the bewildering variformity of life.

The value *of life*

It is appropriate that I turn first to appeals to life's *value*, since that is probably the phraseology of claims having widest currency in the practical debates surrounding life's promotion, protection, and termination. As used in the debates about life's value, there are, I believe, three common understandings of "value":

1.   Value as an *umbrella* concept. Sometimes when we talk about life having value, we intend to ascribe to it nothing more specific than a positive status—whether this status consists in its having value in some narrower sense, or in its being sacred or inviolable (be it in virtue of its inherent properties, its instrumental importance, or its being part of a relational complex), or in its being something to which we have a special right or entitlement.

Using *value* so broadly has little to commend it, except as a categorial label. A book or article titled *The Value of Life* is more likely to consider the regard we should have for life, our treatment of life, than one on *The Origins of Life* or *The Mechanisms of Life*. In this context, talk of life's value functions as a signpost, and, like most signposts, fulfills a useful function. Beyond that, however, it conveys very little. Except as a label, a signpost, a convenient and ubiquitous carry-all—indeed, as the title for this book—I shall not be interested in seeking out some comprehensive, all-encompassing value of life. Although I will generally refer promiscuously to life's "value," I am more interested in an understanding that allows for some differentiation between, say, "the value of life," "the right to life," and "respect for life," and that allows us to ask whether we must value life in order to have a right to it,[2] or, if we wish, to argue that if we are to have a proper respect for life, we should not think in terms of its value.[3]

My point here is not to eschew the possibility of some general or unifying framework within which any legitimate valuings of life should be understood and justified, but to question the usefulness of a discussion which presumes that in talking about the value of life, one might as well be talking about its sanctity, dignity, or worth, of respect for it or a right to it.

2.   The *socioeconomic* valuation of life. The link between "value" and "socioeconomic worth" is very old. Indeed, the oldest uses of "value" seem to come from a commercial context, in the pricing of objects or determination of their monetary equivalents. There is, however, discernible even there something of the ambiguity that has given talk of value a much wider currency. Though value may be determined or measured by the monetary return that an object is able to attract, an object's value is not usually resolved simply into its selling price. It may sell for more or less than its value. Talk of "getting value for money" is not simply tautologous. Thus, implicit in many assertions of economic value is the idea of a *fair* equivalent.

This socioeconomic conception of value—along with its ambiguities—is frequently associated with life. Indeed, a literature search would probably reveal that scholarly discussions of the value of life most commonly revolve round this understanding. Yet the literature is specialized, and the discussion somewhat obliquely connected with what people more commonly have in mind when discussing the value of life. When people oppose abortion or capital punishment or defend wilderness areas, the value they invoke in these causes is not resolvable into some monetary equivalent. Still, as the following examples will show, socioeconomic usages cannot be wholly ignored:

(a) We have inductive knowledge that the introduction of new technology, or employment in certain occupations, will often be accompanied by identifiable risks to human life. These risks can usually be diminished by the investment of additional resources. Those with responsibility for the introduction of the technology or for the conditions under which people work may ask whether the value of individual life is such that, for example, decreasing the death-rate per thousand from ten to seven justifies the injection of, say, an additional ten million dollars into safety devices.

(b) Medical therapies make varied use of social resources. Some are easily provided and make few demands on personnel, or on physical and economic resources. Others are exceedingly costly and may be of questionable effectiveness (say, artificial hearts, heart-lung transplants, treatments for AIDS). Their object is the preservation of human life; but is their cost justified? Is the life that is preserved of sufficient value to justify the utilization of resources that could, perhaps, be otherwise usefully employed (to save many more lives?)?

(c) Where a person has been killed, aggrieved parties may seek compensation for their loss. What value is to be placed on the life lost? Should the compensation for a negligently killed five-year-old be the same as that for a negligently killed fifty-year-old? Should the compensation for a negligently killed doctor be the same as that for a negligently killed janitor? Should the compensation for a good father be the same as that for a bad father? If not, does this show one to have a life of greater value than the other?

At this stage of the discussion, I do not want to get involved with the finer details of these determinations. Some of their complexities will be pursued in chapter 6. However, there are one or two points that bear noting even at this stage. Determinations of socioeconomic value are just that—they need and should not be seen as overall judgments of value. The point of such judgments is not to express a person's monetary value *qua* person or even *qua* individual. Depending on the circumstances, their point might be to provide a fair allocation of scarce resources, or to provide a vehicle for recouping or compensating economic and/or emotional losses precipitated by a loss of life. Although those who write and talk about such socioeconomic value sometimes talk as though that value is the only kind worth talking about, that is not generally what people are concerned about when they talk about life's value.

3. The *affirmative* valuing of life. The two senses of "value" so far considered do not provide us with much insight into what is commonly intended when life is said to have value. Articulating this further sense, however, is no easy matter. Indeed, it has occasioned an extended and frequently polarized debate—some writers focusing on what, for the want of better terms, can be referred to as the personal, subjective, and/or relational character of valuing, and others on its objective and/or nonrelational character. Some even claim that two distinct senses of "value" can be discerned, linguistically displayed in the distinction between "being valued" and "having value." But my own view, which I can sketch only briefly, is that though there are indeed distinctions to be made here, these two foci are best seen as complementary elements within a single "affirmative" sense in which "value" is employed. That which we value, we value because we deem it valuable. It is this Janus-like notion of value that best captures the sense of the appeal to the value of life. When referring to this narrower sense of value, I will generally speak of it as affirmative value, to distinguish it from the convenient carry-all sense in which I often employ it in these pages.

We can understand this affirmative sense of "value" only against a background in which valuers/attributers-of-value are conceived of as choosers. The activity of valuing, and ipso facto affirmative valuing, is the activity of beings confronted by options—not just between alternative acts and courses of conduct but also life-styles—and who can, on the basis of reflective consideration of those options, determine which should be chosen. Ascribing affirmative value to something is, inter alia, to characterize it as choiceworthy in some respect.

This link between affirmative value and choice helps to account for the bifurcation that sometimes occurs between something's "being valued" and its "having value." For someone may affirmatively value X on the basis of features that X does not possess or that do not make X choiceworthy. Standardly, however, statements about "the (affirmative) value of X" refer, on the one hand, to the perspective of a chooser, and on the other hand, to features of X that make it choiceworthy.[4] There is thus no conceptual divorce between something's being valued and its having value. Talk of "the (affirmative) value of life," then, refers, on the one hand, to the interests of a chooser, and, on the other hand, to features of "life" that are deemed to make it choiceworthy. Life valued is life affirmed. This affirmation typically takes the form of some sort of practical commitment to the thing valued.

Although assertions of affirmative value are assertions made from the point of view of a chooser or would-be chooser, they are not to be resolved into what P. H. Nowell-Smith once spoke of as "pro-attitudes."[5] Affirmative valuing does imply a pro-attitude, but it is not the mere impulsion towards something that constitutes it a valued object. Life affirmatively valued is not simply life plumped for or desired. That which is affirmatively valued is so because of features that are believed to make it valuable. Its affirmative value resides in features that render it choiceworthy. It is this that constitutes the so-called objectivity of value—the presence in affirmatively valued things of features which, *from the standpoint of a chooser*, make them choiceworthy.

In speaking of the presence *in* things of features which constitute their value-base, I have tried to remain neutral with respect to two time-honored ways in which those features can be characterized. They may comprise either intrinsic or instrumental (or both) properties of the thing in question. Where the properties inhere in the thing, as component features which the chooser affirmatively values independently of that thing's causal relations with other things, I will speak of them as investing that thing with intrinsic value. Where the properties are valued by virtue of their causal connection with some other valued thing, I will speak of them (and the object) as possessing an instrumental value. "Life" may (in principle) be affirmatively valued intrinsically or instrumentally (or both)—either because of features which are intrinsic to its character as life (or as the particular life it is), or because it is a material precondition for other things that are affirmatively valued (again, either intrinsically or, though not ad infinitum, instrumentally).

I do not, however, want my account to remain neutral with respect to two other ways in which affirmative value may be characterized. A number of writers have made a distinction between "intrinsic" and "inherent" value, and some of them have drawn that distinction as follows. Something is said to have intrinsic value if it is affirmatively valued for its own sake (i.e., not instrumentally). It is said to have inherent value if it is believed to have value-in-itself independently of the existence of valuers. Affirmative value is seen as a property like mass. I do not believe that things have inherent value, though they may be intrinsically valued. To believe that they have inherent value is, I believe, to misunderstand what affirmative valuing is about. It is about the characterization of things—on the basis of their features, certainly—insofar as they are relevant to the perspective of a chooser.

Suppose that valuers (broadly conceived) were never to have existed. Then, even though there would exist some things that valuers would affirmatively value were they to exist, those things would not have affirmative value. For the ascription of affirmative value makes sense only where choice is a possibility. Talk of value generally, and affirmative value in particular, makes sense only in the context of a "form of life" that gives meaning to the enterprise of valuing—one in which choices have to be made. It is only in the context of a set of ultimately practical interests that the selection of these rather than those features of something, as constitutive of its affirmative value, can be understood. Perhaps we should go further. In many cases, it is only in terms of the practical interests that comprise the valuational standpoint that the conceptualization of those features of objects which enter into their affirmative valuation (as value-bases) can be understood. Hume's remark, that "the life of a man is of no greater importance to the universe than an oyster"[6] can, from this point of view, be readily accepted. The universe as such has no valuational standpoint, no practical interests, in terms of which the life of a human might be compared and ranked with the life of an oyster.

A similar—though more general—point is implicit in the quotation from Wittgenstein that prefaces this chapter. In saying that "the sense of the world must lie outside the world," there is, perhaps, a slightly too positivistic edge to his remarks. Nevertheless, the point he goes on to make—that sense and value are *given* to the world—as language users and choosers come to terms with it, captures an essentially relational dimension to meaning, including the attribution of value. Until the interests of choosers are brought to bear on the world, the conjunction of factors that are constitutive of its value does not and cannot exist.

In saying that the attribution of affirmative value to something betokens its choiceworthiness, I prescind—for the time being—from what is surely the sixty-four dollar question concerning those

9

features of things (or, more pointedly, life) that valuers count as comprising their affirmative value. That question—at least in its more pointed form—I will have to confront later. Also, in talking about choiceworthiness, I intend something relatively nondeterminative. It is to affirm that the thing in question possesses certain plus-features so far as practical choice is concerned. In a particular choice situation, that thing may have to compete with other choiceworthy items, or other choice-relevant factors. So, then, to affirm life's value would not ipso facto be to affirm its "absolute," "overriding," or "infinite" value. Nor would the establishment of the former necessarily establish or even provide grounds for the establishment of any of the latter.

The mere appeal to life's affirmative value, therefore, unless uniformly grounded in considerations of a very weighty kind, will not, except in the most straightforward cases, settle the practical dilemmas that it is called upon to resolve. Perhaps those who invoke it believe that life provides or underlies a value-base of such compelling importance, but this cannot be presumed in advance of argument.

The worth *of (a) life*

Assertions of life's worth often parallel those of life's value. Indeed, they are frequently interchangeable. Once again, a threefold distinction can be drawn:

1.   There is a use of "worth" in which it is equivalent to *socioeconomic value*. And in line with that, some discussions of life's worth are concerned with its pricing, either in monetary terms or in terms of more general social resources. Thus, an actuary concerned with risk measurement and the pricing of insurance policies may put the worth/value of a human (or some other) life at $200,000. Others, less impressed by the marvels of economic calculus, may express their distaste for or belief in the inadequacy of such computations by speaking of life as being "priceless" or of "infinite" worth.

2.   A second sense of "worth" displays significant overlap with what I spoke of as *affirmation*, though there is something of a narrowing of focus. Affirmative valuing, I suggested, is two-dimensional, having both a "subjective" and "objective" plane. So too do assertions of worth, but in the case of worth the emphasis is fairly uniformly on what I called the value-base. We speak of valuing, but not of "worthing," though what is often referred to as something's "inherent worth" is not something other than its "intrinsic value."

As this shift in terminology shows, however, judgments of "inherent worth" lend themselves to the understanding I eschewed earlier, that value/worth may be possessed independently of the standpoint of a chooser.

There is a further nuance to assertions of worth that, though lacking formal significance, has some relevance to the present study. Whereas assertions of life's affirmative value are usually characterized by a certain generality (life in general, human life, adult life, etc.), assertions of life's worth more often focus on individual lives. We tend to speak of the worth of *a* life, of *this* or *that* life, rather than of its worth in general. The point is at most one of linguistic convention, since we may also speak of the value of *a* particular life. Yet there lies behind this difference of focus a more important distinction—sometimes referred to as one between "valuing" and "evaluating." To pursue that distinction in any detail here would be distracting, but as a rough characterization the following will do. In (affirmatively) valuing something, we link it up with an interest we have in pursuing/promoting/possessing, etc. that (kind of) thing. Frequently that interest is built into the way we conceptualize the kind in question (from this perspective both "kindness" and "table" can both be seen as value-laden terms). In evaluating, we are concerned to make a certain judgment about the qualities of particular items that fall under a description, generally a description which already picks out an affirmatively valued kind (a "good table," for example).[7]

Individualized assertions of worth can be understood in one of two ways. The first corresponds to what I have termed "evaluation"—a judgment on some particular life by reference to its individual qualities. So, to claim that *a* life has worth, is to affirm its *merits*. Assertions of merit, like assertions of general worth, are usually grounded in features that inhere in the thing in question (here, life); unlike worth, however, merit is generally seen as an assessment of actions, or of the expenditure of effort, and not of inert or unparticularized qualities. Hence assertions of merit are generally made only in relation to particular lives.

3. The second way of understanding individualized assertions of worth is as expressions of a *cost-benefit ratio*. When we speak of something as worthwhile, we generally mean that the effort or cost associated with it is outweighed by its benefits (usually, though not exclusively, to the bearer of that cost). That which is deemed worthwhile is judged worth its while by its deemer. A life may be judged worthwhile in this sense: a sufficient balance of benefits

over burdens is asserted by the person whose life it is. Particular lives are not always judged to be worth their while. A person who is severely depressed or terminally ill may no longer consider his life worth living. The point, in such cases, is not to deny all affirmative (or other) value to such a life, but to claim that the costs of living it, at present and foreseeably, outweigh that value.

Questions arise about the appropriate standpoint for such judgments: To whom must a worthwhile life be worthwhile? And to what end? To make it worth living? Should a judgment of this kind be the exclusive preserve of the person whose life it is? Or could a life be said to be worthwhile, though not worth one's while?

Some writers do not think that judgments of (human) life's worthwhileness need to be made by or from the point of view of the bearer of the life in question. That, presumably, is the view of James Schall, quoted in the Introduction, though his purpose is the innocent-enough one of contradicting those who would judge certain others' lives not to be worth living. But the very concession that this involves—viz., an external or even impersonal standpoint—may, at least in some contexts, give entrance to less innocent claims. This can be seen in the phrase coined by Karl Binding and Alfred Hoche in 1920—*lebensunwertes Leben*,[8] life unworthy of life, a conception that was later to find its outlet in the *Hitlerkammern*. In their view, the costs to others incurred in maintaining certain lives made those lives socially unworthwhile.

The questions I have posed cannot be settled by definitional *fiat*. They raise difficult substantive issues concerning the appropriate standpoint for judgments of value, and will need to be canvassed in greater detail later. Nevertheless, they help us to see why our deliberations seem to pull us in a number of directions.

What is emerging at this juncture is a broad distinction between judgments of affirmative value that are directed generally to life or to some kind of life, and judgments of affirmative value in which individual life or particular lives are assessed. Later, we will need to consider whether, and if so to what extent, these judgments should be interdependent.

Reverence *for life*

The phrase "reverence for life" is most commonly associated with Albert Schweitzer, for whom *Ehrfurcht vor dem Leben* constitutes the foundation of all ethical behavior. But though he uses the terminology deliberately, Schweitzer does not use it exclusively or precisely. He speaks as comfortably of *veneratio vitae*, respect for life, the sacredness of life, and of a devotion to life arising out of a reverence for life.[9] Later we will consider more carefully the details of Schweitzer's own position, and the context in which it arose. For the present, however, it suffices to note that the terminology of "reverence for life" has seeped into the wider debate about life's value, and it behooves us to consider the senses it has acquired in that debate.

1.   Michael Davis has recently argued that reverence involves a "recognition that the thing, class of things, process or what-not in question is, apart from utility, in some way so much better than us or than we can do that we want it to continue to exist."[10] That undoubtedly captures part of what is usually implicit in a reverential attitude, but I think that our most common understanding conveys something stronger—what might be spoken of as a *deferential attitude*. Certainly it is present in the Schweitzerian account, where a certain kind of submissive or yielding attitude toward life is encouraged. Reverence as deference does not cover every such attitude, however, but only as it constitutes a response to what is seen as the exalted character or status of its object. That towards which one has reverence is seen not merely as superior, but as vastly so, and the deferential attitude, though it may be characterized as a kind of respect, might equally well or even better be seen as a form of veneration. *Webster's College Dictionary* captures this well when it speaks of reverence as "profound, adoring, awed respect."

Most of those who speak of "reverence for life" have not wanted to limit their attention to human life. They intend, as one writer suggests of Schweitzer, to advance a "general sense of awe, wonder, and obeisance before the phenomenon of life [rather] than to delineate the distinctly human identity of it."[11] This, however, prompts the question whether life is the kind of object for which it is appropriate to have reverence.

The question is raised acutely in a paper by Lawrence Davis.[12] He begins by distinguishing reverence from awe. Both, he claims, are responses to something believed to be greatly superior to oneself; both include elements of respect (as a disposition to defer to or not to interfere with), and, along with that, fear (or at least the potential for it). But, he goes on to argue, reverence, unlike awe, "includes a disposition to perform *acts* of reverence," acts intended "to *communicate* one's attitude to the object of reverence." What this implies, he believes, is that "only those entities can be revered that are thought capable of noticing and understanding the conventional significance of these acts of reverence." Davis's concern is not directly with the idea of "reverence for life," and he does not comment on it. However, it would follow from his account that although life might evoke a sense of awe, it could not inspire our reverence. Its awesome qualities could not evoke reverence, because our response to them cannot be appreciated by the supposed object of our reverence. For it is the capacity to comprehend the response of others to one's superiority and not merely one's superiority that makes something an appropriate object of reverence.

I think Davis's strictures on the proper objects of reverence may be too severe, though the fact that there is a discernible tendency among those who speak of reverencing life to personify Life suggests some affinity between reverence and responsiveness. Other writers, however, often use "reverence" in more idiosyncratic ways, and avoid the problems that might come from claiming to use it in some "standard" sense.

2. A good example of a nonstandard use can be found in Herbert Richardson's reference to a *sense of identification* with all life. According to Richardson, "the feeling of unity, or sense of participation with others in a larger whole, is technically called reverence for life."[13] This account accentuates a note that runs through most of the "reverence for life" literature, viz., that life, though exalted, is not distanced. There is immanence as well as transcendence. Life engenders not only an attitude of deference, but also of "fellow feeling" with all its other manifestations. But the larger whole of which one is a part is also a greater whole. This does not exclude degrees of identification (a position which Richardson takes), though neither does it imply them. Schweitzer, however, sometimes appears to claim an equality of status among all life forms.

There is little doubt that in Schweitzer's case the postulate of reverence for life is closely intertwined with a sense of life's connectedness with a larger Creative Will. Yet he believes this sense of life's "sacredness" need not depend on the acceptance of a specifically theistic religiosity. Life itself, as a dynamic process, willing its perfection, is seen as evoking a broadly religious response and devotion of its own. It answers to the needs of *homo religiosus* without requiring God.

Respect *for life*

The idea of respect has a somewhat complicated history. The translators of the King James Bible commend God for his lack of "respect of persons" and likewise enjoin us not to "respect persons in judgment."[14] For such respect connoted partiality. That implication has all but vanished from the contemporary demand that we respect the persons or (more problematically) personhood of others—an injunction that has assumed the proportions of a moral truism. Much of the impetus for this refocusing of respect probably lies with Kant, whose insistence that persons should be treated as ends and not only as means has become the touchstone of modern-day humanism.

But this aphoristic summary belies a certain complexity in Kant's own understanding of respect. It has been usefully—if somewhat conjecturally—schematized by Joel Feinberg.[15] Behind the more refined technical uses to which Kant put the idea of respect, Feinberg suggests there lies a premoral root notion, signified by the German word *Respekt*. In *Respekt*, fear played a significant role. To have a *Respekt*-ful attitude toward someone or something was, inter alia, to be cognizant and wary of its power. A key to the *Respekt* one might have for an opponent lay in the *danger* posed by the latter. But *Respekt* could be appropriately shown not only towards opponents whose power made them dangerous, but also towards things of high status, whose status was associated with great power and subject to few moral constraints.

Out of this base notion, Feinberg suggests that Kant developed two distinct accounts of respect. The earliest, for which he used the Latin term *observantia*, associated respect, not with power as such (whether or not grounded in status), but with an attitude appropriate to *authorities*—with those having a right to command and to claim allegiance. On this understanding, respect became an attitude to be shown not only to those with power, but to any who by virtue of their status can make demands of us. Feinberg remarks: "Christianity gave dignity even to the meek and humble. Respect could then be extended to the aged, to women, to the clergy, and then even to offices, symbols, and the dead."[16] It is from this development, he believes, that the "Kantian" notion of respect for persons evolved—the view that all "persons," independent of their merit and talent, have, "not the ability to make demands, backed up by force, but the ability to make claims backed up by reasons."[17] Though distinguishable, this *observantia*-respect need not be incompatible with some kind of *additional* respect (esteem) that might be shown toward some in virtue of their merits, skills, and accomplishments.

Kant's second account, represented by his use of the Latin term *reverentia*, conveys the idea of something morally trumping, something that determines our wills insofar as we are rational beings.

15

For Kant, *reverentia* was appropriately displayed only toward the moral law—or those (like God) in whom that law was exemplified. There are some similarities here between Kantian *reverentia* and Schweitzerian *reverence*, though the differences are probably more significant. Schweitzer did not see himself as taking over the Kantian idea—indicated, perhaps, by the fact that Kant uses the German word *Achtung* to translate *reverentia*, whereas Schweitzer uses the term *Ehrfurcht* for what we translate as "reverence." Even though for both Kant and Schweitzer, *reverentia/Ehrfurcht* had much the same status and import, they are grounded in very different considerations.

Kant's focus is on "respect for persons" rather than "respect for life." This need not indicate any more than the advocacy of a particular (albeit important) moral disposition (or principle) alongside respect for life; but more probably it marks a deliberate choice in favor of "persons" rather than "life" as the proper object of respect. In some modern writers that decision is quite explicit. Respect is viewed as the peculiar stance called for when a being possesses rational capacities. Before seeing how talk of "respect for life" might be understood, then, I shall make some brief observations on the specific character of respect in talk of "respect for persons."

In a helpful paper, Stephen Darwall distinguishes two kinds of respect:

1. *recognition respect*, which consists "in a disposition to weigh appropriately in one's deliberations some feature of [a thing] and to act accordingly."[18] Appropriate objects of this kind of respect may include the law, an individual's feelings, and social institutions, as well as persons. When persons as such are said to be the objects of recognition-respect, we mean that "they are entitled to have other persons take seriously and weigh appropriately the fact that they are persons in deliberating about what to do."[19] Or, as he later puts it, to respect persons as such "is to give appropriate weight to the fact that [they are persons] by being willing to constrain one's behavior in ways required by that fact."[20] Recognition-respect is to be distinguished from

2. *appraisal respect*, which is exclusive to persons, and consists "in an attitude of positive appraisal of a person either judged as a person or as engaged in some more specific pursuit."[21] In the former case, appraisal-respect is said to be grounded in features of a person's *character*, that is, "those features of persons which . . . we think relevant in appraising them as persons."[22] These may include "dispositions to act for particular reasons [e.g., honesty] or a

higher-level disposition to act for the best reasons."[23] In the latter case, character traits will be relevant, but not exhaustive.

Unlike recognition-respect, appraisal-respect may be merited or deserved. Recognition-respect marries features of Kantian *observantia* and *reverentia*, though there is one respect in which Kantian *observantia* is more restricted than recognition-respect. For Kant, *observantia* is grounded in rationality—the capacity for choice—a restriction that does not apply to recognition-respect. Appraisal-respect, which is (according to Darwall) appropriate only to persons, is not warranted simply by the ability to exercise certain rational capacities, but is a form of esteem called for by a person's merits, skills, and accomplishments.

If we turn now to the language of "respect for life," we find "respect" used in ways that correlate closely though not exactly with a number of the senses I have already distinguished:

1.   The *moral considerability* of life.[24] In a number of writers, the idea of respect for life is intended to signal only that vitality is a morally relevant factor when alternative courses of action are being assessed. A person who shows respect for life is one who believes the livingness of things to be a morally relevant consideration, and who will therefore see all killing (or stunting of life) as standing in need of moral justification. To acknowledge the moral considerability of life is to show it recognition-respect.

2.   Life as a *phenomenon to be prized*. This is a much more strongly positive sense of "respect for life." According to it, "life" possesses not some unspecified degree of moral considerability (or affirmative value), but a specially high importance or status; its inherent qualities make it something to be held aloft and even deferred to. Recognition-respect here moves in the direction of *reverentia*.

3.   Life as *something not to be interfered with*. "Respect for life" may be interpreted negatively, as well as positively. It is used to acknowledge a "right to life," where that can be interpreted either as a right not to be killed or as a right to noninterference with the course of a life. The person who shows respect, in this sense, is the person who desists from violating the moral boundaries appropriate to the object of respect.

Is this third sense of "respect for life" simply the converse of the second? Can we say that it is in virtue of the prize-worthiness (or high affirmative value) of life that it is something not to be interfered with? It depends significantly on what we consider to be the grounds of that prizing. If life is believed to warrant prizing in virtue of features inherent in it (and if they are seen as the only basis

17

for such prize-worthiness), then the third sense will not be a simple converse of the second. For the reasons why life may not be interfered with need not be confined to its inherent features. If, as some writers have suggested, the respect due to life is grounded in its being God's creation or property, then its "protected" character will not be a function of what are normally characterized as inherent features.

From this brief discussion of respect we can see why respect for life is not simply a—or a simple—generalization of respect for persons, and why there has been a deliberate shift from talk of respect for life to respect for persons. The respect due to persons (Kantian *observantia*) is seen closely bound up with the perception of persons as choosers or centers of rational consciousness, and "life" does not lend itself so easily to such attributions. But this does not mean that talk of "respect for life" can be given no sense. As Darwall's discussion makes clear, recognition-respect need not be restricted to the outcomes of rational consciousness.

The sanctity *of life*

One of the most popular claims made on behalf of life is that it possesses a special sanctity. Unlike appeals to life's affirmative value, which, apart from indicating some positive appraisal, leave unclear the practical weight that such value is to be given, assertions of life's sanctity often carry with them a religious or quasi-religious overlay, and with it a demand for noninterference. Some of the nuances we can distinguish as follows:

1. The *religious importance* of life. The language of "sanctity" is often used to invest life with a certain kind of religious significance—a sacredness. But there is considerable variety in the way in which this is understood (reflecting the varied understandings of "religious"). For some, the appeal to life's sanctity is intended to mark it out as something set apart for or consecrated to God. It is seen as God's special possession, as something over which God has jurisdiction. But for others, it is not its devotion to God that constitutes or underlies its sanctity, but its own character as life. Vitality is seen as being in itself an awe-inspiring or even divine phenomenon, evoking what must be seen in functional terms as a religious attitude. We may stand before life as we stand before God. So Edward Shils: "Man stands in awe before his own vitality, the vitality of his lineage and of his species. This sense of awe is the attribution and therefore the acknowledgement of his sanctity."[25] To

speak of the sanctity of life, therefore, may be to invest it, either in itself or by virtue of its associations, with a central or pivotal religio-moral importance.

2. The *inviolability* of life. Often closely associated with, though distinct from, the view that life's sanctity is to be understood in religious terms, is the view that life may not be tampered with or violated. Life is thought of as morally secured against (certain kinds of) interference. In this sense, to accord life sanctity is to accord it respect (in the third sense that I distinguished).

Sometimes it is not clear what constitutes a tampering with or violation of life, though people who speak of it as inviolable generally mean to exclude—at the very least—its deliberate extinction. However, it is not only deliberate extinction that may be opposed in appeals to life's sanctity. What are deemed "unnatural" interventions in life processes (e.g., genetic engineering) may also be excluded in its name.

Usually, though not always, sanctity is ascribed to human life. And there is considerable disagreement about whether this carries further limitations—say, to "rational" and "innocent" life. For both proponents *and* opponents of pacifism, capital punishment, and self-defensive killing are likely to appeal to the sanctity (= inviolability) of life in support of their positions.

I have separated sanctity as "religiously important" from sanctity as "inviolable," even though they are often closely associated: the religious significance of life is held to ground its inviolability. But life may be argued to be inviolable apart from any religious significance it is accorded. And its religious associations need not mandate its inviolability.

3. Life as *a phenomenon to be respected*. Sanctity and respect are sometimes distinguished and sometimes identified. When the latter occurs, talk of life's sanctity is intended to indicate a certain prizing, dignifying, or honoring of life, where the intention is to acknowledge life as something to be looked up to, and as having certain claims upon us, but without implying the exaltedness or untouchability that tends to be associated with inviolability. Life is seen as having an elevated status—a high level of moral considerability—but not as awe-inspiring.

W. K. Frankena distinguishes the sanctity of life from respect for it, but sees them as mutually implicative: "If one has respect for life, one believes that life has sanctity, and vice versa. If one believes we should respect life, one believes in the sanctity of life, and vice versa."[26] For Frankena, sanctity is a property of life, whereas respect is a relation, a response to it. The property of sanctity calls for our respect, and respect is properly given to what possesses sanctity. On this view, life's sanctity is understood in something like the first sense I distinguished, as possessing, either in itself or because of its origins/ordination, a religious importance.

Although I have attempted to separate out different nuances of sanctity-talk, I do not want to pass judgment on whether appeals to the sanctity of life are best understood to refer to some feature of life or instead to indicate an attitude appropriate to life. The two are so closely interrelated that a judgment one way or the other would probably distort sanctity's Janus-like character.

The dignity of (a) life

Unlike appeals to the sanctity of life or respect for life, which may refer to life in a fairly inclusive sense, those to "the dignity of life" refer almost exclusively to human life. Indeed, the more likely appeal is to "the dignity of the human being." However, not all human beings are always included, and sometimes the preferred object is "persons"—where the latter may be neither restricted to humans nor appropriately applied to all humans. Dignity tends to be closely connected with rationality and autonomy—with individuality, not human life in general—and the appeal to human dignity is most commonly heard when that rationality or autonomy is being threatened or compromised. For persons, the ultimate indignity is (often claimed to be) the lack of control over one's own life. Hence the frequent appeal to dignity in discussions of human engineering and euthanasia.

According to Elizabeth Maclaren, *dignitas* was originally the prerogative of an elite, and expressed a certain nobility of aspect. It betokened "gravity, sobriety, steadiness through changing circumstance, the capacity to retain [one's] pride, balance in the cultivation of [one's] mental and physical powers."[27] This elitist conception was, she suggests, generalized through the influence of Judeo-Christian egalitarianism. The creation of Man in God's image, and God's indiscriminate love for each individual, whatever his/her station in or condition of life, were taken to invest each person with dignity.[28] Eventually, as in Marxist thought, dignity was secularized, and came to be seen as a status Man has "by virtue of his capacity to transform the world by his labour."[29] In some later writers, this contrast between religious and secular groundings for dignity has been expressed by means of a contrast between Man's "alien" and "inherent" dignity.[30]

Many writers see a bifurcation in contemporary usage, reflecting, perhaps, the "ordained status" and "inherent capacities" strands in the development just outlined.[31] Renaissance humanism has shifted our focus from the species—and Man's superiority to the animals—to the individuality possessed by each person. There has been a shift from the dignity that is ascribed to individuals in virtue of their species membership, to one that is ascribed to those individuals in virtue of their capacities as autonomous beings. Marvin Kohl distinguishes:

1.   *Dignity by association*, whereby an individual is accorded dignity "just because he is a member of a uniquely rational and capable species."[32] Such dignity cannot be lost or destroyed, since it is not based (except associatively) on capacities, abilities, or achievements, but on species membership. This is to be differentiated from

2.   *Dignity as self-possession*, which consists of "having reasonable control over the major and significant aspects of one's life, as well as the ofttimes necessary condition of not being treated disrespectfully."[33] Unlike species-dignity, self-possessive dignity depends crucially on exercisable capacities. It is denied when people are not permitted to exercise control over their life-decisions. And it may be largely lost where people become victims of severely debilitating terminal illnesses. The last dignified act of a terminally ill person might be the refusal of further "treatment." And where that cannot be given, the continuation of treatment may constitute a kind of indignity. So argues Robert Morison:

> There is an implicit indignity in the conception of the meaning of human life revealed by over-vigorous efforts to maintain its outward, visible, and entirely trivial signs. It is not breathing, urinating and defecating that makes a human being important even when he can do these things by himself. How much greater is the indignity when all these things must be done for him, and he can do nothing else. Not only have means thus converted into ends; the very means have themselves become artificial. It is simply an insult to the very idea of humanity to equate it with these mechanically maintained appearances.[34]

At one time, the hiatus between species- and self-possessive understandings of dignity did not attract a great deal of attention. A sharpened appreciation of their differences, at least in the public policy arena, has come about, on the one hand, through the rise of individualism and the exaltation of individual autonomy, and, on the other hand, through developments in technology, which have allowed a wedge to be driven between bodily persistence and purposive living. Such was the dilemma confronted in the Quinlan case. Species-dignity, Kohl believes, has been rightly pushed into the background, and attention is now properly focused on the dignity that attaches to an individual "in his specificity, . . . in his singular concreteness."[35]

Self-possessive dignity is closely associated with respect. As Kohl expresses it, dignity is possessed, respect is shown, and is the appropriate response to a being possessing dignity. In this he follows Kant, who, focusing on "man regarded as a person—that is, as the subject of morally practical reason"—[and therefore] "not to be valued as a mere means to the ends of others or even as his own ends, but as an end in himself," goes on to say: "He possesses, in other words, a dignity (an absolute inner worth) by which he exacts *respect* for himself from all other rational beings in the world: He can measure himself with every other being of this kind and value himself on a footing of equality with them. . . . Autonomy . . . is the basis of dignity of a human and of every rational creature."[36]

Even if, as we may be inclined, we favor self-possessive over associative dignity, it cannot be simply assumed that its grounding is in rationality, autonomy, self-control, self-determination, and suchlike. Maclaren, for example, suggests that nonsubstitutability or "irreplaceability" provides a more appropriate base for its ascription.[37] Unlike rationality, autonomy, etc., which are individual properties, irreplaceability is a relational notion, a value placed on something by others. Referring to certain irretrievably brain-damaged children, she suggests that, though "permanently incapable of gravity, rationality, self control, creativity, they *were* capable of evoking what sounded more like love than pity, and that somehow *was* their dignity."[38] As Maclaren recognizes, even on this understanding self-possessive dignity can be and sometimes is lost or denied, though she does not provide any clear view of the circumstances under which such losses or denials might be appropriate.

The differences between Kohl and Maclaren reflect much larger differences—between individualistic and communitarian approaches to questions of human value, and indicate the extent to which the apparently analytic task of anatomizing notions like dignity is permeated by normative considerations. In the present case, however, Maclaren's communitarian account will not readily do. Our pets, or even family heirlooms, may be nonsubstitutable, but they are not thereby accorded any dignity. Greater subtlety is required if a communitarian account of dignity is to be provided.

The right *to life*

It will be evident from the discussion thus far that what I have re-ferred to in its broadest sense as the language of value serves a variety of practical functions. Sometimes it serves to select for us features of things that, given our practical interests, are to be seen as relevant to our choices. Sometimes, however, the focus is more decidedly on what choosers may do in regard to the objects of their practical attention. Here the language of value tends to be choice-constraining. This contrast of focus and function tends to be clearest between the language of value more narrowly conceived (affirmative valuing) and the language of rights to which I now turn. For some writers, this contrast between choice-relevant and choice-constraining language is of critical importance in normative deliberation.[39]

The language of rights has tended to dominate contemporary socio-political discussion, and in the present context, the appeal to the right to life is now heard as frequently as the appeal to the (affirmative) value of life. Yet, as I noted above, whatever common moral resources they may draw upon, the two appeals serve quite different functions. We can see this by looking at the way in which rights-talk has developed.[40]

Originally an exclusively legal concept, the language of rights was introduced into moral discourse via natural law theory. The main impetus for this conceptual transplant lay with events in the seventeenth century—though there are, of course, earlier intima-tions. A growing disenchantment with traditional authority, and an emerging sense of "the individual" and his moral primacy, gen-erated the need for an appropriate moral vocabulary—one that would designate certain moral claims as politically securable. The language of rights fulfilled that role admirably. Its invocation high-lighted a type of moral consideration that, somewhat analogously to its legal counterpart, could ground a justification for the use of coercive force. Assertions of a *right* to life, liberty, and the pursuit of happiness, were demands for the guaranteed protection of life, liberty, and the pursuit of happiness. In the absence of such guar-antees, political authority lacked legitimacy, and even revolution could be justified.

But to say that rights-talk was well suited to a particular socio-political role is not to specify the character of the moral consider-ations that allowed them to be accorded right-status. The subse-

23

quent evolution of rights-talk has exhibited a certain branching. For most early writers, rights-talk was the language of *human* liberation—a liberation grounded in the human capacity for rational choice. That focus is still championed by H.L.A. Hart and others for whom a right is a discretionary power.[41] Other writers, focusing on the function of rights-talk—to legitimate the use of force (if necessary) in the securing of something deemed morally important—have employed the language of rights whenever they have thought that a morally significant consideration warranted enforcement. Yet others, asking what moral considerations could legitimate coercion, sought to both extend and limit the scope of rights-talk to basic needs or welfare interests.

It is difficult to say which of these different developments should be given pride of place. Each focus has something to be said for it. My own view, about which I will say more in chapter 7, is that since rights-talk is still strongly political in its usage, the avoidance of misunderstanding makes it essential that we reserve it for moral considerations that are believed to be sufficiently weighty to warrant (if necessary) the use of force in their behalf. The question then is: What moral considerations are that important? We could focus on either the capacity for choice, and see rights as marking out a sphere of noninterference, or the possession of welfare interests, and allow for the possibility of positive biotic rights of a more general kind. Here my preference is for the latter view, at the same time recognizing that welfare interests relating to human freedom may have a stronger claim than others. But this will need to be argued for later.

Because the language of rights, like the language of value, has become so dominant in moral discourse, a host of controversial distinctions has developed round it. Positive and negative, protective and welfare, general and special, absolute and relative, alienable and inalienable, prescriptible and imprescriptible rights are differentiated (or challenged) by *aficionados* of rights-talk. This is not the place for their detailed exploration. It is relevant to point out, however, that all these alleged distinctions have played some role in debates about the right to life—in deliberations about the nature and scope of such a right. I shall, therefore, indicate a few of the ways in which they have figured in such discussions, to illustrate the very different ways in which claims for life are supported in moral debate.

In the early days of rights-talk, when rights were appealed to to assert the claims of the individual against ecclesiastical and monarchical authority structures, the right to life (along with other rights) tended to be interpreted negatively or protectively—as a (human) right *not to be killed*. It was, essentially, a right to noninterference: "the right not to be deprived of life, . . . a right that God gave and nature supported."[42] But the freeing of individuals from ecclesiastical and state authoritarianism did not thereby free them from all forms of oppression. The emerging market society served to transfer active social power from a traditional landed aristocracy to an increasingly wealthy mercantile class, and individuals freed from the oppression of church and state found themselves subject to the arbitrariness and unequal bargaining power of the market. Not only so, but the technological progress that catalyzed the market brought with it new possibilities for "the death of individuality." Individuals could be destroyed mentally as well as bodily. Along with the growing recognition of these new social avenues for despotism, there also evolved—as a corrective—an enlarged conception of rights. On the one hand, the scope of the right not to be killed was enlarged to prohibit invasions of personality that would threaten individuality. On the other hand, the right to life came to be formulated in positive terms—not simply as a right not to be interfered with, but as *an assertion directed to the securing of certain minimum conditions of life*, so that life "could not merely persist but be assured of the conditions for its enhancement." This right, sometimes termed a "right of living" or "right to live," is stated by the pre–World War II French League of Rights of Man to imply

> the right of the mother to all consideration, care and supplies which her social role requires; the right of the child to all the prerequisites of his full physical and moral development; the right of woman to complete freedom from exploitation and domination by man; the right of old men, sick men and invalids to the surroundings necessitated by their condition; the right of everyone to profit by all the measures of protection which science makes possible.

> The right to life implies also: the right to work, sufficiently limited to give opportunity for leisure and sufficiently remunerated to permit everyone to profit widely by the well-being which scientific and technological progress is making accessible, and which under an equitable distribution must and can be assured to everyone; the right to a full intellectual, artistic, and technical development according to the capacities of the individual; the right of maintenance for all who are unable to work.[43]

25

Whether it is useful to see the right to life made so encompassing, except as the statement of a general political ideal, I am unsure. If, with Feinberg,[44] we can recognize rights claims as having various levels of generality, and, with that, differing degrees of politico-moral force, then broad invocations of "the right to life" may serve a valued purpose. But there is also the risk that dilutions of this kind will deprive rights-talk of the privileged role that it often claims for itself in politico-moral debate.

Other distinctions within rights-talk—between absolute/relative and alienable/inalienable rights—are no less difficult to pin down. In relation to the right to life, the claim to absoluteness has frequently been heard. The intention is to assert its moral primacy, its overridingness; yet, when pressed, the claim usually contracts into something like "a right of 'innocent' life not to be killed" or "the right not to be killed without due process or just cause." There comes a point in such discussions where the claim to absoluteness is so qualified by the specificity of the right concerned that it invites the charge of posturing.

In the case of alienability, much of the debate has centered on the matter of interpretation—particularly of the commonly voiced claim that the right to life is "inalienable." For some, inalienability has implied indefeasibility/absoluteness,[45] for others it has been interpreted as nonwaivability,[46] for yet others it has been interpreted as "nonforfeitability."[47] These are issues about which I shall have more to say in chapter 7.

What is important to note about rights-claims is that even if they are grounded in considerations that are affirmatively valued, they are not simple assertions of affirmative value. The assertion of a right is intended to determine choice, not because the right-holder is affirmatively valued but because it possesses features that may legitimately constrain our conduct. Rights-talk is action guiding, not because it focuses on factors we consider worthy of affirmation, but because it sets limits to the freedom of choosers.

Review

I have endeavored to display something of the complexity and richness of appeals to what is broadly called "the value of life." When, in the course of a practical argument, life's value is invoked, its invocation may take many forms. It may be appealed to as something having affirmative value or worth, dignity, sanctity, or as something for which respect or reverence is due, or as something to

which there is a right. Although there is some overlap in the way
this terminology is used, it is often used in a deliberate and differential fashion. Just what distinctions are intended, however, is not
always clear, since our normative discourse tends to be hostage to
competing ideologies, and there is no vantage point *sub specie aeternitatis* from which we may resolve such conflicts. Although I have
sometimes indicated my own preferences, this has not been the
place to embark on a full-scale exploration and assessment of these
alternative traditions. It is enough to see something of the conceptual and normative maze hidden by the frequently forthright yet
unreflective appeal to the value of life. Nevertheless, at this stage of
our inquiry, the following gains can be noted:

First, appeals to life often differ in their generality, and sometimes this is reflected in the normative vocabulary used. Appeals to
the right to life, for example, generally focus on the lives of individuals, whereas it is more common for the claims that life is to be
affirmatively valued or reverenced to refer to life of some general
kind. Particular lives are affirmatively valued or reverenced, not as
individual lives but as instantiations of (some kind of) life. True,
there is nothing settled about these observations: species and
group rights are sometimes asserted. But the general tendencies
I've noted reflect something of the conceptual history of these ter-
minologies, and it is important that this not be forgotten.

Second, a few of the terms I have been discussing are more appropriate to some life forms than to others. "Dignity," for example,
is almost exclusively used in relation to developed human life—not
merely to individual human substances, but to humans possessing
individuality—and, as we have seen, there are those who wish to
use "right" in a similarly exclusive way.

Third, terms like "right," "respect," and "reverence" often serve
to delineate a certain stance toward life, rather than to highlight
what might be seen as its affirmative value-making or choice-relevant properties. Their function is choice-constraining rather than
choice-relevant. The latter are signified by "(affirmative) value,"
"worth," and, frequently, "sanctity" and "dignity." These two
broad groupings may sometimes stand in a loose justificandum-
justificans relationship—the justification for according life a right,
respect, or reverence being something like its value, worth, sanctity, or dignity. I suspect, however, that the relationship is often
quite indirect. The focus for choice-relevant attributions is the object as something that might engage the commitment of a chooser.
The focus for choice-constraining attributions is the object per-

ceived as making its own demands of a chooser, quite apart from that chooser's affirmative valuing of it.

Fourth, behind this diversity of terminology there often lurks a deeper diversity in normative and valuational frameworks. There is something proutilitarian in talk about life's worth, something proreligious in talk about its sanctity, and talk of a right to life has an individualistic ring to it. There is, however, nothing hard and fast about these resonances. Language is a social artifact and remarkably adaptable, and a consequence of social evolution has been that terms originating in one context have been partially neutralized by or have learned to function in different normative environments. It is no longer necessary to be theistic to speak about life's sanctity, to be utilitarian to talk about its worth, or to be individualistic in claiming a right to it. Nevertheless, there are deep and diverse ideological commitments informing such appeals and the debates surrounding them, and one of our central tasks in later chapters will be to articulate and to some extent assess those underlying standpoints.

T W O

VALUING *LIFE*

Philosophers, fools and physicists step in where those with some knowledge of the subject have enough sense not to tread and we are still assailed by articles purporting to define or elucidate the nature of life.   —N. W. Pirie[1]

As I have already intimated, the language of "life" is no less problematic than the language of "value." Appeals to the value of life do not have as their object some uniformly cognized *given*, but a phenomenon having varied forms and disputed boundaries. Life—though not necessarily of the same kind—may be predicated of cells, tissues, organs and organisms, of plants, animals, humans and gods, of individuals, groups, species and systems. Some would go further: animism, hylozoism, and panpsychism, though alien to the thought-patterns of twentieth-century scientific rationalists, nevertheless pose a continuing challenge to those who would see the phenomenon of life as unproblematic. In this chapter I propose to articulate some of the understandings of "life" that might and do figure in appeals to it as something of value (broadly understood).

What is it to be alive?

The question is more easily asked than answered. Two sets of contrasts are familiar to us—between the living and the dead, and between the animate and inanimate. What is dead was once alive. That which is inanimate lacks life, and maybe never possessed it. But what makes for being alive rather than dead, for being animate rather than inanimate?

The bacteria, fish, and plants that inhabit a pond possess life; so does my skin, an ovum, a developing fetus, and a comatose human being. We are inclined to contrast these with dried twigs, hair, and corpses, on the one hand, and rocks, clouds, and chemical elements, on the other; the former are said to be dead, the latter inanimate.

At a certain level of everyday experience, these assertions are uncontroversial enough. There are, however, other levels of reflection at which their obviousness is called into question. One level is not too far removed from everyday experience. Phenomena like volcanoes and rivers are sometimes said to be alive or to have a life. This is said of them because they are active and subject to intelligible change—they have what is sometimes called, albeit controversially, "a history." Yet I think most of us would see this way of talking as metaphorical. But there is another level at which such attributions are taken literally, and at which, in addition, life is attributed to sticks and stones, along with those things of which it is ordinarily predicated. Hylozoism, the view that all matter is alive, and panpsychism, the view that consciousness is a universal attribute of matter, had serious followings at the turn of the century, and roots that lead back through some strands of German philosophy to the Stoics and pre-Socratics.[2] In addition to these philosophical doctrines, there have been religious ones, such as animism[3] and Jainism,[4] that see all of the natural world as ensouled or permeated with life.

What is at stake in this controversy? Is it a conception of life, of what something must be to be alive (or conscious . . .)? Or is it a question of the real properties of sticks and stones, of whether their behavior is best understood using vitalistic categories? Or is it perhaps a matter of broader *Weltanschauungen*, of the way in which we conceive of ourselves and our world? There is probably no one answer to the first question. But for contemporary hylozoists and panpsychists, the issue has been chiefly one of overall *Weltanschauung*. The progressive "deanimation" of the cosmos, the reduction of vitality to chemical interaction, and the growing tendency to understand its operations in mechanistic terms, have been perceived as dangerous and decivilizing trends that need to be countered by a view of the world that does not seek to structure itself on a model provided by inert matter, but takes life as the basic interpretative datum. Only so can the world be fit for humans and humans fit for the world.

For the present I shall leave this larger debate to one side—though it is only fair to say that its influence will be seen on the discussion which follows. What is perhaps more pertinent to my present concerns is the observation that where the contemporary hylozoist and panpsychist part company with the naive observer of the world is not so much in their conception of life as in their description of the properties of inanimate nature. Where the naive observer sees an inert and passive stone, the panpsychist sees a responsive and active being. Perhaps, in order to render plausible his claims, the panpsychist has to work with a slightly attenuated conception of vitality and consciousness; nevertheless, his conception is one that takes our naive experience of life as paradigmatic. It is not necessary, therefore, that we engage at depth with the substance of panpsychist and hylozoist claims.

With regard to the views against which they are reacting, however, my discussion will be more obviously counterposed. For it is not with life as a specially complex and subtle interaction of chemical elements or physical particles that I shall be concerned, but with life as a phenomenon whose features cannot be apprehended in purely physicalistic terms. Carl Sagan's "wonder" at the fact "that atoms can be put together in so complex a pattern as to produce man," his *confessio* that "man is a tribute to the subtlety of matter,"[5] is of a different order to the "reverence" that Schweitzer has for life, and the "awe" to which Shils refers, as "man stands . . . before his vitality."[6] There is a fundamentally different apprehension of the character of life in these responses, and the account I shall give will have greater kinship with the second than with the first. To put it crudely, to understand what life is, we need to turn to biology rather than physics. Physics per se has no room for the concept of life. The language of life comes from a different sphere of human discourse.

In offering an account of life *in general*, I shall take as the basic subject of life the living organism. The primary bearers of life, I shall assume, are organic wholes, whether they are simple, like *Amoeba proteus*, or complex, like *Eucalyptus macrocarpa* or *Homo sapiens*. In virtue of what do we characterize all these as *living* organisms? Hans Jonas is one of relatively few to have offered a general account. He provides a subtle and imaginative exploration of the phenomenon of life,[7] and I shall draw heavily on his discussion. In brief, Jonas argues that the livingness of an organism is constituted by its being the site of a self-integrating and self-renewing metabolic process. Each of these elements calls for some comment.

The "processual" aspect is important. Suspension of the process—as is attempted in cryonics—is essentially the suspension of life, a suspension of processes that are constitutive of livingness. And cessation of these processes will mean no less than the death of the organism. Determining when the (relevant) processes have

31

ceased may be problematic—as debate over the determination of death has shown. There are various reasons for this, but among them is the fact that metabolic processes are not sufficient to establish the presence of life. For the processes involved may not be specific to life, or, more importantly, to life when it is predicated of an *organism*. There is more to life, and certainly more to the life of an organism, than metabolic processes. The processes must be self-integrating and self-renewing.

To say that the processes are self-integrating is to draw attention to the way in which, in the constant and complex interchange between the organism and its environment, the organism retains its identity over time. The plant takes in carbon dioxide from the air, water and nutrients from the soil, undergoes numerous internal changes, and releases oxygen into the air, etc., but it does not lose its identity as the particular plant it is. This identity may be retained despite some fairly dramatic metamorphoses: seedling to oak, caterpillar to butterfly. The metabolic processes are structured so as to constitute and preserve certain natural boundaries between the organism and its environment. According to Jonas, the continuous identity of the organism is constituted, not simply by a cognitive synthesis in the mind of an outside observer, but by the ongoing activity of the organism itself.[8] By virtue of this self-integrating activity, the living organism is said to be "spatially self-transcendent."[9] There is an outer environment that exists *for it* in a way that does not hold true of particulars in the inanimate world.

The metabolic activity of a living organism is also self-renewing. The interchange that occurs between organism and environment is directed to the organism's perpetuation. It is a teleological process initiated by the organism itself (whether or not it is capable of sustaining it without assistance), and marks it out as "temporally self-transcendent."[10] When those processes cease, so does life. Jonas speaks of the life process as consisting in the organism's opposing its own being to the environment in the way that "self" is opposed to "other"—in which the other is kept at a distance. Yet at the same time, life's continuation depends on an assimilation of the environment. What is "other" must also be incorporated into the "self." Organism and environment thus stand in a "dialectical" relationship of dependence and independence.[11]

Within the framework provided by this general account of life, Jonas then proceeds to distinguish different levels or orders of life—plant, animal, and human, each having its peculiar character and requirements. He does this by reference to the different ways in which plants, animals, and humans "meet the challenge of the world," ways determined by their inherent structures and capacities.[12] Plants are (generally) immobile, and the metabolic processes that constitute their life must be sustained by elements that exist in close spatial proximity. This is distinctive of their being as plants. Animals, on the other hand, are mobile, a fact that is important to their life, since the sources of their sustenance are not as "available" as those of plants. Animals must search out their sources of sustenance, and this demands of them certain powers of perception. To this Jonas adds "emotion" (feeling)—as that which bridges the gap between the organism and its sources of sustenance. It is "emotion" that moves the animal, and "perception" that directs its movement.[13] Jonas is aware that in speaking of "mobility," "perception," and "emotion," he is speaking of phenomena that are emergent in varying degrees. There is a large gap between the sponge attached to the rock and primitively sensitive to the conditions for its persistence (i.e., without beliefs) and the lion in pursuit of its prey. But he wishes to use such terminology to draw attention to a certain evolutionary continuity (as well as discontinuity) in life. In the case of human life, there is (at least) the additional capacity for imaging, and with it a freedom from the immediate demands and constraints of the environment far in excess of that possessed by other life.[14] Our "imaginative" capacity, our capacity for "symbolic" life—for representation, reflection, and abstraction—brings with it the possibility not only of creative activity, but also of accountability.

There is a great deal to be said for Jonas's account of life. Although somewhat burdened by a linguistic medium that is technical and dense, it is also rich and evocative. Indeed, the characterization he provides is as good as we have. It addresses life as a phenomenon about whose significance we might be genuinely concerned. His discussion is not, perhaps, sufficiently fine-grained to enable us to settle all the borderline questions that demand our response, but its broad brush strokes provide a useful backdrop against which that detailed work can be done.

Of particular importance to Jonas's account, and of relevance to my own discussion, is his contention that one way to conceptualize the development from plant to animal to human is to think of it as an increasing articulation of *freedom*. In the Introduction to *The Phenomenon of Life*, he writes—with evident sensitivity to its strangeness and difficulties—that "it will be the burden of one part of our discourse to show that it is in the dark stirrings of primeval organic

33

substance that a principle of freedom shines forth for the first time within the vast necessity of the universe—a principle foreign to suns, planets and atoms."[15] At its most primitive level, this freedom must

> denote an objectively discernible mode of being, i.e., a manner of executing existence, distinctive of the organic *per se* and thus shared by all members but by no nonmembers of the class; an ontologically descriptive term which can apply to mere physical evidence at first. Yet, even as such it must not be unrelated to the meaning it has in the human sphere whence it is borrowed, else its extended use would be frivolous. For all their physical objectivity, the traits described by it on the primitive level constitute the ontological foundation, and already an adumbration, of those more elevated phenomena that more directly invite and more manifestly qualify for the noble name; and these still remain bound to the humble beginnings as to the condition of their possibility.[16]

In this characterization of life, as a *substratus* or embryonic manifestation of freedom, we find the beginnings of one argument for its positive valuing. At a later point I will consider in greater detail the merits of Jonas's subthesis. At the moment, however, it is sufficient that we see the phenomenon of life as a self-integrating and self-renewing metabolic process.

Levels *of life*

As my exposition of Jonas has already brought out, life is not an undifferentiated phenomenon, but manifests itself with varied richness and complexity. For many thinkers, some dimensions of this variation have carried decisive significance. "Ascending" orders or levels of life (say, plant-animal-human) have been given increasing affirmative value and status, or affirmative value and normative status has been reserved for life at "higher" levels. These levels are seen as having a natural or biological basis, which can be articulated in terms like those already proposed.

We should not automatically and uncritically assume that the tripartite division of the living into plant, animal, and human possesses some valuational significance. The interests that enter into biological differentiations need not correspond—or at least need not correspond exactly—to the interests that directly motivate and inform our practical concerns. This is the burden of what has become known as the naturalistic fallacy. It is not some unbridgeable gap between "fact" and "value" that constitutes the continuing force of this reputed fallacy, but a recognition that conceptualization occurs against a background of sometimes incommensurable interests. Scientific classificatory and explanatory interests lead us to conceptualize the world in a different way to historical, aesthetic, and practical interests. The interests that have led to our distinction between plant, animal, and human may not have been of the same kind that bear on our practical moral choices.[17] At the same time, the incommensurability of our practical and classificatory interests is not something that can be assumed or timelessly settled. It is because *we* are the agents of conceptualization, and our deepest orientations are normative, that we should not be surprised to discover that what sometimes appear to us as normatively neutral enterprises are in fact structured by deep-level normative concerns. To some extent, the debate about models in biology is a debate about how *we* may most appropriately conceive of the world of human experience.

It needs to be remembered that the plant-animal-human division predates scientific biology, and has been traditionally associated with valuational considerations. The rise of modern science, particularly where it has favored materialist/mechanist explanatory models, has brought the significance of this division into question, along with that between organic and inorganic. Where this has occurred, it has prompted an opposite reaction—like that found in hylozoism and panpsychism. The inorganic has been invested with qualities normally associated with the organic. At the cosmic end of this reaction, doctrines of a world soul or *Gaia* have been promulgated. G. T. Fechner's view that "the earth is a creature . . . , a unitary whole in form and substance, in purpose and effect . . . and self-sufficient in its individuality,"[18] has been followed up more recently by the hypothesis of James Lovelock that "living matter, the air, the oceans, the land surface [are] parts of a giant system . . . [exhibiting] the behaviour of a single organism, even a living creature."[19] Though this proliferation of biotic levels may be as problematic as its reductionist opposite, it reinforces the extent to which questions of life and value may be intertwined.

The plant-animal-human trichotomy is usually associated with an order of ascending value or status, in which likeness to humankind (or God) functions as the standard. This can be articulated in terms of freedom (as in Jonas), as a matter of sentience and/or rationality, or as a matter of divine ordering. In some of these cases, experimental and speculative work in the biosciences has cast doubts on the neatness of this trichotomy. There are said to be substantial gray areas on the inorganic-organic, plant-animal and animal-human borderlines, and we are cautioned against appealing to the classification as a basis for differential valuation and treatment.

Dimensions *of life*

My last remarks suggest a more fine-grained approach to the valuing of life. The plant-animal-human trichotomy may be seen as providing at best a crude reflection of those underlying features of particular life-forms which are the true bearers of (different grades of) value. A somewhat different grouping of possibilities could look like the following:

1.   Organismic life. Life may be predicated not only of organisms, but also of cells, tissues, and populations. The claim is sometimes made, however, that the primary bearer of life-value is not the cell or tissue, but the organism—where, in Himsworth's words, the life-bearer "is capable of functioning as an integrated whole and is thus able, or capable of being made able, to support an independent, self-sustaining existence."[20] The capacity for "independent, self-sustaining existence," with its telic overtones, is here seen as a feature of life-bearers that gives them a certain status, some claim to our recognition and deference.

It is not altogether clear what the capacity for "an independent, self-sustaining existence" amounts to. It is arguable that even individual adult humans lack that capacity, and possess it only as members of a social group or even larger bio-community. Himsworth's use of the saving phrase, "or capable of being made able," is intended to get over some of the problems generated by the distinction between "viable" and "pre-viable" fetuses, and therefore to accord a certain normative status to organisms at any stage of their development. The issue of "mere" potentiality is thus not addressed.

The focus on individual organisms as the primary bearers of value (broadly conceived), rather than on populations or species, probably reflects the standpoint of human valuers for whom individual (human) life—however intertwined with that of others—takes a certain normative priority. For when it comes to our valuing of nonhuman organisms the focus often changes. Such lives are often treated as substitutable. We are often inclined to regard one snake or sheep as being much the same as another. But this change of focus may manifest only an anthropocentric prejudice. Ethologists and others who attend closely to animal life are often impressed by the "individuality" of their animal subjects.

2. Conscious life. For many, however, it is not the capacity or potential for "independent, self-sustaining" life that grounds different kinds of value, but "consciousness." An awareness of the world in which they are situated, of being "on the *qui vive*," is said to give special significance or standing to those living organisms which possess it. In consciousness, there is not simply an interaction with the environment, but an apprehension or "grasping" of it.

It is not easy to work out exactly what is involved in the possession of consciousness. Daniel Dennett has offered a helpful systematization of our somewhat confused references to the phenomena to which it is ascribed.[21] We need, he suggests, to distinguish "Intentional" from "non-Intentional" uses of "consciousness." When speaking of consciousness in its Intentional sense, we have in mind locutions such as "conscious *of*" or "aware *that*." We refer to it non-Intentionally when we speak of something's "being conscious" or "being a conscious form of life."

So far as Intentional consciousness is concerned, Dennett claims that our ascriptions are governed by two factors—control over behavior and the ability to make introspective reports. When something adjusts its behavior appropriately in the face of some environmental condition, we are inclined to say that it was conscious or aware of it. Likewise, when someone is able, by introspecting, to report a certain content, we consider him conscious of that content. But although these two factors are usually associated, they need not be, and this leads to a bifurcation in our idea of what it is to be conscious of some X. Animals, according to Dennett, can be conscious in the first, but not the second sense; humans are the primary subjects of consciousness in the second sense. It is to be noted, however, that these two understandings of Intentional consciousness do not rule out the possibility of sophisticated machines being conscious in either or both senses.

In its non-Intentional sense, consciousness may refer to either a capacity to be alert or the state of being alert, where either behavioral control or the ability to make introspective reports may be the capacity referred to.

It is not easy to see how mere consciousness, so understood, serves to invest its possessor with affirmative value or, alternatively, to make normative demands of us. True, certain kinds of affirmative value or normative demands may not be possible unless consciousness can be attributed to the being in question, but this is not the same as saying that consciousness invests a being with valuative or normative status.

3. Self-aware life. A being may be conscious without being self-conscious. Self-consciousness, or self-awareness, requires a capacity for introspection not possessed by some organisms that might in some sense be considered conscious. A self-conscious being must be able to represent *to itself* in some way what it is conscious of. On Dennett's account, self-consciousness in this minimal sense would be attributable to a hypothetical self-scanning language-using machine.[22] A richer notion is more likely to be intended by those for whom self-awareness is a (broadly) value-making characteristic. There needs, in addition, to be some awareness on the part of the organism that it is a "self." Some such view seems to be espoused by Michael Tooley. In his discussion of abortion and infanticide, he argues that for an organism to have a moral right to life or, as he prefers, "a moral right to continued existence," it must at some time have possessed "the concept of a continuing self or mental substance," and of its being such a self or substance.[23] (We must note, however, that Tooley claims only that this is necessary to an organism's possession of the right to life, not that it is also sufficient. For the latter to be the case, the organism must also *desire* to continue to exist as a subject of consciousness. Note too, that what self-consciousness preconditions on this account is not intrinsic affirmative value so much as a claim against interference by others.)

4. Sentient life. Those who write on "the value of life" frequently conflate consciousness with sentience. Sentience can be viewed as consciousness of a particular kind, consciousness characterizable by pleasure/pain discriminations. This may be linked up with value in various ways. One strategy is to argue that valuing—as a choice-oriented practice—is possible only where pleasure and pain can be felt. Affirmative valuing is seen as a form of preference. Note, however, that if this is correct, it does no more than posit a precondition for the capacity *to value*. It does not show the sentient being to be *of value*.

Of course, if other conditions are satisfied, and a sentient being can also be shown to be a valuer, then we are well on our way to establishing it as a being of value. Whatever else we affirmatively value, we value valuing, and respect valuers.

But even if sentience does not serve to invest the life it conditions with affirmative value, it may nevertheless be thought sufficient to constrain the actions of moral agents towards it. This at least has been the contention of hedonistic utilitarians. In a famous footnote, Bentham wrote:

> The day *may* come when the rest of the animal creation may acquire those rights which never could have been withholden from them but by the hand of tyranny. The French have already discovered that the blackness of the skin is no reason why a human being should be abandoned without redress to the caprice of a tormentor. It may one day come to be recognized, that the number of the legs, the villosity of the skin, or the termination of the *os sacrum*, are reasons equally insufficient for abandoning a sensitive being to the same fate. What else is it that should trace the insuperable line? Is it the faculty of reason, or, perhaps, the faculty of discourse? But a full-grown horse or dog is beyond comparison a more rational, as well as a more conversable animal, than an infant of a day, or a week, or even a month, old. But suppose the case were otherwise, what would it avail? the question is not, Can they *reason*? nor, Can they *talk*? but, Can they *suffer*?[24]

Eligibility for (legal) rights, on this view, is not grounded in the eligible being's affirmative value, but in the regard that moral agents should have for the ratio of pleasure to pain that will be produced by their acts or their acceptance of rules governing acts of the contemplated kind.

But the holder of such a view is also committed to believing that no wrong or disvalue will be involved if a life is painlessly snuffed out, unless it can be argued both that (a) the world will thereby be deprived of more pleasure than pain, and (b) there is an obligation to maximize pleasure. We might be able to circumvent problems caused by the first condition by replacing the eliminated being by another, likely to realize as great a surfeit of pleasure over pain. But the second condition is implausible if thought of as an unbounded requirement. Most utilitarians limit the obligation to maximize pleasure to what we might call the "vital" alternatives confronting an agent. An unbounded pleasure-pain calculus would be too strenuous and self-alienating.

5.   Realized life. Affirmative value, it is sometimes argued, is not attributable to life merely in virtue of its organismic character, or its capacity for conscious, self-conscious, or sentient experience. These may provide a framework for limitations on what moral agents may do with or to such life, but this is not the same as according it affirmative value. Value, it may be argued, unlike constraint, must be based in accomplishment of some kind, some fulfillment of *telos* or instrumental purpose. Religious writers who speak of humans as possessing an "alien dignity" sometimes adopt this position. Hans-Walter Wolff, for example, writes: "Everything that is said about breath and blood in the anthropology of the Old Testament is instruction in the ultimate reverence for life. But this reverence is not derived from the manifestation of life itself; it is based on the fact that the breath and blood belong to Yahweh, and therefore life without a steady bond with him and an ultimate tending towards him is not really life at all."[25]

On this view, human life is to be revered because it is animated by, sustained by, and oriented to God. Humans are special repositories of divine creativity—not, however, as mere receptacles, as though they could exist apart from this divine endowment. It is humans as living-beings-who-belong-to-God. Nevertheless, unless humans acknowledge and rightly display this divine ownership, their lives will lack status as an object of *reverence*. However, Wolff does not mean to imply that apostate life may be disposed of at will. From lack of affirmative value, ineligibility for recognition-respect cannot be inferred. For though such "life" does not—or should not—inspire reverence, its deficiencies are remediable, and its destiny belongs to Yahweh.

The idea that human *value* consists in some form of accomplishment seems to have been deeply embedded in classical Greek thought. It was not so much the human capacity or potential for certain kinds of achievement that endowed people with affirmative value, but their actualization of those capacities or potential—in particular, their actualization in conformity to goodness or virtue. It was not mere being that gave humans their value, but their being exemplars. It was not human life that was valuable, but what human life could exemplify.[26]

None of the positions discussed in this section attaches affirmative value or normative status to mere "livingness." It is only as life is characterizable as organismic, conscious, self-aware, sentient, or realized, that it is said to have some valuative or normative standing. To this point, I have not said much by way of assessment of these alternatives. That will come. It is enough for present purposes that we recognize these sources of the plurality that may be involved in broad appeals to life's value.

Lives

In recent discussions of the value of life, it has become fashionable to argue that it is not "life as such" that is the locus of affirmative value or focus of respect, but "lives." Only that which can be said not merely to "live" but to "have a life" is said to possess life of intrinsic affirmative value or to demand our deference. It is *the life* of Mozart, or *the lives* led by American citizens, that ground our normative concern, not the biological processes that constitute something's merely being alive. The focus, as James Rachels puts it, is on biography rather than biology, on history rather than metabolism.[27]

The focus on lives rather than life needs more elaboration. For, as Richard Wollheim has observed, "lots of things which aren't even living have lives, such as alpha-particles, or refrigerators, or the great city of Venice, and of those things which have lives and are living, many don't lead their lives, such as oak trees, or the saints in heaven, or domesticated animals."[28] Some of Wollheim's examples may be controversial, but his remarks indicate a certain looseness in the idea of "having a life." What Rachels is seeking is a class of lives that can be said to be *led*, and not merely *had*. Lives that are led are constituted by purpose and not merely (or at most) natural teleology. Led lives can be spoken of as empty or full, as fulfilled or unfulfilled. We do not think of the life of an oak as characterizable in any of these ways. For that to be the case, the oak would have to live and experience life in a certain way—it would need to have a memory, to have the capacity to be aware of its experiences in certain ways, to be able to connect and foster these experiences. And this it almost certainly does not.

For Rachels, the distinction between "lives" and "life" is crucial to the issue of life's "sanctity"—by which he understands its "value." Understood merely as placing affirmative value on things that are alive, the doctrine of the sanctity of life has no moral bite. Only when it is understood as "placing value on *lives* and on the interests that some creatures, including ourselves, have in virtue of the fact that they are subjects of lives," can the doctrine be sustained.[29] Only the life of lives can be seen as inherently valuable, worthy of nurture, and of being cherished.

This puts quite severe limitations on "life" as an object of value. Since only certain organisms "have the mental wherewithal to have plans, hopes or aspirations,"[30] the doctrine of life's *sanctity* will be fairly restricted in its scope. This is as Rachels intends, though he does not think that animals need be excluded. Nor need his argument be taken to rule out the possibility of according *some* other value, albeit not *sanctity*, to nonbiographical life.

Group *life*

The focus of appeals to life's value may be broad or narrow. Such appeals may be to life in general, where the intention is to encompass any living organism, or they may have in sight some particular individual. But there are, as well, various intermediate possibilities.

In environmental ethics, it is sometimes species-life, no less than (and maybe more than) individual life that is valued (in its broadest sense). What may be thought particularly bad or reprehensible about the killing of bald eagles or whooping cranes is not the death of individual eagles or cranes, but the extinction of the species. Individuals may (up to a point) be replaceable; the species is not.

A variety of factors seem to bear on the valuing of species-life. Many of them are anthropo-utilitarian: economic, aesthetic, scientific, and recreational values. But preservationists, believing such arguments to be too probabilistic, often yearn for a less instrumental approach.[31] Some claim that there is a special affirmative value in *diversity*. Diversity is linked with ideas of complexity, richness, intricacy, stability, etc., whereas its lack is associated with austerity, monotony, instability, shallowness, etc. Human beings, as valuing agents with a penchant for the challenge of complexity, are inspired by nature's diversity, seeing it as inherently preferable to nature with a less complex character.

Other writers focus not so much on species-diversity, as on what they see as an inherent *fitness* in or as the integrity of a self-renewing ecosystem, like the perfection of an intricate mechanism, its interlocking parts and adaptations evoking a sense of wonder and awe. With this approach there often goes as well an attempt to reconceptualize humankind's relation to nature, seeing humans as not standing apart, in some biologically privileged position, but as belonging to a larger whole with a health, and hence a good, of its own.

Obviously there must be limits to such doctrines. Diversity does not automatically imply harmony, and there may need to be some way of ranking species-life when conflicts occur. The elimination of the smallpox virus occasions no mourning, and the same might be said of other scourges, whether it is Dutch elm disease, rabies, or AIDS. Nor need ecosystems be accorded some kind of untouchability. Most ecosystems are in some fairly constant state of flux, and intrusions need to be considered on a case-by-case basis. However, the very admission that these kinds of assessments may be necessary suggests that value of some kind can be attributed to some kinds of life-groupings.

In the human sphere, a special value is sometimes accorded to lineages and ethnic groupings. The perpetuation of a family name is often considered to have an intrinsic affirmative value, and its dying out an unfortunate loss. Interference with a lineage may be accomplished not only through failure to produce progeny (or progeny of the appropriate sex?). Edward Shils has suggested that genetic engineering can also violate the integrity of a lineage. Much the same might be argued of A.I.D. or certain forms of surrogacy, though whether the integrity of a lineage is of such importance to render such practices improper is another matter.

Loss of ethnic identity through cultural assimilation may also be regretted. A certain diversity in human experience has been lost, and human life is seen as being that much the poorer. Of course, here too there is probably a presumption of innocuousness. Cannibalism we can do without—though we may hope that other features of the culture could be perpetuated in some way. In some cases—e.g., the initiation rites of infibulation and clitoridectomy—there may be a serious tension between the values of cultural identity and integrity, on the one hand, and, on the other, values such as sexual enjoyment, freedom from suffering, and equality of status.[32]

We should note, however, that when we speak of cultural life—of its perpetuation or loss—we are speaking of life in a rather different sense to that with which this book is primarily concerned. Although genocide may well destroy a distinctive culture, and with it something of great intrinsic value, a culture may disappear without its bearers losing their lives. Assimilation may be as destructive of distinctive cultural values as genocide.

43

Group life, then, may be of different kinds—it may refer inter alia to species persistence, the perpetuation of lineages, the preservation of a culture, and each of these forms of group life or existence needs to have different arguments made out in its behalf.

Review

When value is attributed to life, it is not necessarily attributed to a single phenomenon. It may be life *in general*—livingness—that is affirmatively valued or deferred to, though more likely it is the life of *organisms* or of some particular kind of organism. Frequently, of course, it is specifically *human* life that is in view—though even then the rubric under which it is being affirmatively valued or deferred to may not be clear. It may be the *lives* led by humans (or others) that is claimed to possess affirmative value or warrant deference; it may even be human *species-life* or, more limitedly, *lineages* to which affirmative value is accorded or deference given.

There need be nothing exclusive about these different valuings of life. Some writers, in fact, explicitly intend life of more than one level or dimension. Shils, for example, writes that "the postulate of the sanctity of life refers to three forms of life: (1) the life of the lineage; (2) the life of the human organism; and (3) the life of the individual human being, as an individuality located in a discrete organism, possessing consciousness of itself as an agent and patient both in the past and present, having the capacity for psychic 'self-locomotion.'"[33] Moreover, it need not follow from such a multiple valuing that each level/dimension is equally valued, or that each is valued for the same reasons.

As we saw in chapter 1, when investigating the vocabulary of value, valuational issues are implicit in the analytic task. That is as true here as it was there. Articulating life-concepts is not a valuatively neutral enterprise, but reflects larger theoretical and practical commitments. Definition or analysis is not something that can be settled prior to an investigation of rationales, but can be provided only in the context of a consideration of rationales.

There is, further, some interdependence to the investigations of chapters 1 and 2. Some value terms are more closely associated with particular kinds of life than others. Dignity is usually associated with human life or lives. Organismic life is not normally claimed as a right, though it may be viewed as an object of reverence. But we have to talk here of "affinities" rather than tight connections. Our moral and conceptual structures in this area are not very tightly organized, and even where connections are reasonably well established, there is nothing to stop the questioning of such alliances. Such questioning may be needed to counter the dead weight of tradition.

We are now in a somewhat better position to look more closely at the substantive questions concerning life's value. I shall begin by considering whether there is anything about organismic life as such that sets it apart as something to be affirmatively valued or deferred to. Then, despite the smudged edges of the distinction, I want to consider in turn plant, animal, and human life as loci of affirmative value or special consideration. In the course of this investigation, I shall discuss in greater and more systematic detail some of the broader *Weltanschauungen* that sustain appeals to life's value.

THREE

ORGANISMIC LIFE

The absolute ethics of the will-to-live must reverence every form of life, seeking so far as possible to refrain from destroying any life.   —Albert Schweitzer[1]

The last two chapters will have made it clear that appeals to "the value of life" may take a variety of forms with a diversity of reference. The rich vocabulary of value reflects the importance of choice to us—the significance attached to directing our conduct along one path rather than another. Yet these value-terms bear on choice in different ways (and with different degrees of directness). Some, as we have already noted, are more concerned with choiceworthiness, others with choice-constraint, and though they are often connected their focus is very different. The appropriateness of a particular value-concept may depend inter alia on the kind of life whose affirmation is in question.

In this chapter I examine those favorings of life that treat life itself or livingness, or, slightly more narrowly, organismic life as a choice-relevant or choice-constraining consideration. This discussion is not intended to exclude some further differentiation based on the kind of life involved. The fact that the life will also be plant, animal, or human may have a bearing of its own on the question of value. These latter differentiations will be taken up in subsequent chapters. At this point I am interested in asking whether there is something about simply *being alive* that calls for our affirmation or our deference.

There are a number of ways in which livingness may be claimed as choice-relevant or choice-constraining. It may be seen as sacred or good, as possessing sanctity or worth, as an object of respect or reverence, or as something rightfully safeguarded. Insofar as life itself is considered a good, it may be thought to be so in itself or instrumentally. And what is favored when livingness is affirmed may be life in some diffuse sense—as that which can be predicated of cells or tissues—or of the kind attributable to organisms, where we are dealing with self-integrating and self-renewing structures. I shall be concerned here with arguments favoring organismic life, whether as a means to the realization of certain goods, or as something intrinsically valuable, as something that possesses sanctity or demands our respect or reverence, and so on.

There can hardly have been a more concerted attempt to establish the importance of organismic life—indeed, of life-in-general—than that associated with Albert Schweitzer in the early part of this century. It is to Schweitzer and the tradition he has fostered that I shall first turn. From Schweitzer I will proceed to the arguments of Hans Jonas, and from there to traditions whose roots are more explicitly religious.

Schweitzer's "reverence for life" ethic

In 1915, while interned in Africa, Schweitzer began writing his critique of civilization, East and West.[2] The proper end and sustaining condition of civilization, he claimed, is "the spiritual and ethical perfecting of the individual."[3] But in the dark shadow cast by World War I, this goal's failure to materialize was painfully obvious. Instead of enlightenment and progress, *decay* and *meaninglessness* seemed everywhere evident. A new start was needed. What was called for, he believed, was a worldview (*Weltanschauung*) that would be world- and life-affirming,[4] and that would give preeminence to its ethical dimensions. In his judgment, past writers and thinkers afforded only limited assistance. Oriental writers tended to be world- and life-denying, and the Western tradition, though world- and life-affirming, had failed to accommodate this within a viable worldview. The ethical dimension had been all but eliminated from it. One reason for this could be found in the attempt to construct a cosmic worldview (*Totalweltanschauung*) on "knowledge"—that is, on the results of rational "discovery and invention"—rather than from "elemental experience."[5] Important though "knowledge" is, particularly in its technological applications, it provides no basis for a cosmic worldview. It is unable to make *sense* of the cosmos: it can reveal no pattern or *telos*. He wrote:

If we take the world as it is, it is impossible to attribute to it a meaning in which the aims and objects of mankind and of individual men have a meaning also. Neither world- nor life-

47

affirmation nor ethics can be founded on what our knowledge of the world can tell us about the world. In the world we can discover nothing of any purposive evolution in which our activities can acquire a meaning. Nor is the ethical to be discovered in any form in the world-process . . . To understand the meaning of the whole—and that is what a world view demands!—is for us an impossibility. The last fact which knowledge can discover is that the world is a manifestation, and in every way a puzzling manifestation, of the universal will to live.[6]

Theories of living that derive from "knowledge" fail to show "individuals how to deal directly and naturally with reality." Such theories remain in an important sense "external" to their experience, where what is needed is something "elementary and inward."[7] At an individual level, Schweitzer believes, this has led to ethical skepticism, and at a societal level to nationalism.

The metatheory that Schweitzer presents here bears significant similarities to the one I adopted in chapter 1. A practical worldview is not given by the world itself, as conceptualized by the sciences. It is only from the standpoint of ourselves as choosers that the world has practical meaning for us. Schweitzer speaks of this as a life-view (*Lebensanschauung*)—a standpoint with respect to the world that has priority over a cosmic worldview (*Totalweltanschauung*): "What is decisive for our life-view is not our knowledge of the world but the certainty of the volition which is given in our will-to-live. The eternal spirit meets us in nature as mysterious creative power. In our will-to-live we experience it within us as volition which is both world- and life-affirming and ethical. . . . Worldview is a product of life-view, not vice versa."[8] In commencing with a life-view, and working out from that to a worldview, Schweitzer believes that he is reversing the order characteristic of European philosophy.[9] That order has its focal point in Kant, whose formalistic approach to morality subordinated the natural feeling of compassion to the sense of duty, and the decline he represented was hastened by Fichte, Hegel, and Schleiermacher. The utilitarians, Schweitzer believes, were no better, and their doctrines led naturally to social Darwinism.[10]

Even so, Schweitzer does see some precursors to the position that he believes he is enunciating with a purity, clarity, and simplicity hitherto unknown. Schopenhauer, for example, recognized the centrality of sympathy, and even postulated an underlying cosmic "will-to-live," but his thought ended in pessimism. Closer to Schweitzer's position is Nietzsche, who shared with Schopenhauer the idea of an underlying "will-to-live," but differed from him in interpreting it as a drive for self-mastery or self-perfection. Where Nietzsche went wrong, Schweitzer thinks, was in his failure to see that the drive for self-mastery required of individuals a certain self-transcendence (that is, "the repressing of natural impulses and natural claims on life"), in which they devoted themselves to the will-to-live as it *universally* manifested itself.[11] Nietzsche focused on self-affirmation to the neglect of world-affirmation. Even closer to his own position Schweitzer acknowledged two virtual unknowns—Fouillée and Guyau.[12]

As I have noted, the centerpiece of Schweitzer's position is a life-view that has its roots in what he speaks of as "will-to-live." For Schweitzer, will-to-live is the basic given in "elemental thinking" or naive experience. Our consciousness of it is not consciousness of an alien drive, an externally determined construct, but of something that is fundamental to the character of all living things:

> If we ask, "What is the immediate fact of my consciousness?" . . . we find the simple fact of consciousness is this, I will to live. Through every stage of life, this is the one thing that I know about myself. I do not say, "I am life"; for life continues to be a mystery too great to understand. I only know that I cling to it. I fear its cessation—death. I dread its diminution— pain. I seek its enlargement—joy.[13]

From this fundamental datum of consciousness Schweitzer develops his "reverence for life" ethic. He speaks of it as being "given inherently in the will-to-live."[14] And he claims that the regard for one's own life that is implicit in the will-to-live must, as a matter of consistency, be shown equally to other lives, other wills-to-live: "What shall be my attitude toward this other life which I see around me? It can only be of a piece with my attitude toward my own life. If I am a thinking being, I must regard other life than my own with equal reverence. For I know that it longs for fullness and deepness of development as deeply as I do myself."[15]

So much for the broader context and contours of Schweitzer's position. It is time to take a closer look at some of the details.

Schweitzer's basic datum is the awareness: "I am will-to-live in the midst of other wills-to-live." What, exactly, is the content of this "will-to-live"? Is it a simple biological "urge"—expressed in the natural impulse for food, the avoidance of danger, the disposition to reproduce, or does he have something more sophisticated in mind—such as the pursuit of certain projects, plans, and purposes? Given the scope of Schweitzer's ethic—its equal reverence for every kind of life—something like the former (the biological urge) would seem to be demanded by his form of argument: one that depends on seeing oneself as will-to-live in the midst of other wills-to-live. Yet even that may be more than his position can support: how are we to conceive of the will-to-live he attributes to plants and ice crystals?[16] This problem aside, there is something worryingly anthropomorphic about the terminology of *will*-to-live, a worry that is given clearer shape when he talks about the dead beetle that "was a living creature, struggling for existence like yourself, rejoicing in the sun like you, knowing fear and pain like you."[17] Or when he claims more generally that all nonhuman forms of life "long for fullness and development as deeply as I do myself."[18]

However, I think we can ignore some of the more contentiously personalistic or anthropomorphic expressions that Schweitzer uses, and can capture the central thrust of his position by speaking instead of the *telē* of living organisms—the patterns of development and activity they are structured or disposed to manifest and in terms of which they can be said to flourish or languish. Each living organism has its own *telos* or pattern of development—whether limited, as in the case of plants, or relatively open-ended, as in the case of humans—and will-to-live may be interpreted as the somewhat anthropomorphized expression of this telic dimension. Whether the example of the ice crystal can be conveniently assimilated even to this understanding is to be doubted, though a teleological account of organic life enables us to understand Schweitzer's extension at least as metaphor.

Insofar as living organisms have a *telos*, they can be said to have a good—they are subject to conditions that will promote or enhance their health or development. However, those things that are good *for* them are not necessarily good *to* them, in the sense of being *recognized as* or taken to be good for them. It is to be doubted whether a plant apprehends its good as such—it is to be doubted whether it "longs for fullness and deepness of development as deeply as I do myself."

Nor does the fact that something *has a good* show that it *is good*. Judging something to be good of its kind does not imply that the kind of thing it is is good. Schweitzer does not show how the fact that every living organism is structured towards its own flourishing, makes it an appropriate object of reverence to other living beings. Although he speaks of the ethic of reverence for life as being "inherently given" in the will-to-live, or even more gnomically of "the ethical mysticism of Reverence for Life" as "rationalism thought to a conclusion,"[19] there is no straight logical connection between the apprehension of oneself as will-to-live in the midst of other wills-to-live and a universalized ethic of reverence for life. Nevertheless, he does consider that some sort of reasonable inference from one to the other can be made.

The general gist of Schweitzer's reasoning seems to be as follows: I am aware within myself of an impulse towards the preservation and enhancement of my life (self-perfection). This impulse is accorded a certain priority in my practical decision-making. I am also aware that other living things are subject to the same kind of impulse or disposition. As a matter of consistency, therefore, I can give their will-to-live no lesser priority than I give my own. Invidious choices may sometimes have to be made, but they cannot be made on the basis of the inherent superiority of my own will-to-live.

If this is a correct rendering of Schweitzer's position, it would seem to involve a number of non sequiturs. From the fact that I am aware of myself as will-to-live and give this impulse a certain priority, it does not follow that other wills-to-live give their self-perfection the same priority, Nor does it follow that *I* should give their will-to-live the same priority as I give my own or equal standing with my own, nor that I *should* give it the priority I do in my own life. Whether or not any of these follow would seem to depend very much on the precise content of the will-to-live.

There is the further problem of deriving *reverence* for (my own) life from the awareness of an inner impulse toward life. It is a serious problem if "life" is thought of biologically—as a self-integrating and self-renewing metabolic process. But Schweitzer tends to view it as something more—as a drive toward "self-perfection." He writes that the will-to-live "carries within it the impulse to realize itself in the highest possible perfection," and of the "craving for perfection" as being "given with our existence. We must act upon it, if we would not be unfaithful to the mysterious will-to-live which is within us."[20] "Perfection," here, can be understood in one of two ways: either (a) as a tendency toward the realization of some inherent end, or (b) as the realization of something intrinsically valued. Schweitzer tends to conflate them: notice the dual overtones of "unfaithful." Only the first kind of perfection can be "given," but

51

the second is needed if the case for reverence is to be established. The second, however, presumes that telic realization is not merely a good for the living organism in question, but also a good thing. To be sure, if for every organism telic realization is a good, then it may seem hard to resist the conclusion that it is also a good thing. But once we get away from the assumption that these ends are compatible, the transition is harder to make.

How far is Schweitzer prepared to go in his defense of life? Sometimes he speaks of his "reverence for life" ethic as "absolute," though he seems to use this term only to indicate the "ideal" character of his ethic: we must always strive to preserve and enhance life, even if it does not always prove possible to achieve; we must never rest content with the deterioration of life.[21] It is in this vein that he speaks disparagingly of men and women today being "haunted" by the question "whether life is worth living," and of the way in which "stoicism" has "suggested" to us that "we are free to choose whether to live or not." Such neutrality, he believes, ignores "the melody of the will-to-live, which compels us to face the mystery, the value, the high trust committed to us in life." This being so, "when we find those who relinquish life, while we may not condemn them, we do pity them for having ceased to be in possession of themselves."[22] Suicide does not gainsay the naturalness and general primacy of will-to-live, though it does, he thinks, represent a failure to appreciate its claim upon us.

Even so, the telic character of Schweitzer's commitment to life means that the affirmative value that life inherently has for him is bound up with the possibility of its realizing itself as the kind of life it is. In *Indian Thought and its Development*, he writes:

> In many ways it may happen that by slavish adherence to the commandment not to kill, compassion is less served than by breaking it. When the suffering of a living creature cannot be alleviated, it is more ethical to end its life by killing it mercifully than it is to stand aloof. It is more cruel to let domestic animals which one can no longer feed die a painful death by starvation than to give them a quick and painless end by violence.[23]

Although Schweitzer here offers what are essentially utilitarian reasons for disposing of life, he is not committed to a utilitarianism of life. The point, rather, is that the creatures concerned can no longer flourish as the kind of creature they are—their afflictions are inimical to any tolerable degree of self-realization.

So, then, for Schweitzer, it is not *merely being alive* that grounds reverence for life—as though reverence would require us to keep a body functioning long after it is able to manifest its character as the distinctive being it is. The attitude of reverence is yoked to the telic character of the life of organisms.

In this respect, as in certain others, Schweitzer's position is similar to Nietzsche's. Nietzsche saw the general questioning of (human) life's value as pathological—as a sign of cultural decadence or "sickness." However, just as Schweitzer was not prepared to accept Nietzsche's vitalistic elitism, he may not have been prepared to go as far as Nietzsche in respect of those who had become invalids. For Nietzsche, where (human) life could no longer be "added to," where it was no longer capable of "ascending," then it no longer retained its character as "life," as something through whose enhancement affirmative value could be created.[24] It no longer retained its character as "life" since, for Nietzsche, the essential character of life is to be found in the "will to power." Such life as remained was to be characterized as "sick." So he speaks of the "indecency" involved in mere vegetation: "The invalid is a parasite on society. In a certain state it is indecent to go on living. To vegetate on in cowardly dependence on physicians and medicaments after the meaning of life, the *right* to life, has been lost ought to entail the profound contempt of society."[25]

Despite their general affinities via a telic conception of life, Nietzsche's vitalistic elitism—or, as Schweitzer would put it, his commitment to life- or self-affirmation at the expense of world-affirmation, probably leads him to different practical conclusions with respect to the maintenance of life. For Schweitzer, although the dependent "invalid" may not be able to ascend, he or she may still manifest some of the distinctive qualities of human existence. The invalid has not been divested of all those qualities that give human life its distinctive values. Nietzsche, with his emphasis on "will to power" and its übermenschlich ideal, has too limited a conception of human life.

Nevertheless, as Schweitzer himself recognized, choices between lives sometimes have to be made, and we may wonder how they are to be made. Not surprisingly, Schweitzer has some difficulty at this point. He does not believe that human beings should submit themselves to the "blind affirmation of life" that is found in nature.[26] Yet his vitalistic egalitarianism seems to preclude him from anything but a survival-lottery in which the fair distribution of life chances is determined by lot. Sometimes indeed he appears to favor a consequentialist maximizing of self-perfection, which would not involve a ranking of the self-perfected beings of different living things, but doing that which is most likely to optimize self-perfection—within, and not across, lives. This, too, could require considerable self-sacrifice or self-abnegation. On yet other occasions he seems to be interested in maximization of "Will-to-Live" in a more abstracted, mystical sense. But he never quite embraces that kind of maximization theory. He does not want to argue that the self-perfection of countless millions of disease germs is to be preferred to the self-perfection of a few thousand human beings.

When Schweitzer eschews the ranking of lives, he does so for epistemological and pragmatic reasons, and not because he cannot accept that some lives may have greater affirmative value or status than others. He is skeptical of the basis on which we would rank wills-to-live. "How can we know what importance other living organisms have in themselves and in terms of the universe?"[27] And he believes that if we start ranking them, we will discount the evil of injuring nonhuman wills-to-live.

There is to be no down-playing of the fact that I am "a mass-murderer of the bacteria which may endanger my life."[28] What is needed is a heightened sensitivity to the wills-to-live around me that may be affected by my choices, and then the responsible choosing of that course of action that best expresses reverence for life: "We must never let ourselves become blunted. We are living in truth, when we experience these conflicts more profoundly. The good conscience is an invention of the devil."[29]

Despite this, Schweitzer frequently accords a certain primacy to the demands of human life. He affirms the "necessity" of taming nature and of "winning fields from the jungle," enterprises that involve sacrificing some life for other. The operative word for Schweitzer is "necessity": "The farmer who has mown down a thousand flowers in his meadow as fodder for his cows, must be careful on his way home not to strike off in wanton pastime the head of a single flower by the roadside, for he thereby commits a wrong against life without being under the pressure of necessity."[30]

It is not clear what precise moral function Schweitzer intends "necessity" to have. In some contexts, the appeal to necessity *excuses*, unlike overriding alternative values, which *justify*. But mostly Schweitzer talks as though the destroyer of life—even when acting under "the pressure of necessity"—is stained. His hands are dirtied. But the situation is not quite the same as that of the public official, who, for the sake of the public interest, "must" act in a way that contravenes ordinary moral expectations. The public/private dichotomy, which tends to bear importantly on regular "dirty hands" cases, plays little part in Schweitzer's thinking.

However, the suggestion of moral stain is not always prominent. Sometimes Schweitzer appears to do no more than remind his reader that necessity does not absolve from accountability: "All through this series of decisions [the Man who is truly ethical] is conscious of acting on subjective grounds and arbitrarily, and knows that he bears the responsibility for the life which is sacrificed."[31] The decision is not removed from the sphere of judgment, but no verdict is delivered. There may also be a suggestion that what is ethically acceptable legitimately varies from person to person. As he says elsewhere: "In ethical conflicts a man can arrive only at subjective decisions. No one can decide for him at what point, on each occasion, lies the extreme limit of possibility for his persistence in the preservation and furtherance of life."[32] It is for this reason that Schweitzer did not prescribe his own lifestyle for others.

I think we have now said enough about Schweitzer's position to appreciate its character and weaknesses. Schweitzer believes that he can identify within living organisms a basic will-to-live—a telic dimension to their existence that may be fostered or frustrated. Living organisms have a good or welfare that can be promoted, endangered, or inhibited. What we do to them may be good or bad for them.

It is tempting to conclude from this, as I believe Schweitzer concludes, that what is good *for* an organism is also good *to it*, and that what is bad for an organism is also an evil to it, that is, is good or bad *from its point of view*. It will also be tempting to conclude, as I believe Schweitzer concludes, that attempts to rank the lives of organisms would almost inevitably be chauvinistic or speciesist—it is natural to rank our own will-to-live more highly than that of others—and that the only rational position to take would be one that gives each life an equal claim to its self-realization. But not all living organisms can be said to have a point of view in terms of which they can be said to *give priority* to their own will-to-live. That they are internally structured so as to realize it is not the same as their *giving it priority*. It is here that Schweitzer's personalistic anthropomorphism misleads him.

In saying this, I do not want to suggest that only human beings have a point of view in terms of which certain factors can be *apprehended* as good or bad for them. My point is the more limited one of suggesting that the very *general* character of Schweitzer's "reverence for life" ethic cannot be sustained on the basis he provides. We cannot assume that a plant is *dedicated* to its flourishing in anything like the same way that humans are dedicated to theirs. *Reverence* for life, one's own as well as that of others, is not a product merely of blind instinct or inherent structure, but rather of a perception of one's life as a source of valued enterprises.

Life as a manifestation of freedom

The difficulty with Schweitzer's position is not that he fails to establish that living things *have* a good, but that they *are* good—and that their good is something we should revere. Further, the fact that we see our own telic fulfillment as affirmatively valuable, as something to be revered, is not sufficient reason for seeing the telic realization of other lives as similarly valuable. It may be that we value or revere our own will-to-live—as against merely recognizing and conforming to the urge to live—because of the character which that fulfilled life possesses or is able to possess—say, its choicemaking character or potential for virtue. But these factors may not be appropriate to other wills-to-live. And even if other living things do seek to further their lives—where the urge to flourish is consciously followed—we cannot conclude that they place the same store by that telic realization as we do. This of course raises some very large questions about what is involved in our varied *valuing* of things and whether or not we can presume that other living things do not value their own lives in the strong senses that we may do. But whatever our response to these questions, the fact remains that there is a less than straightforward connection between Schweitzer's basic intuition and reverence for life.

A way out of some of these difficulties is suggested by those writers who see in organismic life a manifestation, albeit inchoate, of freedom. If we accept, as such writers generally do, that freedom is good, and, moreover, intrinsically good, we have the makings of a case for the intrinsic value of organismic life.

Herbert Spencer appears to tread this path. With Coleridge, he sees in all life a "tendency to individuation,"[33] and he maintains that this is a distinctive mark of organismic life. The presence of and tendency toward increasing "individuality" also provides the foundation for his evolutionary morality,[34] which has as its fundamental requirement the freedom of each living being to develop its individuality without limit, save that constituted by the like freedom of other organisms to develop their own individuality. Spencer believes that the tendency toward individuality is more highly developed in beings with "high degrees of vitality" than in those beings which are structurally simpler. Starting with sponges (*Porifera*) and compound polyps (*Alcyonidae*), he endeavors to show a correlation between "vitality," "structural individuation," and "individuality"—where the last of these refers to a kind of inner freedom. The greater the vitality, the greater the structural individuation and the greater the individuality. Crucially, given the character of morality, such individualities should be permitted to "unfold without limit" to the extent that this does not interfere with the similar unfolding of other individualities.[35]

There is a more subtle exploration and development of this approach in the writings of Hans Jonas. In the last chapter we noted his contention that all life is a manifestation of freedom. Metabolism, he writes, "is itself the first form of freedom,"[36] since the identity of an organism is not reducible to its matter. Despite the constant interchange between the organism and its environment, in which matter is lost and gained, the form remains the same. In the precariousness of this independence that an organism has from its environment—its "self-transcendence"—we have a "germinal freedom" that is progressively elaborated as we ascend the scale of organic evolution.[37] Jonas speaks of the freedom that characterizes organisms at the lower end of the evolutionary scale as "an objectively discernible mode of being," as an "ontologically descriptive" notion which constitutes the "foundation, and already an adumbration, of those more elevated phenomena that more directly invite and more manifestly qualify for the noble name."[38]

Views such as these raise several questions. The first two questions are closely linked: Is it acceptable to say that all organic life is a manifestation of freedom? If so, is the freedom of a kind that we would consider (broadly) valuable? The two questions are closely connected because it is common—though not uncontroversially necessary—to characterize freedom in such a way that it is by definition an affirmatively valued or privileged state of being.

For Jonas, the freedom of organismic life consists essentially in the transcendence of form over matter—the organism's achievement of what he speaks of as its "hazardous independence of the very matter which is yet indispensable to its being."[39] For Spencer, individuality consists in the unfolding and development of distinctive inner powers, a capacity possessed to different degrees by different organisms. Should we grace such conditions of being as manifestations of freedom, albeit embryonic? I see no decisive objection to doing so, though it may be less problematic to speak of organisms as possessing a form of *independence*. Both writers argue with some persuasiveness that what is uncontestably (human) freedom can be seen as an *elaboration* of a feature that is present even in the lowliest organism. There is an observable continuity that is worthy of conceptual bracketing. The fact that in humans this independence is mediated by a vastly more sophisticated sensory apparatus, which enables spatial and temporal boundaries to be much more dramatically transcended, does not gainsay this.

Yet there are also significant dissimilarities that make it appropriate to question the *normative status* of freedom so understood. The problematic character of merely vitalistic freedom can be brought out by comparing the situation of the infant with that of the mature adult human being. Jonas and Spencer are both committed to the view that the infant and the adult, as living organisms, are sites of freedom, albeit to different degrees. Yet the freedom that is "noble" and that demands our respect, does not belong to them equally. Such freedom as the infant has is significantly removed from the creative activity that both writers see as constitutive of the particular nobility of humankind. The infant is not a source of reasons for action that *dignify* it or demand our forbearance. Though we may not remain oblivious to its desires, those desires do not determine our conduct in the way they would were they the desires of a mature adult. Rather, or at best, our conduct with respect to them is largely determined by their being the expressions of an organism who *will come to possess* the peculiar dignity of freedom. It is the prospect rather than presence of "noble" freedom that is action-guiding.

The position looks even more problematic when mature adult humans are compared with organisms that lack the natural capacity to develop into decision-makers. Such organisms we nurture and use for ends of our own devising, even though this may not be compatible with the full realization of their *telē*. What claim does their "freedom" have on us? Are we under some duty to allow or even assist their telic fulfillment?

But we should not too readily treat these questions as rhetorical. For it might be contended that our intuitions in this area display a deep chauvinistic prejudice—an illegitimate discrimination in favor of our own kind—that they are baseless and question-begging, and that other organisms have some claim to their self-development, if not as much as we do.

It will help us to keep our bearings in the swamp we have just reached if we divide up our questions a little more carefully. When talking broadly about the value of freedom, and, more particularly, about the value of the kind of freedom that may be ascribed to any organism by virtue of its livingness, we might have in mind either (a) that by virtue of which a moral constraint is placed on our interference with the organism's realization of its tendencies or desires, or (b) some affirmatively valued property possessed by the organism. And in relation to the latter, we may have in mind either (b_1) an instrumental, or (b_2) an intrinsic good. These are not, of course, exclusive alternatives, and there may in fact be deep-level convergences in their bases. Nevertheless, at the level at which the questions of the previous paragraph were asked, their conflation invites confusion.

(a) When we say of an organism that it manifests the kind of freedom that places a principled moral constraint on interventions by others—a nonderivative right to noninterference—we are ascribing to it freedom of a fairly narrowly defined kind. We generally have in mind what Stanley Benn refers to as "autarchy": a developed capacity for rational choice—an ability to recognize reasons for action, an ability to evaluate these by means of relevant standards of evidence and inference, and the ability to make choices based on these evaluations.[40] The possession of such capacities marks out the organism concerned as a center of rational choice, capable of charting its own course and therefore entitled to others' desistance.

I do not find it plausible to suggest that autarchy is a possession of all living organisms—any more than I find it plausible to ascribe it to all living human organisms. Autarchy is a very specific achievement, an achievement available (so far as we know) only to animals whose cerebral neocortex has developed to a high level of complexity. The respect and dignity that are due to humans at a certain stage of their maturation and nurture are not appropriate to plants, or to animals that lack the wherewithal for this kind of development.

Of course, autarchy may not be the only kind of freedom that generates a claim against interference by others. If the interests of organisms that are constitutive of their "independence" can be said to generate certain kinds of entitlements—welfare rights—those organisms may have a derivative claim to noninterference. There may be some reason to refrain from subverting their telic development. But this is clearly different from the principled forbearance that is mandated by autarchy.

(b) That which constitutes the value of merely vitalistic freedom may not be some exclusively choice-constraining feature, but instead some property or set of properties constitutive of its "independence" that is deemed to give it a measure of choiceworthiness. The issue is not whether there is some *loss* when an organism dies—naturally *it* loses something—but whether vitality as such, and the kind of freedom or independence which that vitality represents, gives valuers some reason to maintain or promote it. There are several possibilities, some focusing on vitalistic freedom's instrumental value, and some on its alleged intrinsic value.

(b$_1$) In the sense that I am using it here, for something to qualify as an instrumental value it must not only be a (good) means to some end, but also be instrumental to an end that is in itself good. Even so, instrumental values possess a contingency that makes generalizations somewhat risky. They may be neither necessary to nor sufficient for the valued ends they serve, and to which their value is yoked. This need not, however, gainsay their—albeit secondary—importance.

Put most comprehensively, vitalistic freedom is partially constitutive of the *adaptability* of organisms, enabling them thereby to realize their *telē*. It is by virtue of their independence that living organisms are able to realize their good. It might appear as though the greater the spatial and temporal restrictions on an organism, the more vulnerable it would be to circumstances that could impede or jeopardize its telic realization. In that case we should expect plants to be more vulnerable than animals, and humans less vulnerable than plants and animals. And this would be a reasonable enough expectation, were it not for the fact that different organisms require very different conditions for their flourishing. Humans, though capable of great independence (autonomy), also require a complex and finely balanced set of conditions for the achievement of their much more complex good. So while, in the abstract, the limited independence of plants might seem to render them especially vulnerable, they also have a relatively limited range of needs, and may do just as well—if not better—than humans in the struggle of life.

But why should organismic flourishing be affirmatively or otherwise valued? What is the good end that vitalistic freedom serves? We need to remember that this question does not magically present itself to human consciousness, but is posed from the standpoint of human consciousness. So the answer we give must be capable of *human* affirmation. Frequently, however, this demand has been interpreted to call for no more than a crudely instrumentalist valuation of nonhuman life: nonhuman organismic life is to be accorded affirmative value only insofar as it contributes to the pursuit of worthy human purposes—those human purposes being the sole bearers of intrinsic value. But the assent of human consciousness need not demand such crude instrumentalism. Human consciousness may acknowledge some kind of value in the *richness* and *diversity* of organismic life, independent of any contribution which that life makes to this or that human end. In other words, it may be valued intrinsically, as an ingredient in the preference-set that constitutes the good for (most?) human consciousness. This is not to exclude the possibility that the complexity and diversity that characterizes organismic life may also have an instrumental value.[41] That which is intrinsically valued may also have instrumental value.

But is the richness and diversity of organismic life, a richness and diversity served by vitalistic "independence," something of intrinsic value? This is not a question to which Jonas devotes himself. However, it has been answered affirmatively by several writers, and I shall pursue that argument further in chapter 7.

(b₂) The controversy that has surrounded the idea of *value* (see sup., pp. 7–9) is at the same time a controversy over the understanding and intelligibility of the idea of *intrinsic value*. The discussion has focused alternately on valuing as an activity of valuing subjects and on value as a property of valued objects. Some writers have gone so far as to distinguish two notions of intrinsic value. However, as I indicated in that earlier discussion, I am reluctant to acquiesce in the polarization that this controversy has engendered. We are not confronted with a simple either/or, in which a choice has to be made between "subjective" and "objective" conceptions of intrinsic value. Conceptualization is an activity, reflecting intersubjective interests, in which the world of human experience is rendered intelligible. Attributions of value reflect the interest in and potential for choice, and ground themselves in those features of the world that are believed to count in the choosing process. In this sense, certain objects are seen as inherently valuable. They are recognized by valuers as having choiceworthy properties.

Does vitalistic freedom or independence possess intrinsic value? In other words, is there something about vitalistic freedom that makes it worth having/experiencing/preserving for its own sake? In the case of specifically human freedom—autarchy—the fact that freedom is constitutive of our sense of ourselves as moral persons ensures its status as intrinsically valuable. This, however, is not the case with the more attenuated vitalistic freedom that inheres in every living organism by virtue of its livingness. There does not seem to be any obvious reason why we should affirmatively value it apart from the contribution it makes to the adaptability of organisms. Though we may affirmatively value their continuance for the richness with which they invest our experience, what we value is not vitalistic freedom as such, but organismic richness and diversity.

But perhaps the connection between organismic richness and diversity and vitalistic freedom is stronger than the previous sentence suggests. Vitalistic freedom is not merely instrumental to organismic diversity, but is a constitutive element in organismic life, and it is organismic life as such that contributes to the diverse experience which human consciousness perceives as intrinsically valuable.

If we are to make this out, I think that we may be required to show that the diversity and richness that are valued for their own sake and in which organismic life is an ingredient, cannot be *mechanically* replicated. Plastic lawn and plastic trees may be too crude to satisfy our expectations, but presumably we could imagine mechanical substitutes of increasing complexity—look-alikes that may be indistinguishable from the real thing, except, perhaps, to the expert eye.

The problem here may be somewhat analogous to that posed by Robert Nozick's "experience machine."[42] Suppose that it is possible to duplicate the *experience* of doing those things we find worth doing for their own sake, by being plugged into an "experience machine." Would there be any loss? Our tendency is to think that there would be. We value our *engagement* in activities over and above the satisfactions gained from the mere experience of engaging in them. Can we—in similar fashion—say that there is a satisfaction involved in knowing that the life of the organism before us is self-regulated (in the vitalistic sense) rather than programmed, that some of the satisfactions of diversity reside in a recognition that objects whose diversity contribute to our satisfaction are *really alive* and not just apparently so? Although there is something technically dazzling about an artificial plant that duplicates the behavior of a living one, the living organism has a depth and nature of its own, to be wondered at and explored, something not perspicuous to us and of our making.

There is probably something to be said for an argument of this form, and I will attempt to press it a little further in chapter 7. We should note, however, that what is valued when we affirmatively value the really alive over the artificially alive is not the vitalistic independence shown by the former, but simply the fact that it is "natural" rather than "artificial." We might have the same preference for real over artificial sand dunes, or a natural over an artificial beach, or a rocky outcrop over a simulated plastic one. It may be more a matter of history than of outcome. If our technology improves to the point where we are able to produce real life and not some mere simulation of it, then only history will distinguish it.

Life as a gift of God

Schweitzer and Jonas both endeavor to avoid theological appeals in establishing their claims for life.[43] Clearly, in a substantially secular environment, there is a tactical advantage in appealing to considerations that have the widest acceptance. But some writers believe that the values to be accorded organismic life arise directly—and even exclusively—out of certain theological commitments. Most often such theological arguments focus on the kinds of value that are to be accorded *human* life. Nevertheless, the forms of argument used have much more general application (and this in fact constitutes one of the common objections to their use in the human case). Two such arguments are commonly employed—one in which life is seen as *God's gift*, the other in which it is seen as *God's property*. Sometimes they are combined. Here I shall discuss them separately.

Those who base the value (in a broad sense) of life on its being a gift of God do not usually think that more needs to be said. The appeal to its origination in God's creative beneficence is taken to be sufficient to establish its value, as something to be treasured, or at least not tampered with. There might be debate about God's existence, and whether life comes from God, but for proponents of the position, once it is granted that life is God's gift, all that needs to be said has been said.[44]

This is not the appropriate place for a general discussion of theism—of whether and what sort of God exists. My interest here is in whether and how the claim that life is a gift of God contributes to the view that livingness is to be valued or respected. For the intelligibility and cogency of the position are not as immediately apparent as its protagonists believe.

One of the things that may alert us to its problematic character is a conceptual awkwardness and complexity involved in speaking of life as a *gift*. A normal precondition of the gift-relationship is the existence of a (personalized) recipient as well as a donor. But where (human) life (in general) is the gift, there is no preexisting recipient. The recipient comes into being with the gift. The gift-relationship seems to presuppose the livingness of the gift's recipient. In this context it makes more sense to speak of *continued* life as a gift, for this can be intelligibly viewed as part of God's providential activity toward the already living. And some of the biblical writers speak of *eternal* (i.e., realized) life as God's gift.[45] For here humans are assumed to preexist the gift that is bestowed. For the same reason it makes sense for parents to speak of their children as a gift of God, for they preexist their children. We do not run into problems if we claim only that life is *given* by God—for that will just be another way of saying that God brought us into being. Not everything that is given is ipso facto a gift.

The gift-relationship presupposes not only a recipient, but also one to whom personal categories can be applied (legal persons may qualify). How then are we to construe the life of plants? As God's gift to them? Not in any perspicuous sense. Insofar as plant—and perhaps animal—life can be seen as God's gift, it must be seen as God's gift to *us*.

In making these slightly pedantic observations, I am trying to draw attention to what Stevenson spoke of as an argumentative "persuasiveness"[46]—in this case in the view that life is to be valued because it is a gift of God. For why talk about life as a gift unless its affirmative value, at least, is already presupposed? The issue is not whether the gift-status of life provides an argument for its value, but whether, because of the value implied in something's having gift-status, life is to be seen as a gift. Schopenhauer thought not. Life, he claimed, is in no sense a gift, but something thrust upon one: "It is evident that one would have declined such a gift if he could have seen it and tested it beforehand."[47] We need not share Schopenhauer's pessimism about life to appreciate the point he is making. In accepting life as a "gift" rather than as a "burden" or "curse," its value tends to be implied. Strictly, perhaps, its gift-status requires only that the donor value it; but if that is so, the question of our valuation of it, because of its gift-status, is left quite open.

There is an ambiguity here, that may help to account for the assurance with which the argument is often propounded. It is not altogether clear whether the position under discussion attaches life's value to its *gift-status* or to its *divine source*. What gives life its affirmative value: its being a *gift*, or its being a gift *of God*? If it is the former, then it behooves us to consider the character of the life referred to: whether it possesses qualities appropriate to an object of value. Mere organismic life may not qualify (except instrumentally). It may be no more than a precondition for the kind of life that is properly subject to positive valuation. Schopenhauer's problem will need to be faced. But if it is the latter, then value need not reside in some quality of the life in question, but in its source. The life may have no inherent value, except as a symbol of a relationship that has value. We may compare it with the trinket or memento given by a lover to a loved one, where the value lies in what is represented by the gift: "it is the thought that counts." It is the giver that is esteemed, and because of that, the gift.

There is, however, more to be said for the view that life's affirmative value lies in its being a gift *of God* than my comments thus far have suggested. For there is a something artificial about the claim that life valued because of its source "may have no inherent value, except as a symbol of a relationship that has value." If life is seen as an expression or manifestation of God's love and goodness—as indeed it is often seen—then its value is not merely "symbolic," as though it had no inherent value. It is worthy of being affirmatively valued as an expression of God's goodness.

Be that as it may, there is still the question of import. Those who see life as a gift or as a manifestation of God's goodness frequently speak as though it establishes life's sanctity or inviolability. But there is no warrant for this in the argument as I have presented it. Indeed, to take such a strong line would create serious internal tensions, for the conclusion covers all forms of life—plant and animal, as well as human. At best, the argument establishes that we should have a certain *regard* for life—see it as being of some moment, to be weighed up or taken into account when choosing our path. And this, moreover, need not imply that all life is to be affirmed equally for such purposes. The (Judeo-Christian) religious tradition at least does not so value it—as can be seen from the different attitudes taken towards plant, animal, and human sacrificial offerings.

In sum, I am inclined to think that the argument from life's gift-status is credible only if the focus is on its being *God's* gift. If the emphasis is on its status as a gift, the question of its affirmative value is begged. But even if its divine source is emphasized, there is uncertainty about how we are to handle it. The latter question is usually thought to be answered more precisely by appeals to the second argument, in which life is seen as *belonging* to God.

Life as God's property

The life that God gives, God may also take away. In this claim, the view that life is God's gift is combined with the view that it remains God's property: it is a gift in trust, a loan, of which we are the stewards. It is in this combined form, indeed, that theological arguments for life's value are most often found. Nevertheless, the two positions can and need to be distinguished. Like the first argument, the second is usually directed to human life. But there is really nothing about its main premises that requires this restriction. And there are traditional sources for a more general interpretation.[48]

According to John Locke, all humans are "the workmanship of one omnipotent and infinitely wise Maker; all the servants of one sovereign Master, sent into the world by His order and about His business; they are His property, whose workmanship they are made to last during His, not another's pleasure."[49] Locke's position may be generalized to cover all living things, to reckon every living (and for that matter nonliving) thing as God's property, to be disposed of only within terms which he has set. For Locke, as for many others in that tradition, this would not have been interpreted to exclude the human disposal of plants and animals, since they were assumed to have been created by God for humankind.[50] Individual humans, however, remained the exclusive property of God, and could not, without God's explicit permission, dispose of themselves or each other.

Although an argument of this kind can be found as far back as Plato's *Phaedo*,[51] there is little doubt that Locke's use of it reflects the burgeoning of capitalist social relations, with their emphasis on private property rights. For Locke, these rights were of fundamental and far-reaching significance, giving the right-holder extensive authority with regard to the use and disposal of the property in question. This gives Locke's position a somewhat paradoxical quality, for he wants to argue not only that God has property in us, but also that we have property in our own persons.[52] We are to be about God's business, but we are also to be about our own. Surely we cannot assume that God's business and ours will always coincide, even if our going about God's business is taken to include living the life of a rational being. Locke resolves the tension to his own satisfaction by positing certain "natural" limits on liberty: certain fundamental limitations placed by God on the conduct of life. Suicide, for example, contravenes this "law of nature," along with assault and murder. In recent secularized versions of Locke's position, exorcised of such natural law, ownership of self has been claimed to give a person absolute right to dispose of himself, so long as this does not constitute a violation of the rights of others.

Those who argue for life by saying that it belongs to God do not necessarily intend to attribute—or succeed in attributing—some intrinsic or even instrumental value to it. If life is God's property, that may be a choice-constraining fact about it, but not something that shows that *we* should affirmatively value it. It may be wrong for us to take it into our hands to interfere with life, but this does not presuppose or establish the goodness of life. The focus in property relationships is primarily one of direction or control.

However, insofar as life is viewed as *God's* property, the position becomes more interesting. If God is affirmatively valued, and along with God, God's workmanship, including life, then life will most likely be valued by those who see it as God's possession. If we are prepared to go along with Locke, this status is reinforced by his labor theory of value and of property. According to Locke, it is by virtue of the labor expended on raw materials that they come to acquire the affirmative and socioeconomic value they have, and, because they thus bear the impress of their enhancer, come to be owned by that individual.[53] The whole structure of Locke's argument for private property rights depends on the valorizing influence of labor. True, what comes to have value, as a result of the labor expended on it, may be affirmatively valuable for and valued by the laborer alone. Nevertheless, in God's case, those who appeal to the argument will almost certainly affirmatively value what God values.

Taken together, the two theological arguments provide a framework for understanding why, within that perspective, life generally is affirmatively valued or deferred to. If it is seen at the expression and manifestation of a loving and benevolent Creator, the handiwork of One who is seen as supremely choiceworthy, its own affirmative value to us and claims upon us seem assured. Of course, such declarations carry little weight outside the theological framework in which they are cast, and we are still left to work out questions of relative value or competing value, but they indicate why it is common, within that framework, to see life as possessing some inherent value or normative standing.

Such arguments, however, are not without their own problems, as we shall see in chapter 6, where the argument that we are God's property has to contend with the claims of human freedom and responsibility.

Review

I have not endeavored to examine every argument that might be advanced in support of the values associated with organismic life. Many arguments that might be adapted to that end are more frequently and naturally associated with the defense of particular forms of life, and I will take them up when those forms are considered. Here I have concentrated on arguments in which the extension to organismic life in general is intended or easily made.

Even so, there have been some built-in restrictions on the scope and thrust of the arguments that I have been exploring. Schweitzer's defense of the affirmative value of all life cannot (despite some of his claims) be read as a defense of the equal and absolute value of all life. Schweitzer's telic conception of the will-to-live allows for a distinction between that which is flourishing, and that which is disintegrating or living-yet-dying, and it is not clear that Schweitzer wants to give life that has found its fulfillment and is now entering into its dying phase the same standing as life that still has its *telos* as a real prospect. He is not an aggressive defender of life, even though he is opposed to its gratuitous destruction.

There is a similar limitation implicit in the life-as-freedom argument. Underlying this argument is a conception of organisms as self-integrating and self-renewing complexes. A dying organism, though still alive, no longer manifests this character, even though it may be artificially maintained as a living structure.

The theological arguments, though perhaps the most common of all, and, under some interpretations, plausible inferences from the tradition within which they are articulated, are even less determinate with respect to what they sustain. If life is God's gift, it still needs to be determined whether there are any strings or qualifications attached to it, to limit or influence our choices with respect to life. If life is God's property, we need to know what rights are thereby implied, and to what extent the exercise of these rights may have been vested in human agents, etc. Some of these argumentative shortfalls we will take up again in later chapters.

Nevertheless, I do not wish to leave the impression that the arguments I have been considering are without merit. In chapter 7 I will endeavor to develop some of the more promising suggestions of Schweitzer and Jonas into an argument for the limited though positive affirmative value of organismic life.

F O U R

PLANT LIFE

God said, "Let the earth produce vegetation: seed-bearing plants, and fruit trees bearing fruit with their seed inside, on the earth." And so it was. The earth produced vegetation: plants bearing seed in their several kinds, and trees bearing fruit with their seed inside in their several kinds. God saw that it was good.   —Genesis 1:11–12[1]

The distinction between plant, animal, and human life has very deep roots. Some would say that it is naturally given, a differentiation that owes nothing to human conceptualizing interests. This probably overstates the case. Nevertheless, the distinction is firmly entrenched in both the Judaic and Hellenistic traditions out of which our culture has developed. The creation stories of Genesis no less than the systematic reflections of classical Greece proclaim a world in which plant, animal, and human life are radically, even if not always rigidly, differentiated. As to the precise significance of this differentiation, there is less agreement, though writers in both traditions tend to treat it as having, beyond its naive descriptive function, some sort of normative import: there is an ascending order of value from plant through animal to human life, in which the value of the former two is viewed instrumentally. As Aristotle put it: "plants exist for the sake of animals, . . . all other animals exist for the sake of man."[2]

But though this is the dominant view, there are other strands to our cultural inheritance, and some of these have gained a greater and more visible following in recent years. The chauvinistic anthropocentrism of the prevailing tradition has been challenged by more integrative and holistic understandings, in which merely instrumental attitudes to plant and animal life have been overtaken, or at least substantially modified. In this chapter I will look at some of these revitalized approaches, as well as traditional arguments, fo-

70

cusing particularly, though not exclusively, on their implications for some kind of valuing of plant life.

Arguments directed to the different valuings of organismic life in general will ipso facto bear on plant life in particular. It would require little effort to orient the arguments of the last chapter to plant life. In developing his "reverence for life" ethic, Schweitzer made frequent and explicit reference to plant life. And Jonas is no less insistent that the dialectic between plants and their environment is an inchoate expression of "freedom." The Judeo-Christian theological tradition likewise will comfortably accommodate, separately or together, the claims that plant life, on the one hand, belongs to God, and, on the other, comes to us as God's gift.

In this chapter, however, I do not want to settle for a simple repetition of these arguments, applying them a fortiori to plant life. Although to do so would probably capture some of the most substantial of such arguments, I wish to focus instead on several more nuanced arguments that are often directed fairly specifically (even if not exclusively) at plant life. Initially I shall discuss several holistic approaches, in which plant life is seen as an important element in a larger or global economy; then I shall consider some species-based or individualistic arguments, in which plants are considered in their own right rather than as part of a larger complex.

Individuals, species, and ecosystems

Focusing attention on the valuative or normative standing of plant life is not a simple or unproblematic matter. For one thing, the phrase "plant life" may encompass several distinct phenomena. It may refer to individual plants (allowing that there will sometimes be difficulties of individuation), to plant colonies (like gardens, crops, stands of trees), to plant species (or families, etc.), or to wilderness, to mention just some of the possibilities. Those who affirmatively or otherwise value plant life will not necessarily value all these equally; indeed, they are frequently in competition. We need, therefore, to be clear as to the precise focus of the arguments advanced.

There is, however, an even more problematic side to the focus on plant life. However time-honored the plant-animal-human division may be, and however natural we may find it, we cannot, at least in the present context, simply assume that it picks out an appropriate—or even the most appropriate—object for our normative consideration. Much contemporary discussion of plant life is focused not on plants *as such* or in vacuo but on something more general—on "nature," or "biotic communities," or "ecological systems," or "the biosphere," of which plants form only an—albeit important—constituent element. It is these larger wholes—which may include animals and humans as well as inanimate phenomena (such as rivers and cliff faces)—that are accorded normative standing. In this context, the affirmative value or standing of individual plants or plant colonies or species may be derivative.

For some writers, the values to be accorded plant life (in its various forms) are totally resolvable into its place within a larger ecological whole, much as an eye or vein acquires its value from its role in a functioning body, or a particular blob of paint gains its significance from the picture of which it is a constituent part. For other writers, however, plant life has a valuative or normative standing which is independent of its contribution to some ecological system, even though a particular plant or plant colony or plant species may have *more* to be said for it by virtue of its place within a larger ecological whole.[3]

There are some writers who construct these alternative foci into opposing metaethical theses—*environmental holism* and *environmental individualism*.[4] In a manner analogous to that found in much social theory, we are made to choose between ecosystems and their individual components as the primary (or sole) bearers of affirmative value or normative force. However, it does not seem necessary to me that we need to structure our investigation in this way (in either environmental or social theory!). There is a case for canvassing the possibility that both the whole and its component parts can be accorded intrinsic value or normative standing, and for treating conflicts that may arise on a case-by-case basis.

In the discussion that follows, therefore, I will not restrict my attention to plant life abstracted from its place in a larger ecological whole, but consider holistic as well as more narrowly focused arguments.

As in other contexts, arguments tend to divide broadly into those that affirmatively value plant life instrumentally, and those that accord it some kind of intrinsic value. The direct or indirect usefulness of plant life to affirmatively valued human ends probably needs little to be said in its defense, so dominant is it in our tradition. Much more problematic—and in some ways more interesting—are arguments designed to establish the claims of plant life in particular, or nature in general, without recourse to its utility. Those will occupy most of my attention. Nevertheless, despite their acknowledged limitations (from the point of view of some environmentalists), instrumentalist (or, as I shall call them, anthropo-utilitarian) arguments are not inherently repugnant, and there is some point to seeing how far they can be deployed in establishing some practical claims for different kinds of plant life. At the end of the chapter, therefore, I shall give some consideration to such arguments.

Since my interest in this project is to look at the whole range of life-related factors having practical import—with what I earlier spoke of as choice-relevant and choice-constraining factors—the instrumental/intrinsic dichotomy is too restrictive to accommodate all the arguments that follow. It may have some point when affirmative value is at issue, but it gets in the way when choice-constraining arguments are being considered.

Nature as sacred theatre

In an article titled "Ecology in Ancient Greece," J. Donald Hughes suggests that among the conceptions of nature current in Homeric and preclassical Greek thought the idea of it as "the theatre of the gods" was widespread and influential.[5] To see nature at work was to see the activity of the gods—Demeter in the grain fields and harvest, Zeus in the weather, and so on. Nature (*physis*) here encompassed more than plant (or even animal) life—storms and earthquakes were as much part of the divine theatre as fields and forests. Not that humans were to be uninvolved spectators. Within this conception, the cultivation of nature—in the form of plowing for food crops—was not precluded but rather given sacred significance. Nevertheless, human interventions required religious precautions, for human actions could have divine consequences in the form of floods or famine, as well as plenty.

It is Hughes' view that this ancient understanding of nature—which had some resonances within ancient Judaism—was fundamentally antithetical to the "consideration of nature *quâ* nature, and interposed between man and the environment a conceptual screen which interpreted phenomena in polytheistic terms."[6] It was not out of a respect for nature that people were reluctant to destroy a grove of trees, but for fear of offending the gods. Only when nature came to be seen as the "theatre of reason" could it be appreciated for its inherent character. True, he concedes, even as the "theatre of reason" nature need not be valued for its intrinsic qualities. The teleological understanding of nature that "reason" perceived could, as in Aristotle, result in a subordination of nature to human purposes; but equally it could, as in Theophrastus, accord to natural phenomena *telē* of their own, "interrelating with man but at the same time autonomous."[7] As the "theatre of reason," there were possibilities to the appreciation of nature that the theistic view precluded.

There is something to be said for Hughes' complaint. Viewed simply as a divine amphitheatrical production, nature's claim to respect was at best derivative. Its claims were also insecure. The further differentiation of some sites as places of special sacredness left other sites vulnerable to desacralization, and the eventual banishment of the gods left nature to the devices of Man. Yet, as John Rodman remarks, the "sacred theatre" view may not have been as alien to an appreciation of the natural environment as Hughes suggests, nor as unfriendly to it as the alternative Hughes champions. Modern conservationism, so far from needing a secularized understanding of nature, was in fact mediated via a sacralized conception of nature.[8] What is more, the championing of scientific reason may have had more to do with an absence of ecological consciousness than the hallowing of nature. Indeed, in the very project of conceiving of Nature as something external to—over against—Man, the major damage may have already been done. What "reason" has set itself against and above, it has also devalued: "With philosophy and science (the theatre of reason) was born that alienation of humanity from a reified Nature that is still preserved in the language of so much of the current ecology movement, most notably in the phrase 'natural environment.'"[9] If desacralization is the peculiar hazard of religious views, *hubris* may be the peculiar temptation of their "rational" counterparts.

Be that as it may, there nevertheless attaches to the "sacred theatre" approach a duo of well-known difficulties. One is evidential: what reason do we have for thinking of nature as sacred theatre? The other is normative: what follows from a sacralized view of nature? For it is only in the context of a developed theology that a sacralized view of nature will come to have normative import. Few of us nowadays are likely to be attracted to Homeric polytheism. But what reason do we have for preferring some other theistic stand? And supposing we do see in nature the stamp of divinity, what kind of normative perspective can be derived from that? Satisfactory answers to these questions *may* be forthcoming, but, unless a full-fledged theology is already presupposed, they are not close at hand.

The inclusiveness of "nature"

Rodman's complaint—that the divorce of Man from Nature that followed the elevation of reason may have been as destructive of a positive appreciation of nature as any theistic conception—suggests an alternative basis for the affirmation of plant life. If, instead of seeing Man as external and somehow superior to Nature, Man is seen as part of and continuous with Nature, the self-affirmation that is implicit in his activity as a valuing being may extend to the rest of Nature.

The character of this extension needs to be spelled out. There are several possibilities. Rodman calls attention to various reincarnationist tendencies in ancient Greek thought. The Empedoclean dictum—that "there is no birth in mortal things, and no end in ruinous death. There is only mingling and interchange of parts, and it is this that we call 'nature'"[10]—envisages, he suggests, "a kind of translation or recycling of cosmic energy from one form to another."[11] This can be seen either as a simple expression of human continuity with nature, or, as in Empedocles' case, as a claim to multiple identities: "In the past I have been a boy and a girl, a bush, a bird, and a dumb water-dwelling fish."[12] Were it possible to establish something like the latter position, there would be some reason for viewing a bush (or other plant), if not as a metamorphosed person, then at least as something into which a person has been transformed or out of which a person may emerge. If the further assumption is made that destructive interference with bushes or birds would be detrimental to the "soul" that animates them, there would be some ground, if not for affirmatively valuing them, at least for respecting them.

The strategic advantage of the Empedoclean position is that it works with what are fundamentally anthropocentric values. It is precisely because bushes and birds are thought of as being animated by person-related souls that they become candidates for respectful treatment. It is doubtful, however, whether the full Empedoclean doctrine of transmigration can be supported. Certainly we do not have any evidence for it. And it would not follow in any strict sense from a theory of the conservation and transformation of energy. Indeed, from the latter it might just as plausibly be argued that Man is no more significant than grass which grows and with-

75

ers,[13] or in more modern vein, the site of a complex chemical reaction.[14] Continuity with Nature might be used either to elevate Nature or to reduce Man. If the doctrine is to be made good, what needs to be established, is not that Man is of a piece with Nature, but that Nature generally, or at least living Nature, also possesses those features that serve to mark out Man as a locus of value (of some sort).

There is a "deep ecological" variant of this inclusivist position that may seem to avoid these problems. According to it, although subjectivity or selfhood (with its normative intimations) is taken as a basic datum, a strict subject-object distinction must be rejected. Subjectivity—whether human or animal—cannot be isolated as a discrete source of value. The position is well-summarized by Arne Naess:

> Deep ecology [involves] rejection of the man-in-environment image in favour of *the relational total-field image*. Organisms [are] knots in the biospherical net or field of intrinsic relations. An intrinsic relation between two things A and B is such that the relation belongs to the definitions or basic constituents of A and B, so that without the relation, A and B are no longer the same things. The total-field model dissolves not only the man-in-environment concept, but every compact thing-in-milieu concept—except when talking at a superficial or preliminary level of communication.[15]

Proponents give a variety of reasons for adopting this kind of image shift. J. Baird Callicott draws on quantum theory. Alan Watts writes out of a Zen Buddhist perspective.[16] But their intention is much the same—to link self and nature so integrally that value of some kind cannot be accorded to self and withheld from nature. Callicott is quite explicit:

> The principle of axiological complementarity posits an essential unity between self and world and establishes the problematic intrinsic value of nature in relation to the axiologically privileged intrinsic value of self. Since nature is the self fully extended and diffused, and the self, complementarily, is nature concentrated and focused in one of the intersections, the "knots," of the web of life or in the trajectory of one of the world lines in the four dimensional space-time continuum, nature is intrinsically valuable, to the extent that the self is intrinsically valuable.[17]

The conditional built into the last sentence betrays the weakness inherent in this position. The intrinsic value of the self is taken for granted. Callicott reports—with approval—that it is "treated very often as a privileged immediate datum of awareness, like the claim that I have a headache."[18] Perhaps so. But the self for which this privileged status is claimed (the self that is set somewhat apart from nature) is not the same as the self from which the intrinsic value of inclusive nature is strictly deduced. It may turn out that "the self fully extended and diffused" will no longer impress us intuitively/immediately with the intrinsic value reputedly possessed—albeit misguidedly—by the "conventional self." If what immediately invests the "conventional self" with its intrinsic value is its capacity for valuing, "the self fully extended and diffused" will take on a different coloration.

Gaia

Among the views recently promulgated to elicit an alternative awareness of—and in some accounts an increasing respect for—nature is the "Gaia" hypothesis. Named after the ancient Greek goddess of the earth, this inclusivist position likens the biosphere to a huge macroorganism, whose various parts interrelate and respond to each other much as do the various cells, tissues, and organs of the body.[19] Although it is not always clear from the descriptions of its advocates what kind of living creature the earth may be likened to, there is often more than a suggestion of personification. And if that were to be the closest analogy, we would have a strong reason for restraint with respect to our use of the earth's resources. The earth's flora (and fauna) would form parts of complex wholes (ecosystems) interacting with other such systems, like the various systems of the human body. They would possess affirmative value and normative status by virtue of their place within the larger organism.

Interpretations and discussions of the "Gaia" hypothesis have proceeded along two distinct but interrelated lines—scientific and moral. James Lovelock, the model's chief protagonist, is more interested in detailing the analogy than in extracting its ethical implications. According to Lovelock, a close examination of the interactions of living creatures, with themselves on the one hand, and the earth, ocean, and atmosphere that environs them on the other, reveals an interdependence and mutuality that is most appropriately construed as the integrative, self-regulating, and self-renewing activity of a single organism: "The entire range of living matter on Earth, from whales to viruses, and from oaks to algae, could be regarded as constituting a single living entity, capable of manipulating the Earth's atmosphere to suit its overall needs and endowed with faculties and powers far beyond those of its constituent parts."[20] In itself, this does not attribute a personal dimension to the biospherical complex. Lovelock accomplishes this further step by suggesting that in humankind Gaia has become self-aware: "The evolution of *Homo sapiens*, with his technological inventiveness and his increasingly subtle communications network, has vastly increased Gaia's range of perception. She is now through us awake and aware of herself."[21]

The scientific adequacy of this account—insofar as it constitutes the conclusion of a "geophysiological" inquiry—has been much disputed. I am not really competent to assess it.[22] But what is of more immediate significance to the present inquiry are the ethical implications, *supposing the Gaian model to be empirically plausible.*

At first blush, they appear to be considerable. If persons are to be accorded respect, and the biosphere is a person or quasi-person, it too should be accorded respect. But this inference—or at least some of its supposed implications—may be much too swift. A major reason lies in the putative relative invulnerability of Gaia. Lovelock, for example, believes that Gaia's homeostatic mechanisms are sufficiently powerful to withstand most of the intrusions that environmentalists abhor—even nuclear war may not cause irreparable damage. True, some actions we might take could be catastrophic to our human survival, and, as the center of Gaia's awareness, this might be thought damaging to Gaia. But with respect to Gaia's ongoing well-being, humans may not be very significant—they constitute the source of Gaia's self-awareness rather than of her self-determination. We are latecomers to Gaia's development, and she may well continue to thrive without us.

But suppose we were Gaia's control center and thus able to determine her progress. Then the possibilities for an anthropocentric approach to the natural environment would be considerable. We could make whatever instrumental use of Gaia we cared to, whether exploitative or conservationist. Gaia would display whatever *persona* we chose to give her. Given her relative invulnerability, the possibilities would be considerable, and there is little to cheer the environmentalist.

Lovelock's picture is in fact more finely nuanced than this. For he does not posit a uniform invulnerability, but suggests that Gaia, like other organisms, has some "vital organs." Tampering with these structures might cripple her or at least set her back. The wet-lands, the continental shelves, and the rain forests are all vital to Gaia's well-being, and may, through human intervention, be dam-aged sufficiently to harm her. Still, this is a much more limited de-fense of nature, and of individual natural things such as trees, than most conservationists—and many others—would be prepared to accept.

There is, moreover, a deep irony in the view that respect for Gaia is grounded in respect for persons. Remember, respect for Gaia is purchased using currency minted for our dealings with each other. But its purchase could have the effect of undermining that basis of respect. For Gaia has no need for this or that individual human—and maybe not any human—and if, as some writers have argued, we should adopt a Gaian ethic in which Gaia's well-being becomes paramount, then respect for *human* individuality could become rel-atively insignificant.[23]

Biocentrism and species-egalitarianism

A feature of all living things is that they have a good of their own.[24] Implicit in our conception of a living being is some idea of its proper functioning, its fruition or fulfillment. This may be furthered or hindered; the being in question may be benefited or harmed. In his impressively argued *Respect for Nature*, Paul Taylor claims that the good or well-being of a living entity such as a plant is something that has "inherent worth." What he means by the latter is that a state of affairs in which a living being's good is realized is better than a similar state of affairs in which it is not realized. And the attribution of inherent worth entails, he believes, "(1) that the en-tity is deserving of moral concern and consideration, . . . and (2) that all moral agents have a prima facie duty to promote or preserve the entity's good as an end in itself and for the sake of the entity whose good it is."[25]

In taking such a view, Taylor claims he is adopting an ultimate moral attitude—what he calls the attitude of "respect for nature." In speaking of it as an ultimate moral attitude, he means to indicate that it is disinterested, universalizable, and not derivable from some higher norm. Even so, it behooves us to ask what consider-ations should persuade us to the adoption of such an attitude. Tay-lor offers an extended defense.

The attitudes we bear toward living things depend crucially on our beliefs concerning them. Taylor therefore endeavors to show that the belief system supporting a respect for nature is internally coherent, well-ordered, consistent with our existing scientific knowledge, and acceptable as a way for "scientifically informed and rational thinkers with a developed capacity of reality awareness" to conceive of their world and of their place in it. He does not pretend to offer a tightly deductive argument: his case is structured like a "picture" or "map," whose various elements combine to form an ordered whole—what he refers to as "the biocentric outlook on nature." This outlook in turn "underlies and supports the attitude of respect for nature." In saying that the biocentric outlook "underlies and supports" the attitude of respect for nature, he intends to convey that "once we do grasp it and shape our world outlook in accordance with it, we immediately understand how and why a person would adopt that attitude as the only appropriate one to have toward nature."[26]

The biocentric outlook has, Taylor suggests, four major components: (1) humans belong to the biotic community "in the same sense and on the same terms" as nonhumans; (2) the earth's ecosystems comprise a complex interconnected web, in which the sound biological functioning of each individual depends not only on its environment but also on its relations to other living things; (3) each individual organism has a good that it pursues in its own way; and (4) humans are not inherently superior to other living things. Each of these components he discusses at length.[27]

1.   Taylor contends that whatever differences there may be between ourselves, other animals, and plants, we nevertheless share a common and fundamentally important biological background: (a) the same biological laws that apply to other living things apply also to us; (b) they as well as we have a good, the conditions of whose realization we cannot always control; (c) to all of us, freedom as absence from constraint is crucial to the realization of our good; (d) we humans are "relative newcomers" and cannot presume that we will last as long as many other species now considered biological failures; and (e) we are more dependent on other living creatures than they are on us. Indeed, it might be better for many of the world's living systems were we to die out.

2.   All of life, Taylor claims, comprises a vast complex of interdependent relationships. The "different ecosystems that make up the Earth's biosphere fit together in such a way that if one is radically changed or totally destroyed, an adjustment takes place in others and the whole structure undergoes a certain shift."[28] This "tightly woven web" view is not easily reconcilable with Taylor's earlier deflationary remarks about the disposability of humans—

though its focus on "adjustment" and "shift" is less conservationist than that taken in an earlier article, where he asserts that "in the long run the integrity of the entire biosphere of our planet is essential to the realization of the good of its constituent communities of life, both human and nonhuman."[29]

3. The third aspect of the biocentric outlook focuses on individual teleology. In the interplay between organisms and their environments, they display not only species-specific behavior, but also individuality. Close observation of a particular plant or animal will cultivate not only an appreciation of its particular way of living out its life cycle, but also a sensitivity to its individual "standpoint," or "perspective," or "point of view," vis-à-vis the world. This language is not intended to suggest that plants have conscious interests or strivings, but only to cultivate a recognition that each living organism "is a unified, coherently ordered system of goal-oriented activities that has a constant tendency to protect and maintain the organism's existence."[30] It is by virtue of this teleological conception that we have the capacity to make judgments about individual organisms from the standpoint of their good.

4. From a consideration of these three aspects of the biocentric outlook, Taylor believes the fourth reasonably follows: humans have the same inherent worth as other living things. To reinforce this, he articulates and criticizes several interpretations of the claim to human superiority. This claim to superiority is generally grounded in *capacities* supposedly possessed by humans but lacking in plants and animals. Let us grant that there are differentiating capacities. How, Taylor asks, do they establish superiority? From what standpoint is this judgment made? Cheetahs have greater speed, eagles greater visual acuity, monkeys greater agility, and trees greater longevity. Why shouldn't these be taken as signs of their superiority over humans? Several possible responses are then canvassed.

(a) Human capacities are more *valuable*. Aesthetic creativity, autonomy, and moral freedom are arguably more valuable than speed, agility, and longevity. But to whom? Taylor agrees that they might be more valuable to human beings, but from the standpoint of an animal or plant, speed or longevity might contribute more to its good.

(b) Humans are more *meritorious*. The intention here is to argue that our judgments of merit are based on standards implicit in the roles and purposes that make up human social life. Within this framework, animals are deficient in merit. But, Taylor asks, why

81

should that be the only standpoint from which to judge merit? May not the good of plants and animals provide us with a standpoint from which their merits may be judged? And who is to say, without begging the question, that the standards embedded in human social life are superior to those implicit in the life of plants and animals?

(c) Humans are *morally* superior. Behind this frequently heard claim there lies, Taylor believes, a serious confusion. Judgments of moral superiority/inferiority can be made only with respect to organisms capable of moral accountability. And since plants cannot be held morally accountable, it makes no sense to attribute moral superiority to humans.

(d) Humans have *greater inherent worth*. To claim this, Taylor contends, is not to claim that humans have greater merit, for inherent worth is independent of merit. An unmeritorious human being may nevertheless possess inherent worth. Instead, it is to claim that there is greater intrinsic value to realizing human good than there is to realizing the good of plants (and animals). However, Taylor believes that no acceptable content can be given to such a claim. Within the human sphere, the idea of differential inherent worth is associated with rigid social classes, now offensive to our democratic egalitarianism. And, he argues, holding that humans have greater inherent worth than plants and animals reintroduces something analogous to the elitism of a class-based society—in which genetic origin rather than family background is used as the basis for ranking.

Taylor canvasses and criticizes several arguments purporting to demonstrate the greater inherent worth of humans before arguing that the first three elements of the biocentric outlook provide a sufficiently solid basis for denying superior human worth. The Greek humanist, Judeo-Christian creationist, Cartesian dualist, and Lombardian capacity-based perspectives, which accord to genetic background a normative significance, are marred by "conceptual confusion and unsound reasoning."[31] The Greek elevation of rationality does no more than establish the affirmative value of rationality for *human* life. The Judeo-Christian commitment to a "Great Chain of Being," in which humans, made in God's image, are given preeminence, is fraught with metaphysical and epistemological difficulties. The Cartesian notion that humans alone are ensouled, insofar as it can be seen as positing affirmative value, indicates something that is intrinsically and instrumentally valuable only to humans. And Lombardi's view that the greater range of human capacities vis-à-vis other living organisms implies their greater worth involves a non sequitur, because it fails to look at those capacities from the perspective of the organism's good. We are left, then, with a claim to superiority based on some arbitrarily selected genetic difference.

The view fostered by the first three elements of the biocentric outlook is, Taylor believes, much more plausible. It enables us to see a deep kinship between ourselves and other living things, each "in many ways like ourselves, responding in its particular manner to environmental circumstances and so pursuing the realization of its own good."[32]

So, in broad outline, runs Taylor's argument for a "principle of species impartiality." There will, he recognizes, sometimes be conflicts of claims between members of the same and different species, and in chapter 6 of *Respect for Nature* he attempts to address some of these conflicts. For the present, however, I shall leave his discussion of these aside and focus on some difficulties in his central thesis.

Despite its lucid presentation, Taylor's argument is not easy to assess. This is because he advances—without keeping them distinct—several different moral theses: (a) because every species forms part of a tightly woven web of living organisms, it has some moral claim to our concern and consideration; (b) the good of every individual organism has intrinsic value and some moral claim to our concern and consideration; (c) every species has equal intrinsic worth and equal moral claim to our concern and consideration; and (d) the good of every individual organism has equal worth and equal claim to our concern and consideration. Taylor's arguments seem to be variously directed to any one of these four positions, even though they are neither conceptually nor practically equivalent. In assessing his account, I shall try to keep these—I think progressively stronger—theses in mind, though difficulties with the first are likely to constitute a stumbling-block for the remainder.

There are problems associated with each of the "coordinates" of Taylor's biocentric "map." We have already hinted at one or two of them. Take first of all his claim that humans belong to the biotic community "in the same sense and on the same terms" as nonhumans. There is some truth in this: we are—unlike angels— "biological" creatures, vulnerable, liable to be stunted by some forms of constraint, dependent on the biosphere, subject to the same biological laws as, and probably possess some sort of evolutionary connectedness with, other living things. Nevertheless, to say that we belong to the biotic community "in the same sense and on the same terms" as other living things obscures some very important differences—for example, the conscious mastery or control that we both need and are able to exert over our environment. That mastery, moreover, is not a simple consequence of maturation, but is developed only after a relatively long period of learning in which constraints on "natural tendencies" may be necessary. Our ability to exercise significant mastery over our lives and environment is of course one of the reasons why we can hold ourselves to account for our treatment of living things. But it is also by virtue of that that we have an evolutionary advantage over other living organisms—albeit an advantage that we could easily squander. If we suffer extinction, that will most likely be our fault. The fact that our participation in the biotic community is grounded in socially acquired knowledge rather than instinct, and is self-conscious and accountable rather than blind or unreflective, may not establish beyond argument the greater inherent worth of human life, but it does call into question the selective leveling down that seems to be implicit in Taylor's presentation.

We should, as well, note that when Taylor speaks of a "community of life" he does not have in mind the shared goals or conceptions that are generally constitutive of community, and that lend to community much of its normative significance, but a more formal sharing, in which independent organisms "tend towards" a good of their own.

Taylor's second coordinate, though expressed in terms of a factual interconnectedness, is also intended to carry some sort of normative weight. The point is not simply that if the web's configuration is changed, there will be consequential changes elsewhere, but that many configurational changes will disenable other living organisms from realizing their *telē*. This is unexceptionable so long as we also recognize the independencies and dynamic tensions that characterize the biotic network. Taylor's own discussion hints at these, without, perhaps, giving them their full weight. On the one hand he believes that humans could vanish from the earth without ecological detriment; on the other he acknowledges the competition for resources between humans and the biotic networks to which they belong. Although that competition may be fiercer than it needs to be, the tensions are probably more deep-seated than Taylor acknowledges. And, given Taylor's principle of species impartiality, the outcomes are likely to be more detrimental to human flourishing than he recognizes.

If the first two coordinates of Taylor's biocentric outlook focus as much on species or populations as on individual organisms, the third, that each individual organism has a good that it pursues in its own way, is unambiguously individualistic. The more familiar we become with individual organisms, he argues, the more aware we become that each is "a teleological center of life, striving to preserve itself and realize its good in its own unique way."[33] It is not clear that Taylor is right about this, at least at the level of plant life. There, the behavior of many organisms seems to be oriented not to their individual survival and well-being, but instead to the survival and well-being of the species. And this may be true not only of particular individual members of a species, but also of classes of members or members in general of the particular species. The members of some plant species focus their energies on reproduction rather than longevity. The species persists through the reproductive capacity of its members rather than their individual resistance to environmental challenge.[34] It is true, as Taylor himself observes, that reproductive fitness demands a healthy organism. Even so, in the case of many plant species it is difficult to perceive the individual member "striving to preserve itself and realize its good" as a means to its "ensuring the continued existence of its genes in future individuals." So, without wishing to deny Taylor's basic teleological conception of organism, it may nevertheless be wondered whether his account has not become too anthropomorphized.[35]

The tension that Taylor recognizes between self-realization and the realization of other ends is heightened by his ethic of species impartiality. For what it requires of humans, who are supposedly able to take the "point of view" of other organisms, is at best a compromise between their "natural" tendency to realize their individual good and the ethical recognition that other living organisms have an equal claim to the realization of their individual good. Reliance on the second coordinate of his biocentric outlook—the web of interdependence—will take him only so far, and in any case it reinforces the earlier tension between courses of action that will enhance the individual's well-being and those that will be conducive to the survival of the species.

What, then, can we say of the fourth, and concluding, element in Taylor's "biocentric outlook"? We should note, first of all, that a commitment to the inherent worth of nature need not imply a doctrine of species/organismic equality. Taylor presses for both, because he has a tendency to conflate two critics: (a) those who accord human life greater inherent worth than nonhuman life; and (b) those who consider that only human life has inherent worth. Perhaps this is an understandable reaction to those who assume that the establishment of human superiority licenses a "free-for-all" attitude towards nature, limited only by the repercussions that it would have for human well-being. It is, in fact, an inference that Taylor himself makes, when he says that if we conceive of animals and plants as inherently inferior beings, it "would mean that whenever a conflict arose between their well-being and the interests of humans, human interests would automatically take priority."[36] This constitutes a non sequitur. To allow that humans have greater inherent worth than plants is not ipso facto to allow that any human interest can take priority over the needs of plants. A person's desire to barbecue his steak over sequoia coals would not justify his felling a thousand-year-old tree.

Taylor tries to take account of something like this objection when discussing Louis Lombardi's position. Lombardi had argued that although all living things possess inherent worth, humans possess greater inherent worth because of their greater capacities. Taylor replies that the greater range of their capacities is not important; what is relevant to inherent worth is the way in which those capacities are organized: "They are interrelated functionally so that the organism as a whole can be said to have a good of its own, which it is seeking to realize."[37] And since, in this respect, there is no difference between humans and other living things, they have the same inherent worth. Lombardi's focus, however, is not simply the range of human capacities, but the content of those capacities; it is the latter that justifies according them greater inherent worth. It is in their character as self-conscious, rational, moral agents that their greater inherent worth resides. To claim, as Taylor does, that this is just what, for humans but not for plants, constitutes their distinctive good, perpetuates a confusion between arguments that support inherent worth, and arguments that support differential inherent worth. We may (for the sake of argument) allow that, by virtue of the teleological organization of the capacities of living things, those who adopt a biocentric outlook will accord them inherent worth.[38] My objection to Taylor's egalitarian position does not need to deny that. For the point of my objection is that it is the *kind* of good available to humans in virtue of the way their capacities are organized that grounds their *greater* inherent worth.

But I think Taylor would be unwilling to concede this point. If I understand his argument, he wishes to claim that, given the other coordinates of the biocentric outlook, all that is relevant to the ascription of inherent worth is teleological organization (something equally shared by all living things). The fact that the capacities needed by one kind of organism to realize its good *differ* from those needed by a different kind of organism has no bearing on their relative inherent worth. Of course, so far as the particular organism is concerned, one capacity might possess greater intrinsic value than another, because that capacity is more central to its realization of its good. But, he continues, to use this as a basis for according to one kind of organism greater inherent worth than another is to confuse inherent worth with intrinsic value. Distinctively human capacities will have greater intrinsic value for humans—but only for humans. It confuses the issue and begs the question if we use this as a basis for the ascription of greater inherent worth to humans. It will betray a deep human chauvinism.

I think, however, that here the charge of chauvinism overreaches itself. Taylor's appeal is (and must be) to beings for whom reasoned moral argument can be expected to count and to count preeminently in practical affairs. As part of that appeal it may be appropriate to enter imaginatively into the "standpoint" of a plant or animal, to try to appreciate the form taken by its teleologically organized energies. But if the results of such imaginative identification are to be given any practical significance, they will need to be assimilated to the perspective of a being for whom reasoned moral argument can be expected to have an authoritative if not decisive place. There is no getting away from this, and Taylor implicitly acknowledges it by choosing to proceed in the way he does. He adopts a moral approach not just because he thinks that humans will find it congenial, but because he feels morally constrained to do so. Certainly we may argue about the kinds of considerations that should be given moral weight, and the weight they should be given. But the crucial relevance of moral considerations will be presupposed.

To ask, as Taylor does, why the capacity for reasoned moral reflection should give the pursuit of human good greater inherent worth than the pursuit of the good of plants, is to call into question the form of argument on which he is himself relying. The point is not just that the development and reasoned exercise of moral capacities is seen as intrinsically valuable by humans, and as part of their good, but that Taylor's very enterprise—of justifying to humans a particular standpoint as morally required—must presuppose the preeminence of moral considerations. The good of organisms that lack the capacity for reasoned moral reflection must, so far as Taylor and those to whom his book is addressed, be regarded as of lesser inherent worth than the good of those organisms that possess such a capacity. How else can Taylor explain the weight he expects the form taken by his appeal to have? To suggest that moral considerations are being appealed to only because those are the considerations that count most for humans, and to assert this without also according greater inherent worth to beings who engage in such moral reflection is to cast a shadow over the significance of the point of view from which the appeal is being made. A certain kind of chauvinism is ineradicable if the goal is to be moral suasion.

Taylor is rightly troubled by elitist traditions among humans, where the grounds for distinction are factors such as ancestry, race, sex, nationality, etc. But this is because the capacities that bind humans—say, self-consciousness, rationality, and moral sensitivity—are believed to be more significant for our treatment of others than those that have traditionally figured in elitist divisions. However, it is just those capacities that elicit our respect for all humans equally that are lacking (albeit, in some cases, controversially so) in the lives of plants (and animals). To Taylor's question: "Why should standards that are based on *human values* be the only valid criteria of merit and accordingly be considered the only true signs of superiority?"[39] we can answer: The point is not that these standards are valued by (and for) human beings, but that they are valued by valuers, for whom alone judgments of value have significance. If there are nonhuman valuers, or human valuers who rate other factors more highly (as Taylor apparently does), then we have a reason to reconsider the value we place on such things as rationality. But it is not good enough to relativize the value of rationality by saying that it is valuable only to human self-realization and not to the flourishing of plants.

The "last person" argument

In a number of writings Routley and Routley have developed a particular thought experiment to support the intrinsic value or inherent worth of wild nature and other environmental objects. What "intrinsic value" and "inherent worth" are generally taken to mean in this context is an affirmative value possessed by these objects independently of any human observers or states of consciousness. The purpose of this thought experiment has been to challenge what are taken as the traditional anthropocentric and anthropo-utilitarian approaches to nature.[40] Routley and Routley's strategy has been to compare two basic scenarios:

(a) The last surviving person, before he/she dies, arranges for the destruction of the earth's biosphere some time after his/her death.

(b) The last surviving person, before he/she dies, does nothing to damage the earth's biosphere.

Their thought experiment has spawned several variants. Robin Attfield, for example, asks us to imagine a last person who chops down "the last tree of its kind, a hitherto healthy elm . . . which could propagate its kind if left unassaulted."[41] Stanley Benn and Elliot Sober have the last person ruining all works of art.[42] And Donald Regan envisages the destruction of the Grand Canyon.[43] But the basic drift of all these scenarios is much the same. We are expected to "see" that outcomes of type (b) are preferable to outcomes of type (a), that there is an intrinsic value (or inherent worth) to the biosphere, trees, works of art or natural formations, and that a last person who acted destructively would act wrongly.

Proponents of this argument have to assume that sincere moral agents will respond as they themselves do, and that they will see as the source of their response a possibly unrecognized belief in the intrinsic value or inherent worth of the biosphere, plant life, etc. Such an expectation, however, would probably not be warranted. True, it is easy to incline to scenario (b), but scrutiny of why this is so will not provide the support it is intended to. An alternative possibility is that what makes the vandalism in scenario (a) so objectionable is the vandalizer's attitude—that is, that it is an act of vandalism—and not the fact that the resultant world would lack some good that it would have independently of there being any one to appreciate it. A valuer, we might consider, would affirmatively value trees and other environmental objects for their own sake; and thus it would betray a base character for a valuer wantonly to destroy a valued environmental object, even were there subsequently to be no valuers present to value it.[44]

There is a further problem with the conclusion that the "last person" argument is supposed to yield. Even were the argument to show that plant life is valued for its own sake, we could not conclude that this affirmative value lay in its character as plant *life*, rather than some other feature it possessed. The fact that the Grand Canyon or a work of art might feature in a "last person" argument indicates that its normative resources need not lie in anything specially connected with life—plant or otherwise. In other words, although the "last person" argument may show us something about the way in which we regard plant life, it is not sufficiently developed to show that its living qualities have much to do with that regard.

The value of originality

In the wake of controversy over the environmental effects of strip mining, some of the mining companies involved have proposed programs of environmental rejuvenation following their exploitation of the underlying mineral resources. Taking the view that one plant is as good as another, or, more abstractly, that plants are substitutable, they have claimed that such restorative programs will return the wilderness to as good condition as, if not better than, it was in before.

Though some environmentalists have accepted this argument, others have felt either that the trade-off could not be justified, or that it missed the issue so far as environmentalist claims are concerned. An extended defense of the latter position has been articulated by Robert Elliot. In "Faking Nature," Elliot argues that wild nature is to be affirmatively valued because it has come about as a result of natural evolutionary processes, independently of human intervention.[45]

In order to make his point, Elliot seeks to construct an analogy between wild and rejuvenated nature, on the one hand, and works of art and forged or fake copies of such, on the other. In much the same way as copies or forgeries lack a dimension of value possessed by the authentic works of which they are copies, replacement "wilderness" or artificial species lack a value possessed by nature, or species that have naturally evolved. The "causal genesis" (as Elliot speaks of it) or history of a biotic community or species has a bearing on its intrinsic value.

In drawing this analogy, it is not Elliot's intention to argue that all wilderness—or all natural species—has (some measure of its) affirmative value in virtue of its being naturally evolved. This is not just because some wilderness areas or species may be quite unpleasant or worse. For it could always be argued in such cases that the affirmative value constituted by their mode of origination has been outweighed by the disvalue of their particular characteristics. His point is rather that some so-called works of art seem to be completely lacking in affirmative value. In other words, the analogy with artworks, even if sustainable, will not by itself establish that all naturally evolved wilderness areas or species possess intrinsic value. He thinks that they may possess such value—but that it would require some additional argument to show it to be so.[46]

But even if we accept the inherent limitations of the analogy, it will not do what Elliot requires of it. For what—in the case of the work of art—gives the original its special value is not simply its originality, but its manifestation of a creativity that the copy lacks. The copy may display the skills of a draftsman; it does not exhibit the creativity of an artist.[47] We can perhaps see this in cases where an artist or composer, taking his cue from a preexisting or inferior work of art, creates something which, though clearly inspired by the "original," manifests greater aesthetic awareness. In such cases we may not discount the "variation" by reference to the original, but see the variant as a work of art in its own right. The problem with the forgery or fake is that it shows no creative talent; at best it displays good draftsmanship. And art is not simply a matter of draftsmanship.

Originality as such, then, does not seem to be a source of affirmative value. It appears to be so only because it is the original, rather than the copy, that is invested with aesthetic creativity. This leaves the support for affirmatively valuing naturally evolved wilderness areas and species above those that have been artificially constructed looking rather weak. Why should not an area that has been rejuvenated after strip mining come to have as much intrinsic value as the original that was destroyed? True, there will be a period of time—perhaps a very long one in some cases—in which the rejuvenated area will lack the natural or unspoilt beauty and richness that some wildernesses possess. And in some cases, no doubt, what is used to replace the original will be aesthetically and ecologically inferior. But this need not be. Replacement vegetation may give the rejuvenated area values that the original area never had. The Wisconsin area restored by Aldo Leopold might constitute an example.[48] Perhaps Elliot would agree, but still argue that the rejuvenated area would have been even better had it come about naturally. Maybe. But the claim needs more than mere statement if it is to be convincing.

But there is a further possibility embedded in Elliot's position, and developed by Eric Katz. Katz claims that "a natural entity possesses intrinsic value to some extent because it is *natural*, an entity that arose through processes that are not artificially human."[49] The anti-Lockean feel of this claim should not sway us, for Locke's labor theory of value has little room for anything but use-value and exchange value. To establish his own case, Katz invokes Elliot, but goes further. He writes that tampering with wild nature—even to increase diversification—"violates the 'naturalness' of the system. . . . It imposes a human ideal on the operations of a nonhuman natural system."[50] There is, Katz believes, affirmative value in preserving a world that has been "given" to us rather than constructed by us.

There may be something to Katz's argument. We may feel awe before a nature that is beyond our ken and control, especially a nature of such manifest intricacy, power, and aesthetic richness, characteristics that often enter into our positive valuations. We may see in it an "achievement" that is not attributable to our own power and creativity. But as Katz develops the argument, it is not clear how the naturalness of nature establishes the independent intrinsic value of wilderness. Wild nature may sometimes have a beauty that is lost to us when we destroy it or limit its natural possibilities. And our tendency to tamper may display an overweening *hubris*, tempered when we come to nature receptively rather than manipulatively. But these are values that wild nature may have *for* us, not clear reasons why we should value it for its own sake. Although such values, as I shall go on to suggest, are not inconsiderable, they still fall short of what is sought by the radical environmentalist.

The anthropo-utility of plant life

So far I have been considering arguments that attempt to justify practical attitudes toward plant life (and nature generally) without recourse to any instrumental value it may possess. The Aristotelian subordination of nature to human ends has been sidestepped in a search for qualities in nature that commend to us its preservation and/or cultivation for its own sake. Our search has been only modestly successful. Yet we should not set utilitarian arguments aside too readily. Such arguments may, within their natural limitations, still carry considerable practical weight, and should not be scorned merely because of their "anthropocentrism." It is to three such arguments that I now turn.

1. *The advancement of human projects.* Humans engage in many projects that they consider affirmatively valuable—either instrumentally or intrinsically. Such projects will in many cases be integral to their conception of a good life. In order to bring such projects to fruition, plant life may have utility. A hedge may serve as a

wind-break; a potted plant as a gift; a particular species as a source of fragrance; and so on. In some cases, of course, human ends will be served by killing plants (though not extinguishing the species). Trees may be chopped down for buildings, paper, fires, etc. In other cases, though, the continued life of the plant may be necessary if the ends are to be achieved.

2. *Contribution to human welfare.*[51] If humans are to advance the various projects that give their lives structure and meaning, they will need the instrumentality of what Rawls refers to as "primary goods"—what we might otherwise call their welfare needs.[52] Food, clothing, shelter, and good health will be important prerequisites to the achievement of many of our individual and collective goals. And plant life may contribute to this in a variety of ways. In recycling stale air, they contribute to a healthy environment. Many plant species have medicinal value, and others of course have nutritional value. Our needs for clothing and shelter may to a considerable extent be satisfied by plants. In some cases the continued life of an individual plant will be required if our welfare needs are to be met; in other cases it will be the species whose persistence will be important. Wilderness may have an affirmative value by providing us with the possibility of "getting away from it all," enabling us to cope with the pressures of urban living.

3. *Enrichment of human experience.* Plant life may also contribute to human life by virtue of its enrichment of our experience. A wilderness area, for example, may be a source of wonder, beauty and awe, affirmatively valued not because of its serviceability, but simply because it evokes in us experiences we find elevating. The same may be said for some individual specimens of plant life—a delicate orchid, perhaps, or a sequoia. A similar kind of argument has been used to justify the preservation of rare species.[53] Just as there may be satisfactions in the contemplation of wild nature, so too there may be aesthetic and other satisfactions in the cultivation of plant life—in gardening, for example.

All of these arguments, though in rather different ways, provide grounds for affirmatively valuing plant life in one form or other. Yet they all have significant limitations, and it is for this reason that environmentalists have sought to locate the value of plant life (at least in some of its forms) in something other than anthropo-utilitarian considerations. Although some human projects are furthered by plant life, others are furthered by its destruction, or by the replacement of one form of plant life (wilderness) by another (crops). And though some plants contribute to human welfare, others detract from it. Some wilderness areas may indeed evoke a sense of wonder and awe, but not all will. And it is at least arguable that some human replacements may in their own way deepen our sense of wonder. Given the form possessed by anthropo-utilitarian arguments, it is not to be expected that they will support a uniform favoring of plant life.

But the contingency of such arguments is not a reason for rejecting them either. For even if it can be argued that plant life possesses intrinsic value, this may not provide a strong enough ground for preserving it, unless anthropo-utilitarian arguments for its preservation can also be advanced to counter what may otherwise be considered overriding anthropo-utilitarian arguments for destroying it.

Review

Arguments affirming the value of plant life move in various directions. They may focus on the affirmative value of individual plants, plant colonies, species, wilderness, ecosystems, or the whole biosphere. Pursuing the good of one may require sacrifices with regard to the other. Such incompatibilities are familiar to all of us, whether we are home-gardeners or involved in the management of wilderness parks.

The affirmative value of individual plants may sometimes be grounded in anthropo-utilitarian considerations, though it is unlikely that these will always provide the kind of protection that their defenders would like for them. Efforts to provide stronger support against their willful destruction frequently have "mystical" overtones: the risk that a particular plant may house a person-related soul; or seeing in the living occupants of nature an extension of self. But there are some arguments that attempt to show in less speculative ways how individual plants might be valued for their own sake. The "last person" thought experiment constitutes one such attempt. And so does the argument that plants have an individual good that is of inherent worth.

Plant colonies, too, may be defended along similar lines. The destruction of particular plant colonies may have ecological repercussions that will be unfavorable to other plants or living things. But the argument may also work in the opposite direction. The failure to destroy some plant colonies may sometimes work to the detriment of particular plants or plant colonies (the failure to weed a garden or crop).

The preservation of species is often defended by appealing to the aesthetic and other values said to be associated with a natural diversity—resources for human well-being, etc. Such arguments will have only limited scope—aesthetically unpleasing and harmful species will not qualify.

But most of the current arguments seem to focus on natural ecosystems—wilderness areas, or at least substantial tracts of vegetation. Some stress the interdependence of members of those systems—including their importance to human good. Others personalize or personify such systems, trading on a taken-for-granted valuing of persons. Yet others see some intrinsic value in the fact that these systems are the product of a natural evolution, unstructured by human purposes. More instrumentally, they will be seen to offer respite from what may be felt as the suffocating hand of Man.

Although I have indicated that I have reservations with most of these arguments, I do not wish to deny all force to them, and in chapter 7 I will suggest ways in which they might be incorporated into an argument for valuing life. Although the strong claims of some environmentalists can probably not be made out, considerations are advanced that should carry some weight with self-reflective evaluators. Diversity, originality, and telic fulfillment, though less than decisive, nevertheless strike a responsive chord.

FIVE

ANIMAL LIFE

All animals are equal, but some animals are more equal than
others.   —George Orwell[1]

In 1973, Peter Singer revitalized a longstanding, but at that time
largely neglected, debate on the moral status of animals.[2] Most of
Singer's discussion centered on "higher" animals—those with a
central nervous system of sufficient complexity to allow for plausible attributions of a capacity for pain. And his primary concern was
not with animal life as such, but animal pain and/or suffering.[3]
However, Singer's arguments and conclusions triggered a more
extensive, general interest in the moral claims, if any, of animals,
including those linked to their status as living beings.

The moral status of animal life has already been given some attention in earlier chapters. Arguments in defense of ecological integrity extend beyond the boundaries of plant life to include,
among other things, various forms of animal life. Biotic communities generally comprise interrelated populations of plant and animal life. And in some cases these arguments display a concern for
the lives of individual animals. Often, however, it is species-life, or
the preservation of a particular animal population that is accorded
moral status.

Nevertheless, arguments grounded in environmental concern
frequently lead in a different direction to those mounted by animal
"liberationists." Environmental integrity, restoration, and/or stability may necessitate the culling of particular animal populations, a
position at odds with one in which individual animals are considered to have strong claims to the "living out" of their lives. Environmentalists and animal liberationists have not always been close
allies.[4]

We might also seek to ground a case for animal life in the general
arguments articulated in chapter 3. Animal life may be set within a
theological framework, or seen as a domain within which freedom

or *tele* struggle to manifest themselves. But for the same reasons that I indicated in the last chapter, a nuanced approach, taking into account the distinctive features of animal life, is likely to carry more weight. Indeed, some of those earlier arguments are but more general—and perhaps less plausible—elaborations of arguments originally intended to establish the affirmative value or claims of animal or human life.

Our "kinship" with animals

It is sometimes maintained that between (other?) animals and human beings there can be found such likenesses that it is appropriate to speak of the existence of a "kinship." And along with the recognition of kinship, it is further claimed, there goes or should go an acknowledgment of comparable worth or regard.

The attribution of a kinship between animals and humans is seductive yet problematic. Generally one's kin are limited to those to whom one is related by blood, and, along with one's kith—friends and neighbors—they constitute a circle of people to whom one is usually thought to have special obligations that go beyond the general duties that one may have toward other human beings. However, the bonds associated with kinship are sometimes extended more loosely to cover ethnic or national ties and occasionally the whole of humanity. Extending kinship to animals not only stretches the concept's normal scope, but invests our relationship to them with considerable normative significance.

Can this extension be justified? We need to see what similarities or likenesses can be established, and then assess their normative implications. Michael Fox has categorized a number of apparent affinities:

1.   Morphological likenesses. Some animals possess brain structures and functions, and central nervous system development, that, even if not identical to, are at least continuous with those of human beings.

2.   Similarities of origin. Most theories of evolution point in the direction of ancestral convergence. Like distant relatives, other animal species are related to us through common ancestors. The distance does not gainsay the reality of the connection.

3.   Likenesses of experience. Animals, Fox suggests, can experience pain and anxiety, pleasure and satisfaction; some are capable of even more complex feelings—of love and jealousy, guilt and embarrassment, sadness, bereavement, and depression.

4. Likenesses in ability. It is possible for animals to have a sense of the future, to conceptualize their death, to know the difference between right and wrong, to possess a sense of self in relation to others, to communicate intentions and ideas.[5]

As I have stated it, the argument is a more refined version of one taken up in the last chapter, in which human continuity with nature is emphasized. But whereas that argument failed because the continuities were purchased at the cost of normative significance, the present one possesses a better prospect for normatively significant connectedness. Between humans and other animals there are richer affinities than between humans and plants. And at least some of those affinities seem to be imbued with normative significance. However, despite the greater specificity of the "continuities" or "affinities" enumerated in the present argument, the problems are not altogether eliminated.

Perhaps the first thing to note about the present argument is its lack of general application. Animals display enormous variations in physiology and capacity, and most of the purported affinities can be ascribed to—at most—a few of the so-called "higher" mammals. Primitive animals, such as sponges and amoebae, are probably less like chimpanzees than chimpanzees are like human beings. There is also, in the above cataloging, a misleading aggregation of affinities, a suggestion that some, many, or most animals or animal species display or could come to display all or most of the characteristics that are said to be constitutive of their kinship with us. At the very most, just a few animals or animal species could be claimed to display any substantial number of the characteristics adduced as showing affinity.

In itself, this does not do the argument irreparable damage. Given the deeply entrenched character of our anthropocentric cultural heritage, it would be no mean achievement to show that even some nonhuman animals were so closely akin to us that their lives should be the object of similar valuations to our own. As it is, those who argue most cogently for the moral claims of animals accord a special standing to a limited number of higher animals, such as whales, dolphins, and chimpanzees—animals that have been systematically mistreated by their human pursuers or captors.

However, the difficulties with the kinship argument do not stop with its restricted reference. There is also a question of the accuracy or even appropriateness of attributing to any nonhuman animals at least some of the characteristics that are claimed to be constitutive of their affinity to us. To what extent are we justified in attributing feelings of jealousy, embarrassment, and guilt, the ability to distinguish between right and wrong, and the capacity to communicate concepts and ideas, to other animals? Is there an illegitimate anthropomorphizing of behavior and experience—a reading into the native or learned responses of animals a form of awareness that allows us to attribute to them morally significant consciousness and intentionality? These questions are not intended to be rhetorical. There is a great deal that we have recently learned about wild animals, and no doubt still a great deal that we do not know. And with respect to domesticated animals, there is much that they can be taught. In all our dealings with animals there is a strong temptation to allow traditional attitudes to prejudice and ignorance to alienate. But equally, when caring about and interpreting animal behavior, there may be a strong temptation to construct their lives and experience analogously to our own, even though the evidence for doing so is at best problematic.

Ants and bees manifest a complex and in some respects inventive social life, and display considerable problem-solving skills. But do we wish to make them the subjects of lives, of a self-aware intentionality and purposiveness? I think not (though it does not follow from that that we may do with them as we please). The evidence for attributing humanlike characteristics to chimpanzees and domestic dogs may be greater, but there is still an ambiguity about their behavior that should make us cautious about attributing to them a consciousness relevantly similar to our own. True, our traditions may well have blinded us to important dimensions of animal life and experience that demand our recognition and regard. But there is an alternative danger of overcompensation, and of reading into animal behavior the sophisticated conceptualization and self-reflective characteristics of our own. Willard Gaylin may go too far when he responds to reports that "monkeys can talk" by saying that he will remain unimpressed until they say something worth quoting,[6] but his retort reminds us that whatever reasonable claims we may make on behalf of animals we are not dealing with a simple continuity from animal to human experience: some differences in degree make for differences in kind. Many animals do have lives of their own, ways of flourishing with which we can acquaint ourselves and with which we can to some extent empathize. But it may be a reflection of our considerable *human* imaginative capacities that we can come to this kind of consciousness rather than of a natural kinship we possess with them. For, from our ability to imagine what it would be like to live the life of an animal, it does not follow that an animal living that life would be conscious of that life as we might be.

Furthermore, we cannot assume that such observed affinities as there are will be of a kind to establish kinship in some evaluatively significant sense. Morphological similarities may count for nothing independently of some capacitative contribution they make. Common origins, in the sense intended in evolutionary theory, may carry no moral weight. And we need some argument or at least some assurance that the affinities noted by ethologists and others bear in some recognizable way on the *affirmative value* or *claims* that animal life is supposed to possess.

Finally, for present purposes, we should note that the argument tends to beg the question about the values—and sources thereof— associated with *human* life. It assumes not only that human life is (broadly) valuable—an assumption that is not, perhaps, too problematic once we have made clear what kind of human life is involved—but also that we are clear about the source(s) of that value. Maybe these two issues cannot be separated—the valuing of human life (of a particular kind) is likely to go hand in hand with an understanding of the factors that make it valuable. Nevertheless, the argument takes as unproblematic what is currently in contention.

The forging of sympathetic bonds is very important to the development of an intrinsic valuing or moral regard for other beings. And to that extent the argument from kinship is a powerful argumentative tool. But the sympathetic identification that is called for does not involve "putting oneself in another's shoes" so much as coming to appreciate what it is to be from the other's standpoint.[7] And that is a much more demanding imaginative exercise. Too often those who recall us to our kinship with animals confuse the process of putting ourselves in another's situation with an empathetic identification with the other's experience. What are held out as underlying affinities between ourselves and animals are overly anthropomorphized, or too remotely related to be recognizable grounds for moral considerability. In such circumstances the claims of kinship must remain less than compelling.[8]

Furthermore, so far as the (broad) valuing of animal *life* is concerned, we need some assurance that established affinities are of the appropriate kind. Animal liberationists can be credited with sensitizing us to the reality of animal pain, its affinities with human pain, and, to some extent, to the contexts in which such pain is experienced. But though this area of kinship provides us with a firm basis for moral concern about animal pain—and an eschewal of cruelty to animals—it does not provide us with a sufficient reason for affirmatively valuing animal *life*. So long as an animal is painlessly killed, why think that something of intrinsic value has been lost, or that some domain has been violated? Were certain other affinities better grounded—for example, that animals have future-oriented interests that would be frustrated were their lives to be prematurely or arbitrarily terminated—this case for the loss of intrinsic value would look somewhat stronger. But the self-reflective and prospective character of animal consciousness needs to be established.

My intention here is not to deny the existence of some appropriate affinities between humans and animals. Animal social life sometimes manifests significant sentimental dependencies and interdependencies that killing would invade, at the cost of considerable suffering to the surviving animals. If, as we may well do, we regard the flourishing of that social life as intrinsically worthwhile, the destruction of participants will be an evil and perhaps wrong. What we should avoid, however, is the easy anthropomorphizing of animals to which the cartoon world of childhood fantasies may incline us.

Possessing a life

In chapter 2 we touched on a distinction between "life" and "a life." James Rachels employs the distinction in a number of writings to accord "intrinsic value," "sanctity," or "a right" to certain instances of animal life and to deny it to certain instances of human life.[9] Not every being that is alive has what he terms "a life." The possession of a life is a matter of "biography" not just of "biology." It is to be the subject of projects and activities, of a social existence made up of interlocking and overlapping stages. The projects and activities that constitute the possession of a life form a backdrop against which the goods and ills to which a being is susceptible may be determined. Thus the evil of death, on this view, consists more in the frustration of projects than in some unpleasant experience. And the good or sanctity of life refers to the affirmative value or claim of a subject of biographical experience. Lives, not life, have a claim to inherent regard.

May animals possess lives? Rachels thinks some do. Monkeys, for example, "are remarkably intelligent, they have families and live together in social groups, and they apparently have forward-

101

looking and backward-looking attitudes. Their lives do not appear to be as emotionally or intellectually complex as the lives of humans; but the more we learn about them, the more impressed we are with the similarities between them and us."[10] Studies of other animals in the wild suggest that some of them, also, have lives in the relevant sense. Although there are large gaps in our knowledge, Rachels thinks it reasonable to believe that the mammals with which we are familiar "have lives in the biographical sense." As we move down the phylogenetic scale, however, "the less confidence we have that there is anything resembling a life."[11] Thus the Jain monk, who sweeps the ground before him, lest an insect be crushed underfoot, has failed to observe the requisite distinction.

What grounds does Rachels have for restricting the scope of the doctrine of life's sanctity in this way? He offers what he suggests is "a simple, but . . . conclusive argument":

> From the point of view of the living individual, there is nothing important about being alive except that it enables one to have a life. In the absence of a conscious life, it is of no consequence to the subject himself whether he lives or dies. Imagine that you are given a choice between dying today and lapsing into a dreamless coma from which you will never awaken, and then dying ten years from now. You might prefer the former because you find the prospect of a vegetable existence undignified. But in the most important sense, the choice is indifferent. In either case, your *life* will end today, and without that, the mere persistence of your body has no importance. Therefore, in so far as we are concerned to protect the interests of the individuals whose welfare is most directly at stake, we should be primarily concerned with lives and only secondarily with life.[12]

There are several things to be said about Rachels' position and argument.

1. First of all, it is not altogether clear what one must have in order to have a life. This is a problem on which we have already touched.[13] Let us assume—with Rachels and against Wollheim—that being alive is a precondition of having a life. What more is required? Rachels has a number of things to say. Speaking of what it is for a human being to have a life, he claims that "it is the sum of one's aspirations, decisions, activities, projects, and human relationships."[14] And insofar as mammals "have emotions and cares and social systems and the rest, although perhaps not in just the

way that humans do," they too can be said to have lives.[15] But this does not give us a very clear picture of the limits of life-possession in Rachels' sense. As he himself recognizes, some mollusks, such as octopi, behave in ways that observers interpret as displaying intelligence, emotion, and a sense of kinship. But he hesitates to draw the conclusion that they "have lives and therefore a right to life."[16] The same kind of point might be made about many other animals, and maybe if we knew more we might also say things about insects (e.g., ants and bees) that could be construed as biographical in some recognizable sense.

Of course, to claim that there is a good deal of vagueness and ignorance here is not to undermine Rachels' argument in any decisive sense. Indeed, he seems to accept the idea of a progressively more ambiguous attribution of a life the further down a being is on the phylogenetic scale. And among beings that possess lives, he is willing to give greater standing to those possessing greater "mental complexity." Nevertheless, his conception does not leave us with any clear conception of what makes for a life, and hence of the source of the moral standing associated with having a life.

2. Rachels' unclarity is to some extent implicitly resolved when he confronts the issue of justification. What sets life-possessors apart, he claims, is the importance *they* attribute to being alive. A being that considers its continued life important to itself ascribes affirmative value to that life and possesses a claim against the life-denying intrusions of others. I say this resolves the unclarity "to some extent," because the notion of ascribing importance to being alive itself stands in some need of explication. Does the amoeba, which "averts itself" or "withdraws" from a noxious stimulus, show that it considers its life to be important to it? I think Rachels would say "no": the amoeba does not possess a consciousness of itself as a discrete center of life. The amoeba may possess a certain kind of consciousness, but not a kind that would make its continued life of concern to it.

Wollheim's suggestion (noted in chapter 2) that what is important is not "possessing a life" but "leading a life (of one's own)" thus seems to capture most of what Rachels is driving at. The insect may sense danger or food, and react appropriately, but it does so instinctively and not out of some conception of what these things mean for its life. It is autobiographical and not merely biographical life that seems to be crucial to Rachels' position.[17]

3. This, however, leaves open the further question whether, even if a living being is incapable of having a concern for its own

life, it should nevertheless be of concern to those living beings who are capable of valuing their own and other lives. Why should the amoeba's standpoint (or lack of standpoint) with respect to its own life determine the stand that we should have toward its life?

Edward Johnson has argued that even if animal lives are characterized by nonreflexivity, this does not undermine their claims to continued life: "If a cow likes to chew her cud, then it is, other things being equal, in her interest to be allowed to do so. She is benefited by having opportunities to satisfy her desires: the more the better. But does this not give the cow an interest in continued life?"[18] Where the lack of reflexivity can make a difference is in our response to unrelieved pain. If "an animal's future will be one of unrelieved pain, then it lacks an interest in life, and should be killed."[19] But humans, because of their reflexivity, can have an independent, nonderivative interest in life, and, even if suffering from unrelieved pain, may prefer continued life.

If Johnson is right, Rachels has drawn the line too conservatively. But is Johnson right? Consider the objection that because humans may have a direct interest in life along with their other desires, they, unlike animals, may *care* not only about what desires they have but also about what happens to them. Death will have a significance for them that it does not have for animals.[20] Johnson believes that this difference fails to distinguish humans from animals sufficiently, since the human second-order interest in life may then be given the same (lack of) normative standing as animals' first-order interests. Unless, of course, humans are capable of indefinitely receding higher-order interests—a position he finds obscure and implausible. But Johnson's response focuses too much on the formalities, and too little on the substance, of the criticism. It is not merely the complexity of human interests that differentiates them from animals—even though that higher-order complexity makes certain things like freedom and accountability possible—it is the fact that humans have an interest in their continued *lives*. They are centers and sources of choice in a way that animals are not, and this imposes on morally reflective actors the constraint that is constitutive of recognition-respect. (Some) animals do not qualify for the egalitarianism of "chooserdom."

The foregoing response to Johnson is not intended to undercut the moral relevance of animals' interests or to deny moral significance to their lives. But what some writers would take it to indicate is the inappropriateness of choice-constraining talk of the *sanctity* of life or the *right* to life. That language, it might be argued, is decisively dependent on the importance accorded to life by its possessor. Unless the subject of the life apprehends itself in a particular way and desires to continue its life, it cannot be said to possess a right to life. Its life lacks "sanctity." For appeals to the sanctity of life or right to life are here concerned with the liberty that choosers may have in their interactions with other lives. Where a being conceives of itself as a discrete center of life and the maintenance of that life is a matter of importance to it, others are morally constrained from frustrating that desire.

Nevertheless, we may still want to argue that even though a being does not see its life as a matter of concern to it, its life possesses intrinsic value. In the eyes of those who are able to value things, it is better that living things continue to live than that they don't. And, where those living beings have desires, it is better ceteris paribus that they be than not be allowed consummation. If it is possible to see an oak or sequoia or even a birch as an object of intrinsic value, then it may be no less reasonable to see a termite's life as something having intrinsic value. A "close-up" of its life-cycle, the complexity of life in a termite colony, and the achievement of such lives, may sustain a judgment that termites are not to be wantonly destroyed. There is something coarse about a person who kicks open a termite hill, destroying its complex structure of tunnels, exposing its occupants to the destructive rays of the sun. True, such affirmative value as termites have may be outweighed by other values. Those that set up their colonies in the timbers of our houses may find their affirmative value of little help to them. But in places where their activities do not interfere with the lives and significant interests of choosers, their continued "being" may be a positive factor in the world of those choosers.

This leaves us some way from Rachels' original position, for he tends to run together "intrinsic value," "sanctity," and "right." The reflexivity of "having a life of one's own" may indeed provide reasons for special consideration, but it need not constitute the only ground for moral considerability.

4. Rachels' "conclusive argument" gets some of what conclusiveness it has from the way in which it is set up. Let us allow that a human being, given the choice between dying there and then and lapsing into a dreamless coma from which there would be no recovery, may see nothing in favor of the latter—nothing added by its continued biological life. This, however, is very different from the situation of the insect that lacks self-consciousness but goes through its normal life-cycle, foraging, eating, mating, reproducing, etc. Even though the insect does not "lead a life of its own" it is not in the same position as the irreversibly comatose human

being. The insect is able to fulfill its *telos*, whereas what is so non-valuable about the life of the irreversibly comatose human being is that it is no longer able to display even the rudiments of its distinctively human *telos*. All Rachels' argument may show is that *mere* biological life has no intrinsic value, not that the currency of value is—in his sense—"biographical life."

It is true that, for at least some of Rachels' purposes—for example, his desire to show the justifiability of euthanasia in certain circumstances—it may be sufficient that the life in question lacks the requisites for telic distinctiveness. But Rachels wishes to employ his argument to distinguish animals having lives of intrinsic value from those whose lives lack intrinsic value—whatever other value they might have. And for this purpose his argument is indecisive. Indeed, there are hints that even with respect to the comatose more can be said. For he allows that the prospect of merely vegetative life might strike us as "undignified." And that, indeed, is one of the major arguments for allowing some form of euthanasia with respect to the permanently comatose. It is an argument, however, precisely because the comatose life is continuous with that of the person whose life it is: it would be undignified for *that person* to be allowed to persist in a merely vegetative state. The person whose life it is may retain rights over it such that previously expressed preferences to remain alive or be permitted to die should be given significant moral weight. The comatose person is occurrently indifferent about his or her life, but is continuous with someone who may not have been indifferent about his or her present condition.

In sum, although Rachels may be right to claim that "possessing a life" carries with it certain normative implications, and, further, that some animals can be said to possess lives, it is not clear that he has established the central significance of this attribution to the intrinsic valuing of lives. Furthermore, although under at least one interpretation of this attribution, some lives may perhaps be said to possess "sanctity," the implications of this for nonhuman animals are unclear. Whether such animals are capable of leading lives of their own needs more argument than he provides.

Equal inherent value and the right to life

Tom Regan, perhaps the foremost defender of animal *rights*, has argued that, if human beings (who are, for this purpose, understood as moral agents) possess a right to life, so too do animals (at least those that qualify as moral patients).[21] For whatever is plausibly proposed as a rationale for the human right to life can with as good reason be advanced in behalf of (some) animal life. Regan limits his argument to "normal mammalian animals, aged one or more," though he does not wish to exclude the possibility of there being other arguments that would embrace animal or other life more generally, or that would sustain the ascription of rights to (some) inorganic nature.

Regan himself grounds rights in what he refers to as "inherent value," something equally possessed by humans and mammals. Inherent value, which he sharply distinguishes from intrinsic value (a quality of experiences), attaches to "subjects-of-a-life":

> Individuals are subjects-of-a-life if they have beliefs and desires; perception, memory, and a sense of the future, including their own future; an emotional life together with feelings of pleasure and pain; preference- and welfare-interests; the ability to initiate action in pursuit of their desires and goals; a psychophysical identity over time; and an individual welfare in the sense that their experiential life fares well or ill for them, logically independently of their utility for others and logically independently of their being the object of anyone else's interests.[22]

As to why subjects-of-a-life have inherent value, and why possessors of inherent value should be viewed as right-holders, Regan is not especially clear. Part of the problem lies with the notion of inherent value itself—the suggestion that "inherent value," like Taylor's "inherent worth," is a property of objects rather than a relational attribution in which a valuer considers something to be worth choosing for its own sake. And there seems to be something of a slide from the view that being the subject-of-a-life makes the attribution of inherent value "intelligible and nonarbitrary"[23] to the view that positing such value is *justified* by the status of being the subject-of-a-life.

Regan's path from inherent value to rights is mediated by the claims of justice. Justice toward subjects-of-a-life, and hence mammals—what is *due* to them—requires that we treat them in ways that respect their inherent value. As a matter of justice we may not harm them. This claim against us they have as a right. And all subjects-of-a-life have this right to respect equally.[24]

Sources of difficulty for Regan's position can be found first, in his initial characterization of the requirements for being the subject-of-a-life and secondly, in his claim that these requirements are satisfied "paradigmatically" by mammals older than a year. Why individual organisms—or even all individual animals—should not be considered subjects-of-a-life is never made clear. His *reductio* of Schweitzer's position does not really deal with this unremarkable position, but focuses instead on the problems posed if cells, blades of grass, and living collectivities are seen as objects of direct duties.[25] The point, perhaps, is that this would expand the notion of a subject-of-a-life too much, and evacuate it of the more restricted content that could plausibly ground some claim to respect. But this raises the second difficulty, for it is not clear that even mammals older than a year generally qualify as subjects-of-a-life. It depends on our willingness to expand our criteria for having beliefs, memories, emotions, a sense of the future, and so on, or on our ability to characterize animal behavior without illicitly anthropomorphizing it.

But these concerns expressed, there is in Regan's impressive statement the wherewithal for a plausible defense of animal rights. Some elements of it were laid out in chapter 1, where the importance of rights-talk and the conditions for rights-possession were briefly considered. Those who want to improve the lot—or protect the lives—of animals have wanted to enshrine their concern in law. Certain questionable attitudes and practices relating to animals and involving the mistreatment of animals are deeply embedded in our culture, and closely tied to the prevailing economic structures. Change with respect to those attitudes and practices is not likely to come about voluntarily, simply as the result of moralizing. This is a case—like slavery and sexism—where morality requires some form of legal backing if the momentum of tradition is to be redirected. But how are we to secure that backing in a democratic community? If it can be argued that animals have rights, and that these are being violated by current practices, then important political ground will be won. The reason for this is to be found in the social function of rights-talk.

As was noted in that earlier chapter, rights-talk was originally confined to the law. What one had a right to at law, one had a legal guarantee to. The force of law could be invoked in its behalf. But in recent centuries, rights-talk has been taken over into the moral sphere, and there has developed the notion of a moral right. The function of this expansion of our moral vocabulary has been to characterize those moral considerations whose realization would justify the invocation of legal support or even (as was historically the case) coercive action. To have a right is to be in a position to require the forbearance or contribution of others. Rights and coercion belong together, or, as Mill—whom Regan follows—puts it: "To have a right . . . is . . . to have something society ought to defend me in the possession of."[26] That is why rights-talk has a special political significance, and why it has become common to cast the case for animals in terms of rights. Not that every argument for legal enforcement can or must be cast in terms of rights, though there is little doubt that rights-talk is the most common currency for expressing the appropriateness of legal backing.

Do animals qualify as subjects of rights, and if they do, do their moral entitlements include a right to life? My own understanding of the requirements for rights-possession are less stringent than Regan's. For I believe rights-possession to be grounded in interests, and it is clear that in some intelligible sense animals possess interests. All animals have a welfare that may be advanced or threatened, and to that extent it is in their interest that certain conditions prevail.

Unfortunately, there is a multiple ambiguity in the notion of an interest, and there is considerable debate about whether the interests possessed by animals are rights-related interests. And that debate is also bound up with disputed understandings of rights—whether they are to be viewed as discretionary powers or specific kinds of advantage/benefit.

Briefly, we can distinguish three well-established senses of "interest":

1. a psychological sense, in which what is indicated is an inclination to attend to something: "I am interested in Melanesian art";
2. a stake sense, in which that in which one has an interest is something from whose outcome one stands to gain or lose: "I have an interest in General Motors"; and
3. a welfare sense, in which one's interests comprise the ingredients of one's welfare: "Exercise is in my interests."

Writers who see rights as discretionary powers generally consider that eligibility for rights-possession requires the possession of interests in sense (2), since the having of interests in that sense generally presupposes the ability to formulate plans and projects which can then be advanced or thwarted by others. But those who take the alternative view of rights, seeing them as requiring simply a capacity to be advantaged or disadvantaged by the actions of others, are inclined to interpret interests in sense (3).

I have already indicated my own preference for the more inclusive approach to rights—for the view that beings possessing a welfare ("interests" in sense [3]) have some claim on others for the protection or securing of that welfare. There is some reason to intervene in the wanton disregard of a living being's welfare. However, even if I am right, and animals can be considered eligible for rights-possession, we will not have established what rights, if any, animals actually possess.

If we follow the lead offered by the third sense of "interest," we might say that a being's rights consist in the ingredients of its welfare. In the case of human beings, this would comprise not only their biological needs, but also the educational, psychological, and other prerequisites for their participation in the world of persons. In their regard, we might be inclined to argue not only for a right to protection against physical harm, but also a right to education, to family life, to opportunities for choice-making, and so on. Animals, with considerably less potential so far as their development is concerned, may have fewer and different rights: plausible candidates might be rights to life, to a certain quality of habitat, and to freedom from suffering.

What would this amount to in practice? Although the function of rights-talk is to pick out those interests of whatever kind that have the strongest moral claim to our protection or advancement, it does not follow from this that rights constitute absolute claims. Rights can conflict, and when they conflict some means must be found for ordering them. The most appropriate way to do this will be to determine and assess the interests underlying the right, giving priority to those interests that have most to be said for them or are under the greatest threat. An examination of this kind might show, for example, that the interests involved in some levels of ownership may be overridden by the interests of others in maintaining a tolerable level of existence (an argument behind welfare taxation), or that the interests in a particular freedom are overridden by the interests of others in communal space (say, prohibiting the sale of a piece of parkland). The interests of animals, too, may come into conflict with those of human beings. There is the food interest, the experimental interest, the recreational interest, and so on. Assuming that animals are not rational choosers, their "claim" to being "let alone" is not as demanding and weighty as that of human beings. But that doesn't subordinate them to every human whim. Their interests cut moral ice, and in many cases should take precedence over the human interests that would jeopardize them. What may be problematic is the impartial weighing of those interests. Humans can be expected to vote in their own favor, and it may take a considerable effort to achieve a standpoint that is not illegitimately or selfishly anthropocentric.

Interspecific justice and animal life

The considerable influence of John Rawls's *A Theory of Justice* has led a number of writers to adapt his position to environmental and animal concerns.[27] The most sophisticated adaptation has come from Donald VanDeVeer, who has argued that, ceteris paribus, to the extent that animals prefer to continue living, it would be unjust to kill them. Their preference should morally constrain the conduct of a just person.

Rawls had argued that the task of devising nondiscriminatory principles of justice could be acceptably accomplished if rational, self-interested interlocutors conducted their inquiry behind a "veil of ignorance." The veil separates out a decision-making environment in which the participants, though knowledgeable concerning human psychology, economics, politics, and sociology, remain ignorant of the details of their own particular psychology, social, and economic position. Their task is to choose principles for a social order without knowing where or in what condition they will find themselves.[28]

VanDeVeer suggests that the veil of ignorance ought to be extended to conceal the species of the participants. A genuinely impartial choice environment would allow for the possibility that participants might turn out to be nonhuman sentient beings. He stops at sentient beings, since they, he suggests, unlike nonsentient beings, are capable of *caring about* their well-being. If this extension sounds farfetched—since the participants, as reasonably knowledgeable rational beings, would know that they possessed capabilities beyond those attributable to sentient animals—VanDeVeer reminds us that in Rawls's "original position" the participants are excluded from knowing whether they are children or adults, normal or retarded, etc., and the participants must realize that *they* are not children or retarded.

It is doubtful whether Rawls's position can be extended in the way VanDeVeer suggests. Although Rawls is not clear at the "margins," there is reason to think that only children, but not most animals, might qualify under the minimum conditions he sets down for being a contracting party in the original position: the capacity for conceiving of one's own good, and the capacity for a sense of justice. Still, the main issue is not Rawlsian scholarship, but a theory of justice that incorporates interspecific relations.

Suppose we allow that species identity is hidden to those behind the veil of ignorance. What principles of justice might be chosen by the primal interlocutors? VanDeVeer does not believe that they would be the same as those chosen behind Rawls's veil. The limited capacities of some members of the sentient community would mandate something short of Rawls's Difference Principle, which permits inequalities only where the least advantaged are benefited. The costs of Medicare for squirrels would cut too deeply into human resources![29] Instead, it is more likely that the participants would adopt a distributive principle in which, within certain limits, the natural opportunities associated with their genetic lot would be accepted. At the same time, however, he believes that they would also accept a "Life Preferability Requirement"—that is, social arrangements prohibiting any rational being from forcing on a sentient creature treatment that would render, on balance, its continuing to live less preferable to its not continuing to live. He further believes that the occupants of the extended original position would accept a corresponding "Creation Requirement," prohibiting rational beings from bringing into existence a sentient being for which no life would have been preferable.

Lying behind these requirements is the assumption that animals generally prefer to live rather than not to live, and that this places a moral constraint on the activities of rational beings in their treatment of them. VanDeVeer's point is not simply that animals' lives have an affirmative value for them but that their preference for continued life should be heeded in a just society. For some animals, death would normally curtail greater satisfactions than for other animals, and this, VanDeVeer suggests, might allow killing in those cases where the loss to the animal would be comparatively small and the gain to rational creatures would be significant.

Even if we accept—what I doubt—that animals generally prefer to live rather than not to live, we might wonder about the stringency of the constraint on killing that is advocated by VanDeVeer's argument. VanDeVeer does not seem to think that animal desires and preferences function as Nozickian "side constraints" on the conduct of rational beings. His emphasis is much more utilitarian: "the disvalue of the loss of life for many animals seems minimal from the standpoint of the magnitude of [human] satisfactions foregone."[30] Humans are likely to care more about forgoing some of their satisfactions than some animals are likely to care about forgoing their lives; though presumably the richer an animal's life experience, the greater the human satisfactions will need to be if that animal's life is to be taken.

Nevertheless, one of the features of VanDeVeer's position that is likely to appeal is the extent to which it mirrors an emerging reflective consensus. On the one hand, it is sensitive to certain deeply entrenched traditional and modern abuses of animals and our pervasive anthropocentric thoughtlessness in regard to animal life. On the other hand, it does not seem to overreact into a radical form of species egalitarianism, in which the "interests" of animals are given equal standing with those of humans.

Even so, I wonder whether VanDeVeer's argument will sustain even the modest conclusions he draws. Do we really have grounds for saying that animals normally *prefer* to continue to live rather than not to live? That they *disvalue* the loss of their lives? That they are sometimes treated in ways that make them *prefer* not continuing to live to their continuing to live? I am not really convinced that most sentient animals are capable of the kind of reflexivity that is necessary to sustain judgments of these kinds. I do not want to deny that sentient animals shrink from pain, and sometimes from anticipated pain, or that their lives are bereft of satisfying experiences. But it seems to involve quite a significant additional step to take the view that they prefer one condition to another, at least when that other condition is death. To have a conception of one's not being alive, such that one might prefer it to continued life, is no mean achievement, not on a par to preferring a life with more rather than fewer satisfactions, or with satisfying rather than unsatisfying experiences.

Review

As we move from livingness in general through plant to animal life, the arguments for life's value (in a broad sense) gain increasing support, and have a much more familiar ring. The reason for this is clear: almost all the arguments here are extensions of arguments used to establish or explain the values associated with human life. The "kinship" argument focuses on alleged continuities and overlaps between human and animal life, experience, and capacities. It is suggestive, though not, I think, conclusive. Where the continuities and overlaps are clearest, the normative implications are questionable; and where the alleged continuities and overlaps have greatest normative significance, the evidence for them is at best ambiguous. Perhaps this overgeneralizes: the category "non-human animals" covers such a diversity of beings that the argument's excesses may blind us to its successes. There may well be a few nonhuman animals whose characteristics qualify them for many of the kinds of value that we are accustomed to accord to human life.

There are similar strengths and weaknesses in Rachels' focus on "possessing a life." Possessors of lives, in Rachels' sense, need to be self-conscious, purposive, with a grasp of past, present, and future. Mature humans are easy and paradigmatic qualifiers. It is not so clear how many, if any, animals pass muster. Again, some of the evidence is suggestive, but not decisive. Tom Regan, whose primary concern is with the rights of animals, makes very explicit the influence exerted by the presumption of human value: that which sustains human rights also enables rights to be ascribed to animals. Like Rachels, he accords primacy not to livingness, consciousness, or even the capacity for pleasure or pain, but to being the subject-of-a-life—a complex notion that may apply to some of the restricted category of animals he includes within his argument, but is probably too restrictive to provide broad moral support for animals. Donald VanDeVeer's less extensive but nonetheless significant claims for animal life are rooted in an argument initially intended to mediate human desires. Professing to find no reason for restricting it so narrowly, he claims that principles of justice ranging over all sentient beings would give some choice-constraining standing to an animal's preference for (affirmative valuing of) its continued life. As with some of the other claims about animal life, this too is more easily claimed than sustained.

I suspect that we are not going to get much further with these arguments until we see how well they, or their prototypes, work when applied to human beings. And so it is to those arguments that I shall now turn.

SIX

HUMAN LIFE

I look up at your heavens, made by your fingers,
at the moon and stars you set in place—
ah, what is man that you should spare a thought for him,
the son of man that you should care for him?
Yet you have made him little less than a god,
you have crowned him with glory and splendor,
made him lord over the work of your hands,
set all things under his feet,
sheep and oxen, all these,
yes, wild animals too,
birds in the air, fish in the sea
traveling the paths of the ocean.
Yahweh, our Lord,
how great your name throughout the earth!
—Psalm 8: 3–9[1]

There is no doubt that the varied appeals to life's value are heard most frequently and insistently where the object is human life. It is here, too, that such appeals have usually seemed most at home. As we have already seen, many of the arguments mounted in favor of other forms of life presume the "value" of human life, and seek to show that whatever it is that gives human life its appropriate values can be attributed in some relevant way to some or all nonhuman life.

At certain periods of human history, the broad appeal to human life's value has appeared so transparently self-evident that its rationale has barely needed articulation. At such times it has been possible to reel off a list of cumulatively overdetermining attributes—rationality, free will, moral accountability, language, ensoulment, *imago dei*—felt to be so persuasive that those who dared question their significance would thereby place themselves beyond the cultural and moral pale. But at other periods of human history, and certainly in recent years, there has been a noticeable degree of

115

skepticism concerning any kind of absolute or unconditional valuing of human life. This skepticism is currently articulated in two main ways. Some have chosen to call into question the very idea that human life *as such* has affirmative value or normative standing. Others have conceded its value and standing, but have treated them as less than absolute—indeed, much less than absolute. The two ways of formulating the issue may not indicate any significant differences of substance—they appear to turn on different understandings of "human life." One position understands by "human life" the life of a member of the species *Homo sapiens*; the other works with a conception of "human life" in which it characterizes the life of a developed member of that species (or possibly some other species). Some of those who take the latter position prefer to speak of "persons" or perhaps of "stages of personhood." The dichotomizing of *humans* and *persons* is intended to avoid confusion and also to cater for the possibility of relevantly similar development in beings that do not belong to the species *Homo sapiens*.

The sources of this recent shift have been manifold. (1) There has been an increasingly public break with a religious tradition that has—in theory—strongly maintained the affirmative value and normative standing of all human life; (2) there has been a growing openness to other traditions of thinking about human life, traditions that have for a long period been given only a culturally marginal status; (3) there have been significant advances in medical technology, that have created a relatively clear division between biological and personal life; and (4) there has been a burgeoning of feminist perspectives and these have created increasing pressure for the legitimation of abortion.

As this brief catalog indicates, behind our contemporary debate about the values associated with human life there lies a complex cluster of material and ideological factors. Technical possibilities raise practical questions and practical issues direct technical effort. Both affect and are affected by *Weltanschauungen* and ideological traditions. Our culture has never been completely homogeneous, and even at those periods of history when one tradition has so dominated the social structure that alternatives have lacked a significant public expression, that dominant tradition has been an unstable and potentially volatile composite. The Judeo-Christian tradition, so much in evidence over the past fifteen hundred years, has always displayed some accommodation to the Hellenistic traditions in which it has grown and diversified. And now, with the diminished political power of Christianity (the demise of Christendom), there has been a reassertion of values and ways of seeing reminiscent of those found in classical writers. I say "reminiscent," because we are not dealing with a return so much as with ancestry—an ideological gene pool that has been modified in transmission.

To give some historical as well as ideological background to the current debate, I commence this chapter with a discussion of approaches to human value articulated during the classical period of Greek culture, followed by a critical exploration of the Judeo-Christian alternatives that subsequently gained the ascendancy. In the latter part of the chapter I review several arguments purporting to provide an appropriate contemporary response to the question of human value.

Classical arguments: value and actualization

We should not expect to find homogeneity in ancient thought. Human creativity and changing cultural and material circumstances are historical constants, albeit less visible or less enthusiastically exploited at some periods than at others. Ancient societies, at least during the periods of which we have any extensive understanding, welded disparate traditions into functional wholes, each whole containing within it possibilities for its own change, each vulnerable to the catalyzing or transforming influence of neighboring cultures. Classical Greek society was no exception. Even though we may hazard certain generalizations about its preeminent self-conception and values, it comprised a plurality of perceptions, sometimes fragmentary, sometimes developed, sometimes cohering, sometimes competing, always in flux.

One generalization we might risk, insofar as it relates to the present subject-matter, is that certain propositions we have till recently formally espoused—the attribution to each human individual of a basic, irreducible affirmative value, the possession by each human individual of certain basic rights, and the moral primacy of the individual—were not only not taken for granted in classical Greek culture, but generally disputed. Instead, human individuals were accorded differential affirmative value (in some cases none), only some could qualify as "right-holders," and normative primacy was often accorded, not to individuals, but to universals such as beauty or the good (Plato), to God, or to objects such as the heavenly bodies.[2] This differential value—or intersubjective estimation—was conceived of and determined in a variety of ways.

There was little incentive in classical thought to ground human value in any affirmative value placed upon it by God. Unlike the Judeo-Christian tradition that subsequently overtook it, the Greek tradition on which the Judeo-Christian tradition was superimposed did not conceive of the gods' relations to humans in a way that gravitated toward the view that they were divinely cherished. Whereas Judeo-Christian belief frequently emphasized the personal quality of the divine-human encounter, and saw it as divinely initiated, Greek religion tended to view such personal encounters as more or less incidental. Though Plato believed that the gods affirmatively valued those who lived uprightly, and recommended imitating them, the affirmative value accorded them which they were enjoined to recognize did not have as its content divine approbation, but an independent goodness that the gods themselves exemplified.[3] Aristotle was even more forthright: by denying Providence, that is, by denying that God had any direct involvement with human beings, he rejected the idea that affirmative human value depended in any way on divine favor.

However, this is not to claim that religious sanctions against the destruction of human life had no place in Greek thought. The pre-Socratic Pythagorean assertion that "we are all soldiers of God, placed in an appointed post of duty, which it is a rebellion against our Maker to desert," pointed to a divine constraint on suicide that was later echoed in Christian thought.[4] But it did not imply any general and individual divine valuing of human life. Such affirmative value that human lives possessed, they possessed by virtue of other considerations.

1. *Value and virtue.* In Plato's Middle Dialogues, the discussion of affirmative human value is closely bound up with his Theory of Forms, and like that theory rings somewhat strangely in the contemporary ear. Briefly, it is Plato's contention that knowledge, a grasping of what is enduringly true, cannot have as its object the world of particulars or sense experience. That sensible world is intelligible only insofar as it "participates in" the world of Forms. These Forms, which, in demythologized garb, function as the universals or concepts of later philosophy, owe their being and knowability to the Form of the Good, which Plato sees as the ultimate source of value.[5]

Against the background provided by this metaphysic, Plato roots human value—and affirmative value generally—in the degree to which a particular (e.g., a person or object) is characterized by "form" (i.e., the Forms), and preeminently the Form of the Good.

In theory, therefore, every object, whether animate or inanimate, ought to possess affirmative value insofar as it is characterized by form. Plato, however, unlike some of those who followed him, does not seem to have drawn this conclusion.

Like Socrates before him, Plato saw the soul or self as the proper locus of human value. It possessed affirmative value insofar as it possessed the goodness appropriate to it (*aretē*, virtue). This goodness was not manifestly present in the human soul, as a concomitant of its *being*, but needed to be realized. A good person would necessarily *act* well: affirmative value required ongoing manifestation, it was not a matter of mere *potentiality, disposition, being*, or *past manifestation*. The Platonic soul, unlike the reflective Aristotelian one, is a cognitive, conative, and affective complex, and Plato believed that its participation in the Forms would necessarily lead to action of an appropriate kind. But the other side of this coin was Plato's contention that good action cannot be divorced from its appropriate disposition. To act well, a person's acts had to flow from his or her goodness; their goodness is not constituted by the detached goodness of the behavior.

In what does acting well consist? Sometimes Plato writes as though it is to be resolved into a matter of social contribution—a matter of playing one's social part. But this is to misunderstand the role he gives to "minding one's business" as the essence of just conduct in his ideal state. For the affirmative value he accords his ideal state is instrumental rather than intrinsic. What the state provides are opportunities for realizing affirmative human value— opportunities for excellence.[6] A person's contribution to the state provides only an index of goodness—of the extent to which that person's soul participates in the Form of the Good—and is not constitutive of that goodness.

Plato's "realizationism" is not, however, to be seen as a tribute to the affirmative value or normative standing of human individuality (as that has come to be understood). It is not in virtue of what gives individuals their distinctiveness that they are to be affirmatively valued—or additionally valued; their affirmative value, rather, resides in a certain qualitative identity or conformity (with or to the Good). Human diversity is not a source of human value but a normatively irrelevant consequence of material or social factors. As G.M.A. Grube remarks, Plato's perfect psyche "remains individual only insofar as it is imperfect."[7]

One important consequence of Plato's linking of affirmative human value and virtue (*aretē*—which is not to be thought of in an

119

exclusively moral sense) is that not all human lives are to be affirmatively valued equally. Different lives will exemplify the Forms to different degrees, and to different degrees will be characterizable by the Form of the Good. In Plato, this is given something of a classist twist, for different classes, by virtue of their different capacities and their different educational opportunities, will differ also in their affirmative value. So, to a significant extent our affirmative value will be independent of our individual efforts, and will be a function of birth and upbringing.

But social background and the opportunities it provides do not constitute for Plato the sole determinants of affirmative human value. There are, in addition, certain general, less class-dependent factors that contribute to the unequal affirmative value of human lives. Children are to be affirmatively valued less than adults—and some, indeed, may be completely lacking in affirmative value. Plato had few qualms about exposing the severely handicapped.[8] Nor did he think it worthwhile to keep alive the incurably incapacitated;[9] and the incorrigibly criminal were deemed to be worthless.[10] Nevertheless, we should, as J. M. Rist warns, be careful about reading this as a Platonic license for the disposal of the socially valueless. Social contribution is not his only source of affirmative human value.[11]

2. *Value and intellectual excellence.* Aristotle rejected Plato's Theory of Forms, and needed therefore to posit an alternative basis for affirmative human value. To this end, he focused on that aspect or function of the psyche/soul most perfectly exemplified by God— *nous* or contemplative mind.[12] Aristotle envisaged a natural order, hierarchically arranged according to the degree to which a being possessed the capacity for and was engaged in intellectual contemplation. Lowest in the order of living things were those capable only of "nutrition and reproduction." Higher in the order were those capable of sensation. At the top were those capable of reason.

But although humans belong to the highest category of affirmative value, for Aristotle they do not all or equally possess the highest kind of affirmative value. Some humans function at the level of "beasts"—incorrigible criminals, lunatics, and freaks.[13] Others are at a stage of development at which only animal traits are possessed—e.g., the human embryo. And children, visibly human, are said to be animals with respect to their moral development.[14] Even among normal, mature humans Aristotle makes important divisions. He distinguishes two kinds of capacity for reason—one involving the ability to comprehend and assent to reasoning, and the other involving the ability to initiate rational activity.[15] Natural slaves, he believed, possessed only the first capacity. And those possessing the second capacity are distinguished even further, according to the use they make of their rational skills: philosophic contemplators are given pride of place, followed by men of practical reason, and those with other skills.[16] Gender is also a determinant of affirmative human value.

Despite his exaltation of rational initiative, Aristotle does not place any value, affirmative or otherwise, on individuality. Affirmative value resides only in the degree to which one approximates to a static ideal of contemplation. The latter, however, is available only to a few, and for most a realization of the lesser (though still valuable) intellectual excellences (*aretai*) will constitute a more realistic aspiration. Like Plato, though not in the same way, Aristotle connects the possibilities for affirmative human value to social position. The laborer, excluded from both contemplative activity and citizenship (and thus political and juridical participation), cannot achieve the same affirmative value as the aristocrat. The contemplative person, on the other hand, unencumbered by the particular, is above citizenship.

In this latter respect Aristotle's conception of affirmative human value differs significantly from Plato's. Plato's ideal person—the philosopher—is eminently practical, and therefore to be urged to accept civic leadership, whereas Aristotle's is contemplative. Aristotle's *nous*—the contemplative part of one's being that is to be especially nurtured—is much more narrowly focused than Plato's *psychē*. In consequence, affirmative human value in Aristotle is less easily characterizable in moral terms. It is, furthermore, less dependent on civil society for its realization.

However, Aristotle's understanding of the role of the state is more complex than this. For the contemplative, to be sure, civil society is unnecessary. But the contemplative life is appropriate to only a few. For other people, civil society provides an essential environment for the development and exercise of the excellences that constitute them human beings of affirmative value. For these, the state will be an even more important arena for self-realization than Plato envisaged—not merely an important means, but a constituting factor: the regular Aristotelian person is a political animal.

3. *Value and independence of convention.* In accounting for affirmative human value, Plato and Aristotle focus on factors having a strong intellectual component. This gives some humans, by virtue of their "breeding," a significant advantage over others with re-

spect to their achievement of affirmative value. Such elitism is less easily attributable to their philosophical forebear, Socrates, for whom "a particular mental orientation, use of the talents one has to tend one's soul, and intellectual honesty" are the crucial determinants of affirmative value.[17] Here, human worth is constituted by a certain independence of convention, a freedom, not so much of the intellect as of the whole self, what we would today speak of as personal autonomy. In taking this position, Socrates differentiates himself not only from those who would intellectualize affirmative value, but also from the aristocratic conception that was embedded in the Homeric tradition.

This Socratic conception, so well demonstrated in his own life and philosophical style, was given even more extreme expression by the Cynics. But their resolute commitment to independence of convention led to a differentiation in affirmative human value no less divisive than that found in Plato and Aristotle. Because they tended to see freedom as an all-or-nothing matter, they considered worthless the large mass of human individuals who were "custom-bound."

Though Socrates, Plato, and Aristotle represent the great presences of classical Hellenistic thought, they do not exhaust it. Other currents are discernible, and some were later to find new life in Christian and, later, post-Enlightenment traditions. For present purposes I mention just one.

4. *Value in being a "spark" of the divine.* According to Stoic metaphysics, the Cosmos is divine, and its ruling principle (*logos*) is instantiated in human beings. The latter, as possessors of reason or moral personality, are capable of ordering their conduct harmoniously with the cosmic ruling principle (God). This they are exhorted to do.

The idea that each of us is a "spark" (*apospasma*) of the divine provides Stoicism with the ingredients for what Rist calls a "democratic" affirmative valuing of the individual.[18] However, the extent to which this found actual expression in Stoic thought depended in some measure on the particular content that was given to the "spark"—whether it was understood narrowly as mind/reason or more broadly as moral personality. As in Plato and Aristotle, the former interpretation was particularly susceptible to elitist applications, since not only the capacity for reason, but also the quality of reasoning, entered into assessments of worth. However, not even the broader conception escaped differential application. Because some individuals were more virtuous than others they possessed an affirmative value over and above that constituted by their status as moral agents. Nevertheless, as Rist notes, invidious or at least harsh discrimination was largely avoided by the Stoic tendency to view moral evil as a sickness of the soul, in need of cure rather than of punishment.[19]

But although the divine "spark" theory found a later expression in liberal individualism, it was not itself sufficient to ground that remote descendant. For it was not the individuality, the haecceity, of Stoic individuals that constituted their distinctive human value, but their conformity to the cosmic order. Indeed, in some Stoic writers the theory dictated a submersion of the individual in the cosmic whole.[20]

To sum up this brief glimpse at classical thought, we may tentatively suggest that it was not in virtue of their uniqueness, their being the particular individuals they were, their being distinctive centers of consciousness and experience, that individuals were affirmatively valued in classical society. Individuality, when not a mark of imperfection, was not itself a source of affirmative value or normative standing. It was the universal and not the individual in humans that gave them their affirmative value. But even the universal characteristics in terms of which humans were valued needed to find concrete expression. There was no intrinsic value merely to being human, to membership of the species *Homo sapiens*. Affirmative value required actualization: it was contingent on some kind of characteristic performance.

The Judeo-Christian heritage: imago dei

The Christian tradition is, on the one hand, an outgrowth of Judaism, sharing with the latter an important body of sacred literature. At the same time, its own distinctive theological commitments have usually been articulated in a Hellenistic thought-world, and many of its most influential theologians conceptualized and debated its doctrines in categories drawn from Hellenistic philosophy. This has led to ambivalence within the Western religious tradition—an ambivalence that can sometimes still be seen in the hiatus that exists between theology and biblical studies. Discussions of life's affirmative value and normative standing reflect this dualism. Biblical language is often spoken with a Hellenistic accent. We shall see evidences of this in the following discussion.

Despite the Hellenistic turn of much Christian theology—its contextualization as we might nowadays speak of it—the Christianization of culture brought with it significant changes in moral perception and practice. This was particularly true so far as the broad issue of human value was concerned. The nineteenth-century historian of morals, W.E.H. Lecky, saw what he spoke of as the "eminently Christian idea of the sanctity of human life" as introducing a "new standard, higher than any which then existed in the world. . . . This minute and scrupulous care for human life and human virtue in the humblest form, in the slave, the gladiator, the savage, or the infant was . . . wholly foreign to the genius of paganism."[21] This probably puts it too strongly, since the high status given to all conditions of human life did have its Hellenistic precedents, and Lecky's reason for this "innovation,"—"the Christian doctrine of the inestimable value of each immortal soul"[22] has a strongly Hellenistic flavor.[23] Nevertheless, the cultural success of Christianity gave precedence to a conception of human life that promised to be less elitist and achievement-oriented than the prevailing Hellenistic tradition. In actual practice, of course, it spawned its own justifications for feudalism and racism: "new age" creeds seldom live up to their deepest intents.

To what factors within that tradition do we owe what Lecky identifies as an elevated and more generalized regard for human life? The religious underpinnings of the tradition do not as such explain the change. Hellenistic culture was no less religious. We need to look at the specific character of the religious tradition—to the character of the relationship alleged to exist between Man and God. This tends to be much more direct, more personal, and more pervasive in Christian understanding. Several ways of characterizing it have been proposed.

In chapter 3 I discussed two arguments commonly used to establish special claims for life, or, more commonly, human life: its status as a gift and its status as the property of God. I do not propose to repeat those arguments here. Though they are not distinctively Judeo-Christian, they were given a special place within that tradition, and constituted one source for the special regard human life was given.

I have already indicated some problems with those arguments. Here I want to broach a further objection to the property argument, particularly as it applies to human life. Some writers have taken offense at the idea of human life as God's property—viewing this idea as an affront to human dignity and autonomy. It is said to reduce humans to chattels, albeit divine chattels. If, as it is usually claimed, personal autonomy is an integral element in individual human worth and/or places significant constraints on others' interventions, then the assertion that we are God's property will compromise that worth or weaken those constraints.

As it stands, however, this objection is too crude, for it accords to the property relationship certain entitlements that cannot be taken for granted. Locke, it is to be noted, though strongly committed to the idea that we are God's property, is equally a champion of human freedom.[24] Our being God's property does not render us passive disposables, but places us under certain obligations whose articulation and fulfillment are subject to our responsible determination. We are to be about God's business, but that business is enunciated in the form of certain moral constraints. We are not marionnettes in a divinely orchestrated show. What is not placed under our (full) control are the times of our entrance and departure from this world. Our own entry, of course, is completely out of our control. Over our departure we may have some practical control, though Locke argues for a moral constraint on the suicidal exercise of that power. If this is all that Locke intends to imply when he says that we are God's property, there may be little at which to take offense.

Something of the same general idea appears to inform Paul Ramsey's avowal that "every human being is a unique, unrepeatable opportunity to praise God. His life is entirely an ordination, a loan, and a stewardship."[25] Here something like a property relationship is postulated, but it is cashed out in moral/religious terms. It challenges humans to take up a particular opportunity—to praise God. Their agent-status is not questioned, but presupposed.

Even so, the argument may be perceived to have coercive overtones, because the traditions which appeal to it often back up the moral constraints in question with the threat of divine punishment: those who do not spend their lives about God's business or who fail to make wise use of their opportunity to praise God will reap the harvest of divine wrath. With respect to some strands of the tradition, this concern is appropriate and the objection well taken. However, for other strands the apprehension confuses the *consequences* of violating divinely sponsored limitations with the *motivation* for adhering to them. If punishment for wrongdoing is justified by desert, i.e., as a just response to that wrongdoing, it does not follow that the threat of punishment should also be taken as an appropriate motivation to right conduct. It may function to stimulate or con-

125

strain, but that does not constitute its raison d'être. Indeed, to the extent that the threat of punishment motivates conformity to the divinely sponsored constraints, the resulting conduct will have questionable moral worth.

There is, however, another way in which the property argument may be considered denigrating, for it can be taken to deny that human worth, human dignity, is inherent to humanity, independently of creaturehood. Daniel Callahan writes that "in the theological problematic . . . it makes no sense to talk of man apart from his creator and redeemer; the 'natural man' does not exist, but only the created and redeemed man. . . . In part this helps to solve the problem of an 'alien dignity' which would denigrate man's worth, but at the same time, it requires that we accept the full theological framework; that is just what many cannot do."[26] The claim is that if there is only "Man as creature," any appeal to human dignity that does not focus on his creatureliness will be misguided. However, as Callahan points out, the assertion of creatureliness is tendentious, and so the argument will have limited appeal. It has a further deficiency, however. Even if Man is always Man-as-Creature, it does not follow that what invests Man-as-Creature with his dignity is the creatureliness (or something integral to that). The dignity-grounding features may be independent of the assertion of creatureliness.

However, it is very likely that those who wish to emphasize creatureliness as a condition for understanding human worth and standing want to focus on some relational feature of Man-as-Creature as the key to that worth or standing. Helmut Thielicke's contention that "God does not love us because we are valuable, we are valuable because God loves us," is one expression of such a position.[27] Here the postulation of affirmative value is tightly yoked to an acceptance of the theological tradition, and may be thought to stand or fall with that tradition. This will seem to offer too narrow a base for the varied valuings of human life—though it would be revealing were no other ground available.

More distinctive than the property argument is the biblical assertion that Man was "made in the image of God," a characterization that was originally used to invest humans with special status within the created order: "And God said: let us make Man in our own image, in the likeness of ourselves, and let them be masters of the fish of the sea, the birds of heaven, the cattle, all the wild beasts and all the reptiles that crawl upon the earth."[28] Later reinforcement of this passage's implications for status is provided when the strong stand taken against murder is explicitly tied to Man's imaging of God: "He who sheds Man's blood, shall have his blood shed by Man, for in the image of God Man was made."[29]

The mere assertion that Man was made in God's image does not take us very far. For wherein does this imaging consist? And in what way does this confer value or status on human beings? Do we look to Man's possession of "a soul," rationality, an original righteousness, free will, the capacity for linguistic communication . . . ? The history of its interpretation tends to be little more than a history of the prevailing philosophical and religious ideas. Each, as it gains ascendancy, tends to mirror its times or theological milieu, so much so that Karl Barth was minded to conclude his survey of the interpretation of *imago dei* with the observation: "One could indeed discuss which of all these and similar interpretations of the term ["image"] is the most beautiful or the most deep or the most serious. One cannot, however, discuss which of them is the *correct* interpretation of Genesis 1:26."[30]

There is a further textual question that has loomed large in some discussions, namely, whether the dual reference to "image" (Heb. *selem*) and "likeness" (Heb. *demut*) is intended to provide emphasis or to mark out two distinct relations. For some of the early Church Fathers, the two were distinct. Irenaeus associated Man's imaging of God with the possession of free will, his likeness with an original righteousness, lost in "the Fall" and to some degree recoverable by obedience.[31] Clement of Alexandria interpreted the image as a capacity for rationality and moral virtue, which, if appropriately exercised, would result in an increasing likeness to God.[32]

Such difficulties noted, I want to canvass three lines of interpretation that are illustrative of the tradition.

1. Few interpretations of *imago dei* have had wider currency than that which sees it, and Man's unique affirmative value and standing, as residing in *the possession of a soul*. However, its ubiquity is somewhat illusory. We might speak more accurately of a cluster of interpretations, for the form of words conceals a great diversity of understanding. Ensoulment has been fertile ground for the blending of Jewish and Hellenistic traditions. Although the Genesis account of creation speaks of Man becoming (rather than being given) "a living soul (*nephesh*)," this does not differentiate humans from animals, who are also characterized in the same manner.[33] It is mainly under Hellenistic influence that ensoulment is taken to

provide a uniquely differentiating status for Man. And even here there are different ways of interpreting it. For easy reference, I shall refer somewhat crudely to "Platonic" and "Aristotelian" understandings of ensoulment.

Those influenced by Platonic philosophy have tended to give a structural emphasis to soul-possession. The soul is conceived of as a discrete entity, immortal, residing within the body for the period of the body's life. Those influenced by Aristotelian philosophy have tended to give a functional emphasis to soul-possession. The soul is seen as the seat of Man's rational, moral, and spiritual capacities, capacities which Man alone in the created order can exercise.

What I have termed the Platonic approach must accommodate a range of problems. Some concern the difficulties of giving an intelligible account of dualism—what Gilbert Ryle provocatively characterized as the doctrine of "the ghost in the machine." Although human beings have properties that cannot easily be reduced to physiological goings-on, it is not obvious that this is best accounted for by positing a ghostly entity—a soul—as their subject. Other problems concern the lack of obvious status and value-implications to ensoulment. Lecky's focus on the soul's supposed immortality does not resolve anything.

When pressed, structural claims tend to give way to functional ones. It is what ensoulment enables that accounts for its normative role. And what it enables is variously described—rationality, the capacity for abstract thought, the possession of a language, self-awareness, free will, individuality, and a moral sense—taken either singly or in some combination. Some writers give their accounts a more explicitly religious cast—Man's addressability by and responsibility to God is taken to capture the evaluative and normative significance of ensoulment.

Some of these capacities are probably shared to a degree with the higher animals, and to that extent there may be some doubt about their adequacy as interpretations of the "image," insofar as our being made in God's image is intended to mark out a unique status for human beings. Possibly the doubt can be resolved, because some differences of degree will amount to significant differences in kind.

Conversely, some human beings seem to be grossly deficient with respect to these capacities. Fetuses and infants will not yet display them, the irreversibly comatose will no longer do so, and some of the profoundly retarded may never do so. This must pose some difficulty for a position that seeks to embrace all human beings on the basis of their ensoulment (to the extent that it is functionally understood).

At this point I do not offer these as decisive objections to the adequacy of *imago dei* as ensoulment—either as an interpretation of the *imago dei* or as providing a basis for some kind of human value. These views will be examined in more detail later. My present purpose is simply to outline one of the traditions of interpretation associated with the Judeo-Christian doctrine of Man as *imago dei*.

2. In recent years there has been a revival of the view that Man's imaging of God was historically and originally understood *morphologically*—a likeness expressed in physical form. Some writers who interpret the phrase "after our likeness" (or as Hans Wildberger translates it: "a being that is like unto us") as intensifying or detailing Man's imaging of God have favored this understanding. The subsequent reference to Adam becoming "the father of a son in his own likeness, after his image"[34] is said to bear this out: it is "natural" to understand this as referring to a physical likeness. But the strongest support for this interpretation has come from students of Ancient Near Eastern sources, who have argued that cognates of "image" (*selem*) are frequently used of an upright statue. Man's upright stance impressed the ancients, and some saw in this Man's special affinity to the deity. Others took a more comprehensive view of morphological similarity.

This morphological likeness would have been given normative significance, since, to abuse a creature made in the divine image would be to cast aspersions on the deity as well. Sometimes, the morphological similarities were accorded normative value indirectly by linking them to other characteristics that were given normative significance. Thus, Man's upright posture, by giving concrete form to his spiritual orientation, was thought to reflect his affinity with the deity:

> Thus, while mute Creation downward bend
> Their Sight, and to their Earthy Mother tend,
> Man looks aloft; and with erected Eyes,
> Beholds his own Hereditary Skies.[36]

With all due respect to poetic imagination, there is a suspicious anthropocentrism in such sentiments. What holds for the direction of Man's gaze should he suddenly find himself on all fours can hardly be said to hold for the animals!

Except as an account of the way in which Man's imaging of God was originally understood, there is relatively little current support for this interpretation among those who continue to espouse the human imaging of God. There is a tendency to see that understanding, no matter how original, as too "primitive," "crude," or "anthropomorphic."[35] Corporeality, though not necessarily eschewed as an attribute of deity, is never made a focal point.

3. In recent biblical scholarship there has been growing support for the view that "the image" is intended to designate Man's *appointed status*. As with the previous account, of central importance to this understanding has been the burgeoning of comparative studies in Ancient Near Eastern religion, and the significance accorded there to concrete images or statues.

In the Ancient Near East an image was no bare representation or symbol, but constituted "the dwelling place of spirit or fluid which derived from the being whose image it was."[37] Where shrines were built for a god, it was believed that the divine fluid entered into the image that had been set up. And in cases where the king himself was designated the image of God, he was believed to be the god's life-long incarnation. Images of the king were in turn given the same respect as the king in person. In fact his person was sometimes spoken of as being present in his image. Images were given an important role by conquering kings—as a means of establishing their continuing presence when they withdrew from newly won territory. Reviling the royal image was tantamount to sedition.

A crucial difference between the Ancient Near Eastern and biblical traditions lies in the designation of those who bear God's image. Almost without exception Ancient Near Eastern religion reserves designation as "God's image" for the king. Only "Tutankhamun" was "the living image of Amun." Imaging God and rulerhood were closely connected. "The king as image of God is his representative."[38] Thus understood, the Genesis designation of Man generally, male and female, as being made in God's image takes on a novel and radical significance. By means of his imaging of God, Man is established as God's representative in the world. He is set in the world as one preeminent, to exercise the rulership of the God who created it. Hence the words which follow the event of human creation "in God's image": "Be fruitful, multiply, fill the earth and conquer it. Be masters of the fish of the sea, the birds of heaven and all living animals on the earth."[39] Arguably, these are not meant to be understood as merely consequential upon Man's creation in God's image, but to be partially constitutive of it. As the final act of creation God places his image, his vice-regent, on earth. He can then "rest."[40]

If we understand Man's imaging of God as his possession of a designated status, then we appear to be back with the idea that Man possesses an "alien dignity"—a status and affirmative value vested not in his intrinsic qualities or capacities but in his being set apart and affirmatively valued or at least elevated by God. That may smack of parochialism in a culture committed to secular traditions of value. And no doubt its appeal is limited. However, there is embedded within the religious tradition the seeds of a more ecumenical appreciation. For there is no attempt to divorce Man's divine appointment from the means necessary to its satisfactory fulfillment. With the image there goes the likeness. What Man needs to carry out his task as God's representative on earth—control over and care for the created world—he is given.

But this still leaves us with the problem of those who, though human, lack the capacity to exercise a commanding role within the world—who are unable to be fruitful or to have dominion over the animal world. It is a problem to which we shall need to return.

Human life as self-evidently valuable

With the rise of Christendom, there was imprinted on western culture a high conception of human life's value. But Christendom has now shed many of its political supports, and the prevalent liberalism of recent centuries has been accompanied by a widespread unwillingness to yoke the valuing of human life to theological premises. For some, that has led to a much more conditional valuing than in the theological tradition; others, however, have wished to retain that tradition's sense of human value without its theistic underpinnings. In some circles this has been accommodated by speaking of human life's value as "self-evident."

Edward Shils gives articulate expression to this latter tendency. Writing in what he conceives to be a post-religious era, he asks why so many of us experience something ranging from a vague uneasiness to a passionate revulsion when contemplating what humans are sometimes prepared to perpetrate in relation to themselves. It may be something as brutal as genocide or as scientific and aseptic as genetic manipulation. Does the aversion simply reflect a residual religiosity—a hangover from those early years of our lives or an absorption from slow-changing cultural institutions? He thinks not. It is, rather, the expression of "a deeper, protoreligious 'natural metaphysic'" that affirms the sacredness of life.[41] This "primordial attachment to the elemental fact of vitality," this "natural" recognition of life's sacredness or sanctity, is not grounded in a commitment to some transcendent sacred power.[42] If anything,

> the transcendent sacred is a construction which the human mind itself has created to account for and to place in a necessary order the primordial experience—and vicissitudes—of the actual embodiment of vitality to which it attributes sacredness. . . . If man did not prize his own vitality, the sacred and its vast symbolic elaboration into cosmogonies and theologies would not exist. . . . If life were not viewed and experienced as sacred, then nothing else would be.[43]

The basic datum, then, is Man's prizing of his own vitality—not as an inferential response to divine ordering, but as the "natural" outcome of "the primordial experience of being alive, of experiencing the elemental fear of its extinction. Man stands in awe before his own vitality, the vitality of his lineage and of his species. The sense of awe is the attribution and therefore the acknowledgement of sanctity."[44]

Shils recognizes that the apprehension and/or abhorrence of genetic engineering or mass killing is not shared by everyone. Nevertheless, he does not think that this shows the ascription of sanctity to human life to be merely a "learned cultural response" needing, perhaps, to be unlearned. Our realization that some humans lack a sense of human life's sanctity serves only to accentuate the concern of those who have this sense. Likewise, the fact that humans are so often careless of life calls not for a reappraisal of the doctrine of sanctity, but only for an explanation of our insensitivity. As illustrations of such insensitivity, he refers to the way we sometimes commit ourselves to institutions to which we then come to ascribe false sacredness (e.g., the state), to the existence of competing dispositions within the human psyche, to the unequal distribution of sensitivity to the sacred among the members of any given society, and to the thinning effect of biological and/or social distance.[45]

Skepticism about the sanctity of human life has no place, Shils believes, except as a subject for explanation. To the question: "Is human life really sacred?" Shils answers unequivocally: "It is, self-evidently. Its sacredness is the most primordial of experiences, and the fact that many human beings act contrarily, or do not apprehend it, does not impugn the sacredness of life."[46] The numbers do not count, any more than the prevalence of lying counts against the obligatoriness of truthfulness.[47] The importance of numbers lies only in the social and political weight they carry: unless there is "a widespread affirmation of the sanctity of life . . . as a basic and guiding principle of social life, we will be hopelessly adrift . . . it provides the only ultimate foundation for the protection by public and professional opinion and by legislatures and courts against sadism in its more crude and brutal forms or in the more refined form of allegedly 'scientific' curiosity."[48]

But despite the strong language of "sacredness" and "sanctity," Shils does not want to be too conservative about the implications of his position for day-to-day decision-making: "the proposition that life is sacred is no more than a guiding principle," or, as he later puts it, it is "an equivocal criterion."[49] The sacredness of human life marks it out as worthy of preservation and promotion, though not to the exclusion of moral dilemmas. Indeed, some of those dilemmas are internally generated. This is because "the postulate of the sanctity of life refers to three forms of life: (1) the life of the lineage, (2) the life of the human organism, and (3) the life of the individual human being."[50] In particular cases, these may make competing claims, and choices between them will need to be made.

At first blush, Shils's position is very similar to Schweitzer's. Both appeal to "a primordial attachment to the elemental fact of vitality." But it soon becomes apparent that Shils's primordial experience is much more narrowly focused than Schweitzer's. Whereas Schweitzer's consciousness brings all of life within a reverential compass, Shils is drawn only to human life in its various dimensions. How do we account for this difference? It is one of the difficulties of appeals to self-evidence that it can offer us no workable decision procedure for dealing with conflicts in intuition. Is Shils too, along with those whose defective sensitivity he criticizes, guilty of contracted or distorted moral discernment—another human chauvinist? Perhaps the question can be answered, and should be answered negatively, but its answer cannot be given from within the justificatory framework that Shils provides.

Schweitzer's difficulties attach also to Shils's account. Were Shils to see the "natural recognition of life's sacredness" as placing an absolute bar on all life-compromising behavior, we would know more or less what was required of us. True, we would still need to determine what constituted life-compromising conduct. But there would be no conflicts of principle to resolve. However, by making sacredness only a guiding principle—and an equivocal one at that—we may be left in something of a moral quagmire when it comes to settling competing claims, whether between conflicts of principle or between the various dimensions of the "primordial attachment." *Perhaps* that is just the best we can do, and, given what human beings do do, a moral advance. But I doubt whether most of us would be prepared to leave it at that. These are not obviously issues that lie beyond the horizon of deliberative consciousness. Controversial and inchoate though our reasoning in such areas may be, deliberation is not out of place—it is not a piece of what Bishop Butler viewed as reflective disingenuousness, an attempt to wriggle out of the morally obvious.[51]

No doubt there is some point in human experience and moral reflection beyond which we find it impossible to go. Our argumentative resources are stretched to the limit, and what we wish to assert does not seem to be the sort of thing any thinking and morally sensitive person would want to challenge. But it seems very difficult to specify in advance or for others what that point would be. A commitment to life's sanctity no longer seems persuasive as such a limit. Our human finitude, which imposes these limits upon us, also prevents us from being privy to them.

It is in the context of cultural homogeneity that appeals to self-evidence are most likely to be suasive, for there the appeal, like that to shared axioms, reminds interlocutors of their common traditions. In that context, an appeal to self-evidence may be appropriate. The justificatory enterprise is not pursued in a vacuum but in response to specific criticism—some alleged hiatus between belief or conduct and a standard against which that belief or conduct is being assessed. Persons asked to justify their beliefs/conduct are not being asked to respond to every possible objection that might be raised, but to quite determinate difficulties perceived by the questioner.[52] Justification is essentially an open-ended enterprise: transcendental justifications (following Kant), which close off further justificatory questioning, are few and far between.

But cultural homogeneity is a fragile phenomenon, and so too will be appeals—like the appeal to self-evidence—that frequently depend on it. What is seen as self-evident in one context may not look so unproblematic in another. In twentieth-century industrialized societies, characterized by rapid change and cultural pluralism, the appeal to self-evidence is likely to have a very limited value, except as a form of retreat. This is certainly true of appeals to the value of life—even human life. Indeed, it is precisely because such appeals have lost their value that there is so much controversy over the various kinds and conditions of human life. There are those who do not see any intrinsic value in human life, those who do not consider its value to be self-evident, and those who accord it some self-evident value, but stop short of attributions of "sacred-ness" and "sanctity."

Shils acknowledges that there are many whose sense of life's sa-credness fails to match his own. But, as was noted earlier, he does not see this as a decisive objection to his belief in its primordiality. It is no more so than would be an argument to the effect that the prevalence of lying gainsays its wrongness. However, the analogy is problematic. Certainly the mere commonness of lying provides no reason for revising our views about lying. And insofar as those who do lie feel uneasy or guilty about their lying, the movement is in the opposite direction. But suppose lying were not accompanied by such internal discomfort. Then, even though it would not show lying to be an acceptable practice, it might give us pause, and cause us to rethink our opposition to it. And if those who lied sought to justify their lying, it would be incumbent on us to reconsider our opposition. That we have not—in general—changed our views on lying has more to do with the fact that we remain unpersuaded by such justifications, and continue to believe that the arguments against lying are stronger. This strategy is not available to Shils. True, there is a range of cases in which those who kill or otherwise interfere with life will experience guilt. But what can be said to those who believe that human life possesses no inherent sanctity, and who consider that whether or not it warrants our protection depends not on its status as human life, but on its particular poten-tialities or achievements? Why should we follow Shils rather than accept this? No reasons can be given beyond the invocation of self-evidence—an empty echo in this context. It is only because the case against lying does not rely on an appeal to self-evidence that we can have confidence in the face of its practical rejection; Shils has denied us that ground for confidence in the case of life's sanctity.

Appealing to the self-evidence of human life's sacredness is not the way to go about making good life's credentials. Even were it the universal primordial experience of humans that human life is sa-cred, this would not show it to be so; it would only show that sa-credness constitutes a universal feature of human experience. Of course, it would not be an insignificant datum of our experience, and we would probably not be under any strong pressure to chal-lenge it. But there is no denying that its universality and primordi-ality would not ipso facto insulate it against rational scrutiny.[53]

Where the self-evidence of human life's value is not universally accepted, and is even challenged by people of seemingly reflective goodwill, the appeal to self-evidence takes on the character of what

William Warren Bartley III has dubbed as "the retreat to commitment."[54] For here, what the appeal displays are the limits of our own understanding posing as the limits of reason, and purporting to tell us something about the truth-status of the beliefs in question. It is not too difficult to see this as a sign of philosophical *hubris*, a willingness to vest in our own perceptions and experience a presumptuous incorrigibility.

The value of human life given in the activity of valuing

There is, however, a different way to interpret Shils's position. If his appeal to the primordial experience of life's sacredness is not taken to express a way of knowing the truth of a particular proposition—viz., that human life is sacred—but is taken instead to manifest a conception of life in which the activity of valuing can have significance, it begins to play a quite different dialectical role. Like the foundational significance of the external world, and the epistemological role this plays, the "postulate" of human life's value may play a similarly presuppositional role in our activity as valuing beings. Such, at least, appears to have been Nietzsche's position.

Nietzsche left little doubt as to the foundational character of human value: "For a philosopher to see a problem in the *value* of life . . . constitutes an objection to him, a question-mark as to his wisdom, a piece of unwisdom."[55] The issue of life's value is not a conclusion so much as a premise, or perhaps better, a framework: "value judgments concerning life, for or against, can in the last resort never be true: they possess value only as symptoms."[56] The denial of life's value is a symptom of "decadence," of "sickness"; and even its affirmation is misguided: *"the value of life cannot be estimated."*[57] Why not? He responds: "Not by a living man, because he is a party to the dispute, indeed its object, and not the judge of it; not by a dead one, for another reason."[58]

These gnomic remarks do not readily yield their sense. It is not too difficult to see why Nietzsche thinks a dead person cannot estimate the value of life: the dead person isn't in a position to make any estimations. But why not a living person? Is he saying that the living person, as an interested party, cannot maintain the impartiality that judgment requires: one may not be both judge and supplicant? If that is what he means, then the impossibility seems to be at most a psychological one. What will be required is the overcoming of a certain kind of subjectivity—a propensity to self-bias—no doubt a difficult, but hardly an insuperable task.

But Nietzsche seems to have something more fundamental in mind—what he thinks of as the pathological character of such inquiries. Later in his discussion he focuses on what he regards as the denigration of life by Christian thinkers, and remarks: "a condemnation of life by the living is . . . no more than a symptom of a certain kind of life."[59] His own judgment, he notes, is not to be confused with a judgment on the justice or injustice of their condemnation: "the question whether the condemnation is just or unjust has not been raised at all." And *that* question cannot be raised:

> One would have to be situated *outside* life, and on the other hand to know it as thoroughly as any, as many, as all who have experienced it, to be permitted to touch on the problem of the *value* of life at all: sufficient reason for understanding that this problem is for us an inaccessible problem. When we speak of values we do so under the inspiration and from the perspective of life: life itself evaluates through us *when* we establish values.[60]

Once more, Nietzsche's meaning is not transparent. What he says in the first sentence seems to raise again the issue of an impartial standpoint. The question must be asked and answered by one situated outside—at a distance from—life, yet at the same time by one who could appreciate how it is to all those who have experienced it. Why so? Again, it looks as though the problem is one of partiality. If that is so, then cannot some effort be made to counteract it? And if the problem is that of being both valuer and valued, there is a problem only if valuation cannot be authentically self-reflexive. And do we have to know life as thoroughly as all who have experienced it?

I think such questioning misses the more subtle point Nietzsche articulates in the second sentence. It is that the *activity of valuing* is prompted ("inspired") by life, and, moreover, is engaged in from the standpoint ("perspective") of life. Valuing is something that humans engage in and engage in out of their livingness. What is more it is precisely through that valuing activity, by means of which they seek to enhance their lives, that "life itself evaluates through us." A being committed to evaluation—to the enhancement of life—has already adopted a framework within which the question of life's value has been rendered redundant. Thus in the section immediately preceding the one from which the last quotation was taken, he writes: "All naturalism in morality, that is all *healthy* morality, is dominated by an instinct of life—some commandment of life is fulfilled through a certain canon of 'shall' and 'shall not,' some hindrance and hostile element on life's road is thereby removed."[61]

The import of Nietzsche's position is brought out when he considers the case of human life that can no longer be enhanced or "added to," life no longer capable of "ascending." Such lives no longer retain their character as "life," as something through which value may be realized. Human life's central possibility as "will to power" has been lost. Its perpetuation constitutes an "indecency."[62]

For Nietzsche, then, human life is not an abstraction that lends itself to evaluation from some external standpoint, but is properly expressed in the will to power whose self-enhancement is constitutive of value and hence of life's value. Life is what you make of it, not an independently evaluable object. It is for that reason that the denigration of life is a pathological condition, and not simply a mistake. Nietzsche's strategy is very similar to that of those who claim that it makes no sense to attribute meaning to life, since meaning is created within life, as a dimension of living out a life.

This general picture is confirmed by and developed in Nietzsche's other writings. It is not human life as such that has value, but "life raised to the highest degree of potency."[63] In himself, Man bears only the possibility for value, a possibility actualized by only the few who manage to rise above the "herd." Most humans are merely "domesticated" or (equally pejoratively) "civilized" reflections of their social milieu. They have an instrumental value—as providers of the perquisites of "life," but lacking in life's substance. They have value for life; but not lives of value. The life of value is marked by an excess of creative power in which values are established and not merely mirrored: "Not 'mankind' but *Übermensch* is the goal."[64] The "higher man" does not stand apart from the world, weighing it, assessing its value, but exerts himself through the world, giving it and life value. For such a person the value of life is no longer problematical.[65]

There is no doubt that Nietzsche has captured something of importance for our reflections on the value of human life. There is a way of posing the question that fails to appreciate its import and subverts the attempt to answer it. There is a valuing of life in the activity of valuing, directed as it is to the enhancement of life (albeit in other-than-Nietzschean terms). But there are other ways of posing the question that do not conform as readily to Nietzsche's diagnosis. Where we are faced with choices that involve other lives, we find that questions of value (broadly speaking) cannot be so easily set aside. Whether it is the introduction of a social measure whose benefits will be purchased at the cost of a number of statistical lives, or a choice whether to expend substantial social resources to save a particular life, or a decision about capital punishment, we will want to include in our deliberations considerations which broadly address the value of the life or lives at stake. From such valuing Nietzsche does not prescind. He writes that "the invalid is a parasite on society. In a certain state it is indecent to go on living. To vegetate on in cowardly dependence on physicians and medicaments after the meaning of life, the *right* to life, has been lost ought to entail the profound contempt of society."[66] Here he offers a third person valuation of life which is neither presuppositional nor uncontroversial. It raises profound questions about the nature and importance of the will to power in human life, not only as a differentiating feature of human life, but also as the locus of its value. Perhaps the question of the value of my own life does not arise for me so long as I pursue value in life; but Nietzsche has said nothing to prevent it being raised in relation to other lives. And there the question is not redundant and the answer not immediately evident.

Maybe Nietzsche would claim that the two valuations are not disconnected. What makes for the indecency of the "invalid's" clinging to life is the detachment of the will to live from the will to power—life is no longer seen by the "invalid" as an arena for valuational activity, for assertions of the self. Instead it is only a cowardly refusal to come to terms with one's condition.

Human life as preconditionally valuable

Although Nietzsche's dark utterances about the givenness of life's value presuppose a somewhat idiosyncratic conception of human being, his position, along with most of the others that we have so far canvassed, grounds life's value in certain features that are taken to be internal to its characterization as human life. Only to the extent that that relatively rich conception of human life is plausible is it also plausible to value that life intrinsically. This creates a problem, for some humans appear to lack lives that are characterizable in these ways. Infants, the comatose, the profoundly retarded, anencephalic newborns, and perhaps others, may qualify as human, and alive, though not in ways that are, except biologically, characteristically "human." Can their lives be accorded value, and if so of what kind and on what basis? More generally,

139

does the life of human beings, stripped of its enculturated expressions, have value?

To the latter question, many contemporary writers have answered "no"—or perhaps more helpfully, "only an instrumental value." It is claimed that human biological life is only a *bonum utile*—it is not valuable in itself but only as a means to or as a precondition of the actualization of human achievements that are valuable in themselves. Where the human biological life is of a kind that is lacking in the capacity for such intrinsically valuable achievement, it lacks even instrumental value. So Richard McCormick asserts that biological life "is a value to be preserved precisely as a condition for other values, and therefore insofar as these other values remain attainable."[67] Where the values for which human biological life is instrumental can no longer be realized through it, it loses what value it previously may have had. This returns us, to some extent, to the classical arguments surveyed at the beginning of this chapter, though McCormick in fact writes (albeit not doctrinairely) from within the Roman Catholic tradition. What may be crucial to distinguishing his position from the classical ones will be the particular values for which that biological life is a precondition.

His general position seems to be paralleled by other contemporary writers. Paul Johnson is more detailed: "Life is valuable in relation to the attainment and exercise of other values. . . . Life is valuable in its relation to higher values, in particular to the values of human relationships and relation to the transcendent, through relation to neighbor.[68] And Michael Bayles writes in a similar, albeit utilitarian, vein. What gives human life its value, he suggests, are pleasure, physical movement, and relations of personal affection. It does not have value in itself, but only as a necessary condition for these satisfactions.[69]

There is, however, a subtle though important difference between Bayles's position and that of McCormick and (probably) Johnson. For Bayles, what is important to the actual value of a human life are the actual satisfactions it yields. Mere conscious human biological life is not enough; the consciousness must be one that its possessor values. As Seneca put it: *non enim vivere bonum sed bene vivere.*[70] McCormick, on the other hand, formulates his position in terms of "capacity": human biological life has value to the extent that it provides a realistic base for the actualization of (intrinsic) values. There does not seem to be the requirement that the human biological life in question actually embody the values. These views might be expected to diverge practically over issues such as abortion.

Despite their differences, all the authors just cited believe that human lives may lose whatever value they once had—when those lives have lost the capacity to support the values to which life is a precondition. But not all writers sharing that general understanding of the context of value have been willing to draw this conclusion. Holmes Rolston, for example, writing of irreversibly comatose human life, claims that "whatever is biologically *vital* also carries ethical *value*."[71] Although there is some question whether Rolston wishes his argument to extend beyond human life to life in general,[72] he means at least that individual lives should be viewed not as temporally segmented and detached entities, but as continuants with histories, with pasts and futures.

Rolston distinguishes "subjective" (self-aware, conscious) and "objective" (biological) life, and sees the irreversibly comatose as persons whose subjective life has lapsed. Their objective life continues nevertheless. This is of no little significance: such life is no mere "precondition" but the "natural spontaneous face" of life. It constitutes life's "deep structure," from which subjective life emerges. Where subjective life is present, it is "inseparably interlocked with objective life."[73] Those of us able to reflect on the issue have at some stage in our personal histories crossed the border from embryonic to adult life; the comatose have recrossed that border in the opposite direction. Nevertheless, they need not do so in a completely disintegrative way. The body may retain its "intelligibility" as a living organism: somatically, the individual still fights for life and health.[74] The affirmative value and claims of that life may not be equal to those of subjective life, but it is not valueless, and we have real though limited responsibilities to it.

Rolston's arguments can be interpreted in two ways. On the one hand, he can be understood as claiming that in itself objective life possesses value—a value over and above that which it possesses as the precondition of subjective life. On the other hand, he can be understood as claiming that objective life has a symbolic value. The fact that fetal or comatose life is continuous with a subjective life to which respect is owed, in which so much value is invested, means that we accord it, too, a place among our action-guiding considerations. According to Stanley Benn, although such symbolic reasons derive from our notions of respect and affirmative value, they cannot be identical with them, and may sometimes conflict with them.[75]

In chapter 8 I will argue that although there are serious deficiencies in Rolston's argument, his focus on history and continuities is

141

important to our conception of human being, and that viewing human biological life in detachment from its future and past, from its potential and accomplishment, narrows our moral vision too severely.

The preferential argument for human life

The forms of argumentation employed by welfare economists have provided the tools for a recent attempt to establish the value of human life. In "The Value of Life," T. G. Roupas argues for three propositions which, he believes, conjointly explicate the claim that human life is "objectively" valuable:

Ceteris paribus:

1. the longer anyone lives, the better;
2. the more people there are, the better; and
3. *who* the people are makes no difference so far as value is concerned.[76]

Roupas's notion of "objective value" requires clarification. Take first his view of what it is to make a judgment of value. Such judgments, he believes, are constituted by preferences and attach to "complete states of affairs"—what some writers refer to as "possible worlds." That is, the judgment that a particular state of affairs is best can be determinately made only when every possibility has been taken into account—a prodigious demand, but, he thinks, not unsatisfiable where only comparative judgments are involved—viz., that state of affairs S_1 is better than state of affairs S_2. Such judgments may be either "subjective" or "objective." They are subjective when determined by preferences that an individual actually has, and objective when equal status is given to the preferences of others. Roupas considers that human life is both subjectively and objectively valuable—though he believes that only objective value has *moral* standing.

Subjectively speaking, Roupas claims, a person will prefer a complete state of affairs in which, other things being equal, he lives a longer time to one in which he lives a shorter time; and he will prefer a complete state of affairs in which, other things being equal, he puts in an appearance at some point to one in which he never shows up at all. Only where his preferences have been irrationally distorted will this not be the case.[77] Roupas attempts to establish this negatively, by maintaining that certain counterarguments are unsuccessful. For example, to the charge that the first preference is irrational, since a person whose life ends early will not be aware of what he has missed, Roupas responds by claiming that since his *welfare* may be affected by that of which he is unaware, it would not be irrational for a person to prefer a longer to a shorter life. And to the charge that the second preference is irrational, since a person who never existed in the first place would not miss anything, Roupas responds by allowing the observation but denying the conclusion: for the person who *actually* exists and contemplates the alternatives, it would not be irrational to prefer to have existed rather than not to have existed. Roupas's only proviso is that the person be glad to be alive in the context of the complete state of affairs within which he appears.[78]

When it comes to objective value—a context of evaluation that, Roupas claims, is blind to the distinction between hypothetical and actual individuals—the strategy he adopts is derived from one developed by decision theorists for choice-making under conditions of uncertainty. The individual expresses a preference for one complete state of affairs over another without knowing where *he* or *she* might figure in the states of affairs being compared. Roupas believes that the adoption of this strategy will yield the following two principles:

1. Let S_1 and S_2 be complete states of affairs, and let A_1, A_2, A_3, . . . be all the individuals, actual or hypothetical, in either S_1 or S_2. Assume that for some individual i, A_i lives longer in S_1 than in S_2 and continues to be glad he is alive as long as he lives in S_1. Assume also that for every $j \neq i$, A_j fares at least as well in S_1 as he fares in S_2. Then S_1 is objectively better than S_2.

2. Let S_1 and S_2 be complete states of affairs, and let A_1, A_2, A_3, . . . again be all the individuals, actual or hypothetical, in either S_1 or S_2. Assume that for some individual i, A_i appears in S_1, whereas A_i does not show up at all in S_2. Assume also that for every $j \neq i$, A_j fares at least as well in S_1 as he fares in S_2. Then S_1 is objectively better than S_2.[79]

After rejecting what he sees as an alternative Rawlsian understanding of what the choice-making situation would yield, Roupas posits his third principle:

3. Let S_1 and S_2 be complete states of affairs, and let A_i and A_j be individuals, actual or hypothetical, involved in S_1 or S_2. If S_1 is like S_2, except that A_i appears in S_1 while A_j appears in S_2, and there are no morally relevant differences between A_i and A_j, then S_1 and S_2 are equal in objective value.[80]

Taken together, these three principles add up to the conclusion that "although human life is valuable the individual as such is not."[81]

143

There are several difficulties in Roupas's position. One set of difficulties, developed by Michael Tooley and Derek Parfit, concerns Roupas's move from subjective to objective preferences.[82] Is it reasonable to hold that objective preference is a construct from subjective preferences? Imagine two states of affairs, S_1 and S_2. S_1 comprises 100 individuals, each enjoying 100 units of happiness. S_2 comprises the same 100 individuals—but now each enjoying 120 units of happiness—together with an additional 100 individuals, each of whom enjoys only 1 unit of happiness. The first group enjoys its additional happiness in S_2 because members of the second group are serfs to the first group, performing all the unpleasant tasks. Nevertheless, members of the second group prefer to be alive than not to exist at all. Would S_2 be objectively better than S_1? On Roupas's view it should be; yet such a conclusion is counterintuitive.

Consider again: a state of affairs S_1, comprising 100 individuals, each enjoying 100 units of happiness; S_2, a state of affairs differing from S_1 only in that it contains 100 additional people, each enjoying 10 units of happiness—their existence does not affect the happiness of the first 100; and S_3, a state of affairs containing the same 200 individuals as in S_2, but in which they each enjoy 60 units of happiness. Using Roupas's methodology, assuming that all the individuals concerned are glad to be alive, state of affairs S_2 will be objectively better than S_1. What about S_2 and S_3? Although Roupas does not provide a ready-made method for comparing the two states of affairs, any plausible principle concerning rational choice under conditions of uncertainty will, Parfit and Tooley think, result in S_3 being preferred to S_2. Given the transitivity of preferences, it should follow that S_3 is objectively better than S_1. Is it? The argument can be repeated, with more and more people enjoying successively lower levels of happiness, until the position is arrived at in which a state of affairs S_n, containing a massive number of people, only just glad to be alive, is claimed to be better than one like S_1, containing relatively few people, each of whom enjoys a very satisfying life.

As Tooley points out, the argument can be varied to bear on the length of life as well as the number of lives.[83] Roupas's methodology allows it to be argued that a state of affairs containing a massive number of individuals living extremely short and minimally happy lives is better than one containing a small number of people living long and very satisfying lives.

What has gone wrong? Tooley suggests that there is a flaw in

Roupas's assumption that, in comparing two complete states of affairs, there is "an equal likelihood of one's being any of the individuals who is actual in *at least one* of those states of affairs."[84] That assumption, however, is unnecessary. Were the comparison to be between two complete states of affairs, in which the likelihood of being any one of the individuals was equal in *each* of those states of affairs, the preferences would most likely be different. This "Rawlsian" alternative is not satisfactorily disposed of by Roupas.

However, I think there are even more fundamental problems in Roupas's argument. These concern the *reduction* of value to a matter of preference, albeit—in his sense—objective preference. Let us allow that individuals' preferences are such that longer life and more lives are preferred. Is it inappropriate to ask whether such preferences are justified? Or whether such preferences are for the better? Roupas appears to assume that because the preferences in question are the preferences of rational individuals, they are therefore rational preferences. There is no strong reason for assuming this. Or perhaps he assumes only that whatever people prefer, they prefer under the description "better." But that seems to be false. People do not always prefer what they believe to be better.[85] Furthermore, even if their preferences do show what they value, they do not ipso facto establish the value of what they value. Even if everyone values life, that will not show life to be valuable, for what we may (universally) value may lack value. Even if value is something attributed by valuers, "objectivity" in valuing is not a simple matter of the universal congruence of subjective preferences.

The socioeconomic valuation of human life

Although the term "value" had its genesis in economics, it was taken over into nontechnical vocabulary as part of a universal discourse of appraisal. The choice-oriented character of human life, with its civilized antipathy to mere plumping and its demand for reasons, accords a central place to valuing. But even if "theory of value" is now more closely associated with appraisal generally than with economic estimations, the economic links have not been entirely lost. And that is also true where "the value of life" is at issue.

Indeed, although attempts to estimate the socioeconomic value of (human) life go back to the late eighteenth century, most of these discussions belong to the last sixty years, and the burgeoning of personal insurance and compensation for injury and death. Louis I.

145

Dublin and Alfred J. Lotka, whose book, *The Money Value of a Man*,[86] is often accorded a seminal status in this area, both worked in the insurance industry. And since that work, first published in 1930, there has been a vigorous and often highly technical debate about ways of assessing "the value of (a) human life."

Risk is endemic to human existence, for we are vulnerable beings. Few, if any, of our projects are guaranteed. In some cases the risk we run is not simply the risk of failure in some specific enterprise, but a more general risk to ourselves—a risk to life and limb. In some of our doings the risk to life and limb is negligible. In others it may be very substantial. Composing Haiku carries few risks; playing Russian roulette is very risky. The risk to life and limb attaches not only to our solitary doings, but also to our interpersonal and social interactions. What Jack and Jill do together may create or involve certain risks for each and for others. The promulgation of social policy, whether it takes the form of prohibition, regulation, or assistance, will carry certain risks with it. There will be different degrees of risk, depending not only on the kind of activity under consideration, but also on the particular untoward outcomes that are being contemplated. In some cases the untoward outcome will be loss of life.

The degree of risk involved in an activity may be quantifiable in certain ways. On inductive grounds we may be able to say that engagement in activity a or the promulgation of policy b can be expected to lead to x deaths in, say, every 10,000 members of a given population. In some of these cases, the risks (of various kinds) involved in a particular activity may be considered unacceptably high. That is, in relation to the various values realized by the activity, the costs may be deemed too steep. This judgment can operate at the level of either interpersonal transactions or social policy. At an interpersonal level, Jack's engagement in activity a may be claimed to create undue risks for others, so that if Jill is damaged as a result of Jack's engagement in a, Jack ought to be made to bear (some of) the costs of Jill's loss. At a policy level, the risks involved in permitting people to engage freely in activity b (say, owning handguns or self-prescribing drugs) may be thought excessive in comparison to the benefits thereof. The response may be to prohibit or regulate such activities.

Judgments of the reasonableness/unreasonableness of particular acts/policies seem to depend on the possibility of making cost-benefit calculations, in which factors such as convenience, the public interest, economic advantage, and loss of life and limb are probabilized, expressed in a common currency, and then aggregated. Commensurability seems to require that life and limb be given some monetary (our most neutral medium of exchange) equivalent.

But the very idea of giving human life a monetary value has struck many as not merely difficult but repugnant. A 1976 US House of Representatives subcommittee report, in which it was recommended that sprinkler systems be installed in all nursing homes (at an estimated cost of at least $86,000 per year of life saved), stated: "The value of human life cannot be measured in terms of dollars and cents. . . . We cannot, and will not, attempt to prepare a cost benefit analysis which will compare the cost of an automatic sprinkler system to the benefit of saving lives."[87] Such sentiments have frequently been expressed. But can valuations of this kind be avoided? How else is a cost-benefit analysis to be undertaken or an aggrieved party to be compensated? In a world of scarce resources, programs have to be assessed, at least in part, in terms of their effects on human life. If it costs $10,000 per worker/year to improve equipment safety to the point where five fatalities per 10,000 workers/year can be anticipated, but a further $250,000 per worker/year to decrease fatalities to three per 10,000 workers/year, and another $1 million per worker/year to decrease it to two per 10,000 workers/year, then those in charge of workplace conditions will need to decide whether, in view of the benefits involved, it is worth investing the sums required to lower the anticipated fatality rate from five to three or two.

The view that "the value of human life cannot be measured in terms of dollars and cents" can be taken in more than one way. On the one hand, as I noted above, the House subcommittee may be taken to be making a moral point: that there is something degrading about putting a price on human life. If that is so, it may depend on the context. To see lives as objects of economic exchange—as in the slave trade or baby selling—may indeed be to devalue them. But if it is a matter of allocating scarce resources or compensating someone for the loss of a loved one, then giving human life a monetary value may be better than nothing. On the other hand, the subcommittee's assertion may be understood as a statement of impossibility: there is no way that the value that human life has can be "cashed" out. And this can further be understood either as a claim that the kind of value it has is not amenable to monetary equivalents, or as a claim that human life is of inestimable value (like a priceless work of art). The former claim is factually incorrect whatever we may think about its propriety—the marketing of human lives has a long if ignoble history. The second claim will be taken up a bit later.

Before I say more about these questions, and seek to provide some overall assessment of claims about the socioeconomic valuation of life, I want to look more closely at both the theoretical background to, and the details of such assessments. These issues have been subject to lively debate. Dublin and Lotka developed an approach that assessed a person's "worth" as his/her "discounted future earnings" (DFE) less personal consumption, with some allowance made for "intangibles" (e.g., the significance of that person's presence for others).[88] This approach, a particular specification of the view that humans can be viewed as "capital," had many variants, and is still espoused in some contexts.[89] Economists, however, as distinct from actuaries, have not generally been as favorable to the DFE approach, and have favored another, usually dubbed "willingness to pay" (WTP). The latter involves an assessment based on the willingness of all those affected by a program to pay for risk reduction, or, alternatively, to accept greater risk for greater income. This view, popular since the 1960s, has become closely associated with the names of Thomas Schelling and Ezra Mishan. Like the DFE model, it too has spawned numerous variations. Indeed, the variety generated by each model makes it unhelpful to think in terms of a simple DFE/WTP dichotomy. In addition, the volatility of judgments in this area, and the values at stake, have led to the development of several other models or strategies for "value of life determination." Here I shall restrict myself to some of the main options and their variants, focusing less on their technical details than on their theoretical structures.[90]

Statistical vs. identifiable lives

But there is one other theoretical division that I would like to consider before turning to the closer inspection of the various socioeconomic models. Economists and actuaries approach the valuational task from one of two different directions—some focusing on *ex ante* and others on *ex post* judgments. Where *ex ante* judgments are made, statistical lives are normally involved; where *ex post* judgments of human value are made, the identity of those whose lives are being valued is usually known. One of the interesting anomalies of socioeconomic valuations is the considerably greater value usually accorded to identifiable than to statistical individuals. Does this reflect some sustainable moral difference, or at most a psychological bias? The anomaly deserves some further comment.[91]

To focus on the problem, consider two related scenarios. In the first, a choice has to be made between two policies, A and B. The risks associated with policy A project five deaths per year for every 100,000 members of a population, but the identity of these people is not known. Policy B has the same risks associated with it, but in this case the victims can be identified beforehand. Are the policies morally equivalent? Our intuitions tend to favor policy A. In the second scenario, the choice is between policy B (as stated) and policy C, which statistically projects ten deaths per year for every 100,000 members of the population. Where does this leave our intuitions? No doubt some people will be moved solely by the numbers, and for them the anomaly will not exist. For most, however, I suspect that policy C will be favored over policy B, despite the larger number of lives that will thereby be lost. Can such intuitions be sustained? And if so, do they indicate the inadequacy of a utilitarianism of life, in which the numbers may play a decisive role? Charles Fried has canvassed several possibilities:

1. Perhaps there is a subtle consequentialism that distinguishes the two cases. If, for example, we associate greater certainty with knowing the identity of the victims, as in policy B, we may believe that maximization favors either A or C, despite, in the latter case, a greater loss of life.

It is certainly possible that we are misled by the identifiability of the victims in B into thinking that their deaths are more certain, and that if we were to be as sure in the other cases our judgments would be altered. But I doubt whether this is adequate to explain the aversion to B. The statistics may be just as well founded in one as in the other cases, and the probabilities identical, and we may be aware that this is so. Yet our preferences are not likely to change. There seems to be something specific to the *identifiability* of the victims in policy B that makes its adoption morally problematic. Perhaps there is a figure at which the statistical individuals will come to assert as strong a claim on our investments as identifiable ones—after all, the numbers are not likely to be totally irrelevant—but even so, our favoring of policies A or C over B will not be explicable in terms of a probabilistic utilitarianism.

2. It is arguable that simple consequentialist arguments for preferring either A or C over B fail because they leave out of account our capacities for sympathetic identification. Because identifiable individuals "touch our hearts" more than statistical individuals,

life-threatening situations in which they are involved are able to evoke from us a greater investment of social resources. Adoption of policy B would limit our responsiveness in a way that would alienate us from our sympathies. It would artificially limit the resources we are prepared to invest in life-saving. The prospect of an identifiable person's death draws upon our "reserves of energy, resourcefulness, courage, and willingness to sacrifice"[92] in a way not found where merely statistical lives are involved.

This may indeed explain our preference for policies A or C over B, even though they are not life-maximizing. But that our sympathies are more adequately accommodated that way does not constitute a justification for our having those sympathies. Why should we not be moved to prefer more lives or fewer deaths, even when those lives cannot be identified?

3.   Perhaps there are symbolic reasons for favoring identifiable over statistical individuals. Identifiable lives are, at the time of their identifiability, particular in a way that merely statistical lives, at the time of their determination, are not. Our commitment to individual life in its particularity (rather than its generality) is, it may be claimed, shown in the preference for identifiable lives.

There is something to be said for this, though it might be thought perverse to appeal to such symbolism as a reason for favoring policy C over policy B. After all, the statistical lives will, if policy C is adopted, eventually materialize as particular lives. But though that is so, what we are choosing between in choosing policies, is not policies in which five and ten identifiable lives, respectively, will be lost, but policies in which five identifiable and ten statistical lives will be lost. That is the choice at that point, and the symbolic significance of the choice is not destroyed by the recognition that at some future time the statistical lives will become particular lives.

Fried claims that the symbolic significance of choosing policy C in preference to policy B , that is, of preferring to save ten statistical lives over the five identifiable lives, would be the indication of a preference for human life (in general) over particular human lives. The alternative policy, on the other hand, would not have the effect of denigrating or devaluing human life in general, but simply of prioritizing its particularity.

4.   Reasons of fairness might seem to provide additional support for policies A and C over B. At first blush, there is a fortuitousness about the distribution of risk in policies A and C that is absent from B. The burden of victimhood is distributed more randomly—

and, it might be thought, therefore more fairly—in the former policies than in the latter. The point is not to value identifiable lives more highly than statistical lives, but to affirm that, if lives are to be lost, it is fairer that they be selected out randomly.

This argument appears to work better for situations in which the choice is between life-threatening policies, though even there it does not seem to follow that identifiability indicates nonrandomness. But if the argument is applied to the distribution of resources for rescue, it seems to work counterintuitively. If I have available x resources, and can predict that its random distribution (by means, say, of a ceiling) would enable the rescue of ten statistical people, and its devotion to five identifiable people would exhaust those resources, then fairness would seem—counterintuitively—to demand that they be distributed to the statistical ten. It is true, of course, that the statistical individuals will eventually become identifiable individuals; nevertheless, policies A and C, unlike B, randomly determine who they will be.

A problem with this objection is that it counterfactually holds the distributable resources constant. We are dealing with a choice that, depending on the alternative chosen, determines what social resources will be made available. If, as it was suggested above, the plight of identifiable individuals evokes from us a greater response, then the choice will not be between the rescue of ten randomly determined individuals and five identifiable individuals, but between ten randomly determined individuals and an undetermined number of identifiable individuals—perhaps more than the ten who would otherwise have been rescued.

There is a further problem with the argument. It assumes that statistical individuals are subject to "a rough equality of exposure to risk," and that, clearly, is not always the case.[93] Particular groups— the young, elderly, the poor, etc.—are often disproportionately affected by the risks associated with social policies. Nevertheless, some accommodations may be made to handle this problem without sacrificing the argument's initial thrust. It can be conceded that the less random a distribution, the less the weight that can be given to considerations of fairness in favoring policies that pose life-threatening risks to statistical over identifiable individuals.

5. Fried gives serious consideration to the possibility that the priority we give to identifiable lives stems from the fact that relations of love and friendship (as distinct from those of justice and fairness) can be entered into only with actual and not with statisti-

cal individuals.[94] In respect of such relations we are prepared to make much greater sacrifices than would be the case were we constrained only by the demands of fairness.

Once again, the reasoning seems to be explanatory rather than justificatory. It indicates why we may sometimes go beyond what fairness can require, but does not provide a reason for its obligatoriness. Moreover, it assumes that the identifiable individuals of policy *B* are people we love or count as friends. But the fact that we can love or count as friends only identifiable individuals does not guarantee that we will regard identifiable individuals in those ways. They may be strangers to us. Why, then, prefer them to statistical individuals?

Fried believes that more can be said: "If we say no to the particular stranger we are saying to him that though we can see plainly enough that he is a particular person, not just a statistical possible person, we refuse to take that particularity into account."[95] And this, he believes, would be a horrible thing to do. But even so, Fried claims, the argument fails, for we will ultimately stand in exactly the same relation to the statistical individuals as we now do to the identifiable ones before us: "Love and friendship can not justify one in disregarding principles of justice and fairness, the beneficiaries of which are, after all, real persons too."[96]

6. Fried's final consideration—one that weighs heavily with him—derives from the common belief that some ways of dying are to be preferred to others. In particular, we prefer not to suffer in dying—whether the suffering in question be caused by dying or by the knowledge that one is marked out for death. The former is indifferent between statistical and identifiable individuals. The latter is not. And so policy *B*, in which the identity of the victims is known beforehand, will be the agent of a worse kind of death.[97]

This argument, of course, assumes that the identifiable individuals of policy *B* will themselves be aware that they are marked out for death. In rescue cases that may sometimes be so, but there does not seem to be any reason why this should generally be the case. And even in those instances where they are not aware of their identity (assume they are small children), we might still think it wrong to adopt policy *B*.

The general preference for identifiable individuals over statistical individuals is difficult to justify, but equally difficult to set aside. Perhaps it is, as some would hold, simply a prejudice, without any significant moral basis; or maybe, as I think is more likely, there is no one decisive consideration that establishes the prior claim of identifiable individuals, but a number of considerations, like those we have considered, that edge us in that direction, but which may be too inconsiderable should the numbers be radically different. Were policy C to result in the loss of one hundred or a thousand statistical lives, our moral intuitions might well favor policy B. Though even here, one possibility might be to choose not to have a policy where B is the alternative to the revised C. Social policymakers, however, may not always have that luxury available to them, and in such circumstances, I doubt whether C would be preferable to B.

It is time to return to the various models for determining socioeconomic value.

Models of socioeconomic value

Market value

Keeping close to the economic milieu in which "value" has its home, it may be suggested that the socioeconomic value of human life is most appropriately understood as what it would fetch in the marketplace. Just as the market value of a house is constituted by what it could be expected to sell for if offered on the "open market," so the market value of human life is constituted by what it could be expected to fetch if offered on some (hypothetical or actual) open market.

There is nothing incoherent about the idea of trading in human lives. The system of slavery depended on it, the dowry system has sometimes approached it, and babyselling still occurs. There is, however, a strong moral repugnance towards treating lives as tradable commodities, with a worth vulnerable to the vagaries of supply-and-demand. It does not comport with what we perceive as the dignity of a (mature or maturing) chooser that he be treated as the object of other people's transactions.[98] The repugnance would not entirely disappear even were the person whose life was to be traded to offer it himself. If people wish to regard themselves in that way we may not wish to prevent them—but may still consider it unseemly for others to be a party to their conduct. Nor, it might also be added, would it do to ask the question only hypothetically. For the whole idea of using market considerations to determine human value instrumentalizes human life in a way that only denigrates it.

Nevertheless, there are elements of the market-value model that figure in other accounts of socioeconomic value. If we ask, not: "What will this life fetch in the marketplace?" but: "What factors would be likely to weigh in any decision to buy human life?" we would probably want to make some reference to the labor invested in it or the contribution that the individual could be expected to make. And it is the "investment" or "contribution" made—or likely to be made—by individuals that has figured prominently in some of the other socioeconomic accounts of human value.

Invested value

One way of conceiving of the socioeconomic value of an item is to think of it as an aggregate of various investments. Human lives may be seen as the products of various social resources—talents, effort, material goods, and so on—dedicated to their sustenance and nurture. These, translated into economic terms, might then be thought to yield the socioeconomic value of human lives. Using this model, such lives might be valued individually, or, perhaps by means of averaging, generally.

There is an initial plausibility to this approach, harking back, no doubt, to its origins in a labor theory of value. But unless it is modified, or there is a careful selection of the kinds of investments that could count towards such value, the understanding it offers leads to some unusual conclusions. If individualized, it would probably accord a severely retarded or disabled or even a violently criminal life a greater socioeconomic value than an enterprising, trouble-free one. That may not be inappropriate if the purpose of such an assessment is simply to compensate those who have invested their time, energies, and resources in those lives (e.g., parents who have lost a child). But it does seem strange to speak of this understanding as providing a measure of that life's value—albeit socioeconomic value. An averaging approach would conceal these large differences in investment, but just because it did that, it would probably not serve the differentiating purposes for which the invested value approach is usually mooted.

Productive value

Rather than looking at the resources invested in a human life as a way of gauging its socioeconomic value, we might focus instead on that individual's social contribution—actual and/or prospective. A version of this approach has been adopted in many compensation cases. It lies at the back of the "discounted future earnings" criterion. The family of a deceased breadwinner is awarded damages based on the income that might reasonably have been expected, had the breadwinner continued to earn. Those earnings are seen as an index of the person's social contribution—an index of the wealth he/she created. The assumption is that what a person is paid is what "society," through the mechanism of the market, considers him/her to be worth. (In its actual implementation, of course, the DFE approach is usually supplemented by other factors—some addition for the pain, grief, and suffering the individual's death has caused.)

A common complaint concerning this approach has been that it is elitist (and maybe racist) and sexist. On the one hand, the talented who have managed to "make it" are valued more highly than those who for one reason or other have not achieved economic success. On the other hand, housewives, because they are not paid for their labor, will be compensated at domestic rates. What is more, certain groups—the severely retarded, the chronically disabled, the senile—will be accorded a negative socioeconomic value, perhaps encouraging policies that would put them at risk. There is, it might be claimed, a certain kind of egalitarianism—the equal moral value of all individuals—that would be eroded were productive value to be taken as an index of "the value of human life."

No doubt a defender of the "productive value" approach could insist that there is a firm distinction to be drawn between equal value and equal respect, and that an unproblematic egalitarianism is directed only to the latter. Just as unequal wages may indicate unequal achievement and the unequal "social value" of a person's work, without thereby calling into question the moral equality of those human individuals, so too might the differential assessments of productive value be made without invidious discrimination being implied. But the issue is not quite as simple as this suggests. On the one hand, in market-oriented societies, it is socially and psychologically very easy to slide from economic to personal worth: an aristocracy of earning power comes to replace an aristocracy of bloodline. And on the other hand, by conceiving of such judgments of socioeconomic value as judgments of "the value of life," there is a tendency to focus away from the various other features of human life that give that life its standing.

Nevertheless, the suggestion that productive value is inherently elitist or discriminatory seems too strong. For the background to this position is compensation, not reward. Productive value is an estimate of the economic and social loss that others have suffered—usually through the negligence of others—and is generally employed only to recompense them for that loss. There is nothing particularly elitist about this, even if such compensation will generally reflect an existing discriminatory social status quo.

Surrender value

To ask: "What is life worth?" invites the counter-question: "To whom?" And responses to the latter question often reduce to a conflict between those who believe that the answer must be "To the person whose life it is" and those who favor some "external" standard. Such conflicts are replicated in debates about the socioeconomic value of human life. One body of opinion believes the value of human life is determined by its worth to its owner—by what its owner is willing to trade it for. Just as we are willing to trade our possessions for some kind of economic benefit, so too, if the price is right, we might be willing to trade our lives.

For obvious reasons, people will normally place a high surrender value on their lives. Indeed, they may place such a high value on them as to be unwilling to part with them "at any price." They may see their lives as "priceless" or as having "infinite value." That is understandable, given that for most of us, life is a precondition for the enjoyment of whatever (else?) we value. This is translated into a social policy measure by John Broome, who argues from the premise that every individual will regard his/her life as being of infinite value to the conclusion that any social policy whose implementation could reliably be expected to result in the loss of life should be eschewed.[99] A cost-benefit analysis would always favor life. To the objection that any lives threatened by such a policy would be only statistical and not identifiable lives, Broome replies that over a period of time statistical lives will become actual identifiable deaths, and that the persons concerned, were they able at that time to make their will known, would have individually said: "I should never have agreed to this project at any price."

However, it is simply an assumption on Broome's part that rational individuals would never trade their lives for money—whatever the amount involved. His assumption is given the plausibility it has by two constraints that he builds into his argument—that the death must be immediate and the money nonbequestable. Except in those rare cases in which a person does not think his/her life worth living, it probably would be irrational to trade immediate death for nonbequestable money. But Broome's restrictions have an ad hoc character: he does not establish their appropriateness.

A person may be willing to trade certain death for a sufficiently large sum of money provided that he/she can first enjoy it, or, alternatively, can devote it to some chosen project. A person who is fiercely committed to a social cause may be willing to sacrifice his/her life if it will guarantee, say, a $15 million donation to that cause.

What is more, as soon as we get away from a direct trade (and conditions of certainty), and consider instead only a probable loss of life, a certain kind of personal pricing of life becomes almost commonplace. For guaranteed economic rewards or expanded benefits, most of us are quite willing to assume an increased risk to our lives. Such agreements are explicit where people consent to participate in dangerous experiments or especially hazardous working conditions, but the acceptance of risk is more widespread than that. True, as Broome observes, statistical deaths eventually become the actual deaths of identifiable people, and it may be that the person who becomes the victim of a policy will, at the point at which *he/she* becomes a victim, regret having consented to death. But that does not gainsay the legitimacy of the consent originally given. *At that time*, consent to the policy may have been both responsible and rational.

Mishan argues for the even stronger conclusion that Broome's position is irrational: "If there is a 1 in 50 million chance of person *A* being killed, Broomian rationality requires that person *A* act as if that person is actually going to be him, *A*, and therefore he should not accept that miniscule risk for all the treasure in Aladdin's cave."[100] Broome's position, he thinks, would spell the death of almost every social policy, since it is hard to think of any policy—or anything that an individual might do—that would not result in some risk to life ("even staying at home in bed bears some risk of mishap—the bed might collapse, the wind might blow the roof in, a marauder might enter"[101]).

Maybe Broome could reply that Mishan's conclusion would follow only if all social policies resulted in an increased risk of death. Generally, however, they are—in the broader view—enhancing rather than diminishing of life prospects. Introducing a social policy that results in three deaths/year for every 10,000 of a given population, to replace one that results in five deaths/year, or to meet a situation in which there has not previously existed a policy and in which fifteen are killed/year, avoids Mishan's *reductio*. However, the reply still does not sit comfortably with Broome's point of departure, viz., that any actual victim would, at the point of becoming a victim, eschew the policy. It is that point of departure that I have called into question.

Except for circumstances like those envisaged by Broome, in which it is assumed or argued that every individual will regard his/her own life as being of infinite value, the "surrender value" approach is not likely to provide a workable model for *social* policy, and the *socio*-economic valuation of human life. For the value that individuals will put on their lives will differ, and this may reflect a great variety of considerations, both rational and irrational. Social policies, especially where compensatory, are usually designed to minimize rather than capitulate to the effects of merely subjective factors, and the "surrender value" approach does not provide an appropriate control. This is not to deny the relevance of personal estimates to socioeconomic valuations, but for social policy purposes, they will need to be directed toward *policies* rather than individual assessments.

But even if personal surrender value does not lend itself to incorporation into social policy, there are other ways in which it may be given institutional expression.

Insurance value

In the last few decades, the surrender value approach has been given a workable institutionalized form, measured by individuals' willingness to pay for security of life or for compensation on loss of life. In 1965, Gary Fromm argued that if the probability of being killed in air travel could be reduced from the existing figure of .0000017 per trip of five hundred miles to zero, a person who valued his life at $400,000 should be willing to pay sixty-eight cents to reduce the existing risk to zero.[102] Using the same general approach, it seems as if it should be possible to work back from the premium an individual is willing to pay to the value he places on his life.

A strong motivating factor in this approach was the desire to take some account of the "personal"—as distinct from strictly economic—costs of loss of life. This is something that was inadequately accommodated by the "invested" and "productive" value approaches. And here, along with the "surrender value" model, some attempt is made to give a socioeconomic representation of life's value from the point of view of the individual whose life it is. Insurance value can be gauged individually via the insurance premium an individual is willing to pay, or collectively via the political process or questionnaire surveys. There are numerous variations and refinements—to take account of voluntary and involuntary risk, direct and indirect risk, and so on.

But whatever the theoretical merits of this approach—the place it gives to self-assessments of value—it has not been without its critics—even among its proponents. One difficulty has concerned the common assumption of linearity. In a high-risk activity, the amount that a person is willing to pay will almost certainly not be a simple multiple of what he/she is prepared to pay to insure against death in a low-risk activity. At a certain point, the willingness to pay will rise ever more steeply than the risk. There is, in addition, an assumption that the person who pays a premium to cover such risks is implicitly valuing his own life rather than—what is more likely—indicating the risk he is prepared to run for *others*, say, a family.[103] The person is not valuing his life, but the loss of his life to others whom he values. Furthermore, a person's willingness to pay will be significantly influenced by what he can afford (along with other factors). The wealthy will almost certainly "value" their lives more highly than the poor, not because they are prepared to invest a larger proportion of their resources in insurance, but because they have more resources than the poor. And finally, because there is some doubt about the extent to which individuals are able to appreciate small risk differentials, there is likely to be a good deal of variability to costing judgments. This difficulty is likely to be magnified by the remoteness of the calculations required by these judgments from those of ordinary experience.

Is the idea of socioeconomic life-valuation chimerical?

As the preceding discussion indicates, attempts to give human life a socioeconomic value are marked by competing conceptions of what is appropriately relevant to such valuations. There are reasons to ask whether the inquiry is a coherent one. We can formulate these questionings in at least two ways. First, we may query the appropriateness of seeking *a* socioeconomic value for human life; and second, we may wonder whether what is referred to as "the value of life" in socioeconomic contexts is a single thing.

Nicholas Rescher takes the first path. Looking for the socioeconomic value of a human life, he says, is like searching for the price of an item in a department store. There is no unique price. Different articles have different prices, and a search for some general price is the wrong kind of search.[104]

Rescher's point is not to eschew all efforts at giving some nonarbitrary monetary value to a life, but rather to challenge the view that some general value can be computed. How we value a life depends significantly on contextual features. Where people lose their lives from engaging in activities possessing equal risk—say, driving four thousand miles, drinking a bottle of vodka, or jogging four miles—there is, he believes, little temptation to think that insurance policies covering each eventuality should offer the same terms. How we appraise the value of a particular life threatened or lost depends significantly on "the exact nature of the death being risked or the mode by which it is risked."[105] What is more—to raise a point to which we will return—a threat to life that is psychically proximate to us is likely to attract a much greater investment of life-saving forces than one that is only statistical. If an improvement to vehicular design can be expected to save five lives, though only at a cost of $1 million, we might decide that it is too costly for the few benefits it will bring. However, if a particular known individual is trapped in a car because of the defect, we may not hesitate to spend what it takes to get him/her out—even if it exceeds $200,000. In addition, where a threat to life is produced involuntarily, we may be prepared to expend more resources to prevent or compensate it than would be the case were it inherent in some voluntarily chosen activity.

The situation is even more problematic than Rescher's department-store analogy suggests. Searching for *the* value of a human life is not even like searching for *the* price of an item in a department store. Although there is no such thing as the price of an item-in-general, each item nevertheless has its price. In the case of each human life, however, there is not even a fixed price. Context will determine its socioeconomic valuation: the kind of activity that threatens it, whether other lives are also threatened/lost, and so on. Indeed, for the most part, compensation judgments are not made after deliberation on the merits or worth of a particular life, but after a consideration of what, in the circumstances, the loss has been, and how its burden is best distributed. The judge makes a decision, "not an estimate of a preexisting—stable and well-defined—quantity."[106]

Where, then, does this leave the assessments that usually rely on some appeal to the value of a human life? Rescher believes that for the most part they can be made without recourse to some nominated "value of human life." This is because costing decisions can be made on a comparative basis: e.g., option *A* may save fifty lives but cost $100,000 to implement; option *B* may save only fifteen lives, though at a cost of $85,000. In order to choose between these options it shouldn't require that we know "the value of a life." But it may not be possible to avoid judgments of the "value of human life" in all cases. If the options are between saving two human lives for $100,000 and spending that $100,000 on a program to eradicate boll weevils, it will be necessary to make a judgment of the kind that Rescher seeks to avoid.

The second doubt concerning socioeconomic valuations is more fundamental. It calls into question whether what goes under the rubric of "the value of a human life" is really that. What we call "the value of a life" is so-called only as a convenient shorthand for other things. For example, what is being assessed on the market model is probably the value of a person's labor or services to someone else. One dimension of a person's life is quantified and its importance to another is indicated by the financial outlay that that person is prepared to make. The invested-value model is compensatory in intent. It does not really purport to value a particular life, but to recompense others for a loss, to repay them for an investment that has come to naught. The productive-value model is also compensatory: the purpose, again, is not so much to determine the socioeconomic value of a life, as to compensate certain others who were (usually) its beneficiaries and who may have relied on its material and other resources. Compensation also looms large in the surrender and insurance approaches to life-valuation. The individual who, by payment of a premium or acceptance of risk-loading, contracts to "receive" a certain financial benefit in the event of the loss of that life or for undertaking the risk, is not generally valuing that life—even to him/herself—but expressing a regard for the needs of others should that life be prematurely foreshortened.

Why, we might ask, should the various compensatory schemes detailed in the foregoing discussion be denominated schemes for the "valuing of human life"? The most benign answer is that this way of talking is a convenient shorthand for a range of more complex valuations—e.g., supplemented estimates of the financial needs of dependants of a prematurely killed person, and means-based expressions of the regard that a risk-taker has for the beneficiaries of an insurance policy. But a less generous response is also possible. It may be that the ease with which this way of talking has been adopted reflects a tendency towards the commodification of human life, in which human life is seen as a social resource and social value is measured from the perspective of either consumption or production. If that is so, and to the extent that it is, there is every reason to protest the routinizing of trade-offs between resource allocations and human lives.

Review

In reviewing the various arguments concerning the value of human life, it becomes clear that the reference of "human life" is variously understood. Sometimes the subject of value is *Homo sapiens* collectively, sometimes the focus is on individual members of the species, and at other times it is some more restricted grouping whose members are said to possess a basic or intrinsic value. Some such groupings—particularly that to which the term "person" is often ascribed—comprise members who are only contingently members of the species *Homo sapiens*.

But the problem of determining whether—and if so, why—human life is valuable is not settled through disambiguation. There are deep ideological commitments woven into some of these distinctions—or at least into the significance that is accorded to them.

I have attempted to review these commitments both historically and ideologically. Classical Greek writers, for example, seem not to have discerned any value in human life as such—in either its species-specific or individual manifestations. Value was not so much an endowment as an achievement, and as an achievement it was often the particular preserve of elites. Even for these elites, value did not reside in their individuality, but for the most part in conformity to some supra-human ideal. The Judeo-Christian tradition, to which classical Hellenism largely succumbed in the succeeding centuries, sought to generalize the regard that the classical writers had restricted. It was, ultimately, in God's creative dispensation that human value was located—Man as *imago dei*—and though this was variously understood, it tended to universalize human value, not only collectively but also individually. The purpose was not to sustain a crude egalitarianism but to ensure an equality of basic respect.

But if the Judeo-Christian tradition accorded a basic moral standing to all, it did so primarily in terms of a theology whose appeal for many has waned. And contemporary moralists have been faced either with finding an alternative foundation for valuing each human being or with specifying and defending a subset of human beings or some other restricted grouping.

Except, perhaps, for those whose embeddedness in a moral tradition has enabled them to "intuit" the basic and intrinsic worth of every human being, most writers have followed the second path. They have argued for the value of a human life in terms that need not confine eligibility to members of the species *Homo sapiens*. The problem has been to find a basis for valuation that does not draw the lines too broadly or narrowly—that neither erases morally significant distinctions nor creates invidious ones. Appeals to the capacity for self-awareness, language-possession, rationality, a moral sense, free will, and so on, possess some initial appeal, but are notoriously difficult to articulate without a reliance on ideology just as significant and problematic as that involved in the Judeo-Christianity it rejects.

What can we conclude from this discussion? I doubt whether any ideologically neutral conclusions are available. Although I draw back from the view that would have us trapped within competing yet incommensurable ideological frameworks, it is very difficult to speak on these matters without some accent.

It may assist some convergence, however, if we do not see the issue of human value as unidimensional. In chapter 1, we noted something of the complexity of the discourse of value, and it is not unreasonable to imagine that different human beings may be eligible for different kinds of value attributions. For example, what I called choice-constraining attributions may be most appropriately applied to human beings with a sense of self and capacity for some self-determination. That does not prevent their extension to others, but we may need to recognize that this will involve a degree of reconceptualization. Choice-relevant attributions, on the other hand, may be more generally applicable to humans, and help to mediate between a position that places an equal moral burden of care, no matter what the condition of life, and one that evacuates some human lives of any considerability.

SEVEN

TOWARDS A MORALITY OF LIFE

I believe one should trust problems over solutions, intuition over arguments, and pluralistic discord over systematic harmony. —Thomas Nagel[1]

To a significant extent, the past six chapters have been devoted to clarification, classification, and critique. I have endeavored to provide some insight into the considerable variety of concerns that lie behind and inform appeals to "the value of life." I have sought to organize these appeals in a reasonably systematic or at least a structured way. And I have offered the beginnings of a critical analysis of those appeals. Some arguments I have rejected completely; others I have pursued only so far, because to take them further would have immersed us in much wider debates in metaphysics, epistemology, ethics, and the philosophy of mind. Still other lines of argument I have found promising, if not decisive. There are many loose ends, and though this may be an affront to tidy and evangelistic minds, I do not think it a bad thing that a particular philosophical inquiry should have this outcome. On the contrary. I believe it to be a peculiar form of philosophical *hubris* that we presume to raise ourselves so far above the horizons of our particular age, culture, and assumptions that we purport to speak with the voice of eternal Reason.

Nevertheless, I want to make an effort to pull some of these disparate threads together—to indicate where I, at least, think the arguments are most promising, and to provide some suggestions for further reflection. I begin as I did at the beginning, with some general remarks about different kinds of valuing, and then I reconsider some of the most promising arguments for according to life-in-general and then particular forms of life some positive value-status. I conclude with further consideration of the place of different value-categories in discussions about particular life-forms and life-conditions, and of the varying weight that these different attributions may have in moral argument.

Valuing revisited

As I indicated in chapter 1, valuing (broadly conceived) is a vari-
form and essentially practical activity. We engage in it by virtue of
our achievement and status as choosers, as beings whose futures
are not and are not conceived of as the outcome of intersecting
forces and limiting structures beyond our control. We are, rather,
beings whose self-awareness, imaginative sensibilities, and capacities enable us, both individually and collectively, to shape our
future for ourselves. As choosers, we have devised a complex
structure of practically oriented conceptualizations that enable us
to confront our world in terms of what, as choosers, we would
choose it to be, and that help to organize and fine-tune our day-to-
day decision-making.

For ourselves, as valuers, valuing is a complex and nuanced enterprise. It represents one of our most characteristic and central
activities, and there has developed round it a rich and diverse—
though not necessarily consistent—structure of conceptual discriminations. Some elements within that complex structure of
conceptualization were surveyed in chapter 1, where notions of affirmative value, worth, dignity, respect, reverence, right, and sanctity were differentiated and discussed. Later in this chapter I will
return to these. But for the present I want to emphasize just three
points about our valuational activity.

1. Its *provisional* nature. Because choice, and the valuational activity that mediates a great deal of it, is so important to us, we are
strongly tempted to attribute to the valuational structures we adopt
an "objectivity" they cannot bear. If J. L. Mackie errs too much in
one direction in claiming that right and wrong are "invented," it is
no less an error to say that they are "discovered." Sinai notwith-
standing, there is no fixed and permanent valuational structure,
etched in stone, to which we can appeal, and from which we can
read off what it would be good, best, or obligatory for us to do. We
do not have any final understanding of what, as choosers, we
would choose our world to be, or even of what should be the appropriate vocabulary for our engagement in that task. The imaginative
enterprise of world making and self-understanding is an ongoing
and contested one.[2]

The point of the foregoing remarks is not to champion some form
of nasty subjectivism or relativism in ethics, but to insist that valuing is a human activity; it is something engaged in *sub specie humanitatis* and not *sub specie aeternitatis*. That is our human predicament.

165

The value judgments we make (be they judgments concerning what is good, bad, virtuous, right, obligatory, or inviolable) and the decisions we base upon them need be no more or less subjective or relativistic than any other of our determinations. What makes them appear more difficult, and disagreements less amenable to rational resolution, is the fact that they are concerned with what it is appropriate for us, as humans, to choose, and uncontaminated self-understanding does not come easily to us.

Provisionality, however, is not incompatible with firm views, with better and worse arguments, with an unwillingness to tolerate certain practices. In his debate with Judge Learned Hand, Justice Holmes expressed concern that Hand's toleration of opposing opinions would undermine "the sacred right to kill the other fellow when he disagrees." Not so, replied Hand, "kill him for the love of Christ and in the name of God, but always remember that he may be the saint and you the devil."[3] There was of course a subversiveness about Hand's response, but it brings out well the fruitful tension that may exist between robust opinions and a recognition of fallibility. What provisionality is incompatible with is authoritarianism and a closed mind, the refusal to reconsider beliefs in the light of opposition.

2.   The *diversity* of valuational language. Although I am not persuaded to Alasdair MacIntyre's perception of an irremediably fragmented and even contradictory moral discourse, it nevertheless behooves us to recognize the diversity of that discourse, and the differing and complex ways in which valuational concepts bear on practical choice. As something of a simplification, I have suggested a three-fold division into choice-relevant, choice-constraining, and choice-determining valuational discourse.

I have conjectured that the language of worth and affirmative value, and of good and bad, is used to portray selected aspects of our world in a primarily *choice-relevant* but not ipso facto choice-determining way. The old *Oxford English Dictionary* characterization of "good" as "the most general adjective of commendation" gets it about right, so long as we do not understand "commendation" in the way it became fashionable to do *post*–R. M. Hare.[4]

The language of respect and rights, however, tends to have a much more *choice-constraining* function. Assertions of respect, etc., tend to render certain choices inappropriate. They have, inter alia, a protective, "hands off" function. As was indicated in the earlier discussion, that is too simple a characterization of the rich implications of such discourse, but it captures one very important role that it has historically played.

The role of *choice-determination* is discharged primarily by the language of right and wrong, justified and unjustified. The assertion that a particular course of action is right or wrong is not merely action-guiding but *action-prescribing*. The person who asserts thus is expected to do or eschew.

I do not pretend that this classification of practical language is exhaustive. It offers at best a unidimensional division of part of our valuational world. As I have stated it, it takes little account of much nonmoral practical discourse; and the important language of virtue is also ignored. Nor have I offered any account of the relations that exist between these different kinds of valuational discourse. I have introduced the classification simply because it provides us with some assistance in understanding the diversity of life-affirming and life-supporting discourse. It helps to explain why talk of a "right to life" is sometimes favored over talk of the "value of life," why talk of human "dignity" may be more closely associated with "respect for life" than human "worth," and so on.

3.   Its *anthropogenesis*. Valuing, whether understood as a choice-relevant, choice-constraining, or choice-determining activity, is, so far as we know, a human- or person-centered enterprise, and it may be, as some have said, the most human of all activities. With the exception of God, the angels, and other denizens of a supernatural world, judgments of affirmative value and worth, of sanctity and respect, of right and wrong, are the preserve of human agents. We are the valuers of our world, not simply as the articulators of value, but as the shapers of value. However much and in whatever ways we may choose to ground different kinds of value in the features of a world external to us, nevertheless it is only as that world is comprehended *sub specie humanitatis* that it may qualify as a bearer of value, affirmative and otherwise. One of the great mistakes we make, a mistake made by those who see the world or parts of it as having inherent affirmative value/worth independent of any valuer (human or divine), is that of presuming that our perception of the world is or can be as neutral as a camera's. Rather, the world of language, the world of communication, is a world structured by human interests, albeit shared ones.

I am, of course, excluding animals from the class of valuers. I do so contingently, rather than as a matter of doctrine. It is not beyond my imagination that some animals should be discovered to have the powers that make them not merely choosers, but choosers who can base the choices they make on some evaluation of alternatives. And some animals, I grant, display the rudiments of such valuational activity. Yet it is my present view that the differences are

167

more significant than the similarities, and that we do better to concentrate on improving the accountability of humans for their treatment of animals than on wondering whether we ought to punish animals or seek to engage in moral dialogue with them.

Moral reflection and appraisal are part of a broader valuational activity in which humans, by virtue of their chooserhood, are regularly involved. The more restricted domain of moral reflection and appraisal is distinguished by its primary focus on *what we are in our relations with each other*, whether those relations are construed interpersonally, collectively, or structurally. In another context I would argue that as one of the products of our self-awareness we recognize ourselves as beings whose flourishing consists in a rich communal as well as individual life, and that this demands of us that we see and respond to each other in certain relatively determinate ways. Further, I would argue that what we are in our relations to each other is not necessarily limited to what we are in direct dealings. A person who is indifferent to the sufferings of others or of animals or to the destruction of the environment may show him/herself to be a person with sensitivities unworthy of human society.

What is relevant to note is that even though valuing in general and moral valuing in particular are the special—and almost exclusive—preserve of human agents, and are intended to reflect on and guide the conduct of those agents, they need not be confined to direct agent-agent relations. There is nothing about the anthropogenetic character of the different kinds of valuing that rules out the possibility of trees or animals or other living things being valued for their own sake.

Valuing organismic life

Ought the fact of an organism's being *alive* to weigh with us, and if so to what extent? Ought we, after the fashion of a Schweitzer, to have a "reverence for life"? Ought we to see in livingness something precious, something to be preserved or nurtured? These questions are not identical, but they point our inquiry in much the same direction. They ask us whether the livingness of some organism—its being the site of a self-integrating and self-renewing metabolic process—is something to be intrinsically valued or accorded normative status.

The arguments that have most going for them are those that try to make something of the "affinity" between human beings and other organisms that is supposedly constituted by their living-ness—an affinity that is absent from our relations with the inanimate world. This affinity in "life" is then said to make a difference to the way in which we ought to take the world of living things into account in our decision-making.

It is not surprising that an argument for the broad valuing of life should seek to draw on some affinity that we have to other forms of life. For life is something we experience and cherish from the inside; it is something with which we, as valuing beings, can easily identify. Livingness is not merely the condition of our own being, and a precondition of our valuing activity, but it provides the milieu within which our valuing makes sense—chooserhood is the privilege only of the living (though not all the living). By virtue of that affinity, then, it might be thought that there is something special to acknowledge in the humblest organism, a reason to see in its continuation at least an intrinsic (even if not an overriding) good.

But mere talk of an affinity is hardly perspicuous. Might we not equally speak of an affinity between ourselves and the inanimate world by virtue of our physical nature—the chemical elements we share? Perhaps not. There is more implied by the idea of affinity than some shared elements—its origins have to do with neighbor-relations and alliance by marriage. Still, that does not explicate any relevant affinity in this case. Why should the fact that we are all alive make more difference than the fact that our fundamental chemistry is continuous with that of the rest of nature? I want to consider four possibilities:

1.   The strongest—though least plausible—statement of affinity would posit something like a "kinship" between living things, drawing upon what we usually acknowledge to be the special affinities and obligations of consanguinity. The kin-child is not merely a child but my child, the kin-parent is not merely a parent but my parent, and there are sometimes said to flow from these kinship relations particular obligations—especially those of care and protection. Does the livingness of plants and animals make them comparably "of us"?

As I argued in chapter 5, when considering animal life, we cannot easily push the special bonds and obligations of kinship—supposing there to be such obligations[5]—as widely as this, to cover all of life. It is difficult enough (though admittedly not impossible) to extend this way of thinking to all human life. When we go beyond that, then, absent some unrecognized connection, it loses its plausibility. Talk of evolutionary links does not convey the necessary intimacy. A metaphor that relies heavily—as this one does—on certain discriminations made within human life will tend to lose its power if extended to cover all of life.

2. A somewhat different way of characterizing the affinity is suggested by some arguments of Robert Goodin, who happens to oppose the view that even for humans there are special kinship obligations. Instead he argues for the moral significance of vulnerability, and claims that our obligations to others, including those obligations that appear to arise out of kinship, are grounded in the vulnerability of others to what we do. Can we, then, maintain that living things possess a choice-relevant affinity by virtue of their vulnerability?

There is some plausibility to this. Since all living things are capable of flourishing or declining, they possess a welfare that can be promoted or diminished, they can be benefited or injured. Their welfare is vulnerable to what we do. Might this fact about them lay upon us certain burdens of care, or certain constraints on our invasions?

It is not hard to accept that living things have, with few if any exceptions, a welfare that is vulnerable. And I guess it can be maintained that all living things *have a good*. But as I argued in chapter 4, it doesn't follow from the fact that something has a good that it is good. From the fact that X has a good, it does not follow that X is a good thing to be. At least, *how* that is meant to follow needs to be made clear. If anything, the argument moves in the opposite direction. It seems more plausible to argue that any obligations we may have in virtue of the vulnerability of living organisms will presuppose a prior valuing of them, the very thing that we need to establish. In the case of human beings, for example, it might be argued that the good that their lives represent, and the obligations that arise out of their vulnerability, stem not from their livingness as such, but from what their lives are capable of being. The argument's conclusion is not so much false as undetermined.

In any case, vulnerability does not seem to be exclusive to living beings. Art objects, rockscapes, and the atmosphere are vulnerable to forces of destruction, and we may think that in at least some of these cases their destruction would be the destruction of something inherently valuable. But the value would not reside in their livingness, despite their vulnerability.

3. The views of Hans Jonas—already discussed in chapter 3— suggest a different kind of affinity. This is constituted by the stirrings—even in the most primitive forms of life—of freedom. Using some traditional terminology, Jonas argues that all life manifests

the contingent assertion of being against nonbeing. And, he believes, in that assertion there are the rudimentary or nascent stirrings of freedom. That freedom, so highly valued by ourselves, thus finds its progenitor in the struggle of every living being.

In my earlier discussion, I suggested that using the language of freedom as a means of distinguishing the processes of organic life from those of inorganic reaction was too strong. We can grant that the kind of self-integrating and self-renewing activity that is constitutive of an organism's livingness is also a material condition for what we ordinarily consider—and broadly value—to be an expression of freedom. But to speak of this, as Jonas does, as in itself an inchoate or embryonic assertion of freedom overdescribes the phenomenon. Even for human beings, freedom is an achievement rather than an endowment.

But it is possible to argue that this criticism was too heavy-handed, and fails to acknowledge part of what Jonas is attempting to say. For even though it may be misleading to speak about life as such manifesting an embryonic freedom—at least in anything but a metaphorical sense—there may nevertheless be something sufficiently akin to freedom to elicit from us an acknowledgment of the value (broadly conceived) of livingness. There is manifest in living organisms a distinctive *independence* of their environment that may evoke our affirmation and regard. By virtue of their self-integrating and self-renewing character, living organisms actively maintain their identity in a world that is constantly impinging upon them. Unlike inert substances, which passively retain an identity over time, and unlike inorganic matter, which offers no resistance to the impersonal forces of nature, the ability of a living organism to maintain its being—both individually and reproductively—in a dynamic interaction with its environment may be seen as an achievement, an accomplishment, something that we can marvel at or esteem.

We can see in the achievement of other living things the seeds of our own achievement, a certain triumphing over the forces of "nonbeing." To the extent that we do not affirmatively value this achievement, it might be argued, we detract also from our own. Of course, the achievement represented by subhuman life is in certain important respects quite different from our own. We might be cautious about using the language of dignity, respect, or sanctity when referring to a plant or insect: their independence is not of that kind. But we need not think that the whole valuational discourse needs to be applicable for some of it to be. We may affirmatively value livingness without seeing it as demanding our respect. We may see

171

in it a reason for having certain attitudes and for acting in certain ways toward it, without seeing it as placing side-constraints or other restrictions on our conduct.

I would suggest, then, that one source of affirmative value for livingness may lie in the fact that life represents some kind of accomplishment, in which a being succeeds in maintaining its identity in tension with the vast cosmic forces that both sustain and threaten it. This fact of our own existence we celebrate; we may also applaud it in the achievement of other living organisms.

We should, however, beware of inappropriate personification in characterizing this accomplishment. Very often, an organism's achievement in rising above the forces of destruction, will not be the result of conscious effort, but of an integration and organization of internal organic processes, both adaptive and responsive, to the external world that impinges on it. The achievement is better compared to the achievement of the unconscious human body, ravaged by injury or disease, but nevertheless able to marshall its internal resources to keep it functioning as a more or less unified whole.

4. A related but different kind of affinity shared by living things, and which we may see as a good, can be found in their possession of a *telos*. A characteristic of most, if not all, living things is that they have a *telos*—they are beings whose fulfillment is embodied in a life-cycle. Their livingness is not constituted by *stasis* but by the dynamic outworking of an end, a maturation or consummation, and this, it might be argued, represents a good, albeit—again—not an overriding one. In telic development of this kind it might be claimed that we and other living organisms are at one. It is of course true that different living organisms possess different *telē*, that some *telē* are much more rigidly determined than others, and that in some cases the outworking of those *telē* may interfere with the capacity of other organisms to fulfill their *telē*. Nevertheless, it might be maintained that by virtue of their telic nature we have some reason to leave them be, some reason not to be indifferent to the unfolding of their lives.

In chapter 3 I suggested that this is probably one of the subterranean impulses of Schweitzer's thought. What troubles him is not so much "the farmer who has mown down a thousand flowers in his meadow as fodder for his cows," as that same farmer who on his way home "strikes off in wanton pastime the head of a single flower by the roadside."[6] In one case the farmer is acting in recognition of the will-to-live; in the other case he does not. The telic will-to-live is not overriding; but neither is it to be treated with indifference. The harvesting is "necessitated" by the well-being of his cows, and the lives they serve. Though a thousand flowers are destroyed, the wrong done is not to be compared to that when a single flower is wantonly plucked.

I think this teleological dimension to life suggests a further affinity through which living things can be affirmatively valued for what they are. Human life is not seen as a static thing, but rather as a growth toward maturity, in which all our capacities come to be realized. It is usually seen as something of a tragedy when an individual dies before he or she is able to reach that maturity, or when some defect prevents a full expression of those capacities. To a lesser degree, but not therefore trivially, we might value the flourishing of other living things. True, their maturity does not promise as much as their human counterparts. But we can still respond to and admire the way in which their lives unfold.[7]

This telic character of human life also provides us with a way of making a connection that puzzled us earlier—between an organism's having a good and its realization of that good being itself a good thing. It is not simply that other living organisms have a good—a welfare—which may be well- or ill-served, but that this welfare is part of a developmental trajectory, something they share with us. They are not inert objects, whose *haecceity* can be represented in mechanical or electronic terms, and is therefore transparent to us, but centers of directed activity, whose dealings with the world are self-generated and self-fulfilling.[8]

I don't want to make too much of this argument. It is not intended to demonstrate some "equality of living things" or even to provide a watertight argument for their being accorded some intrinsic value. It is, rather, intended to display a perception of living things that, if absent, tends to leave a shadow over our own achievement and significance as living organisms.

Valuing diverse forms of life

Although all living organisms share something in common—viz., their livingness—it is not as the bare expressions of a generalized phenomenon that we encounter them. It is, rather, as manifestations of a particular form of life that we must first respond to and make decisions concerning living things.

So we might want to consider whether, beyond any value we may accord them by virtue of their livingness, they are amenable to

173

some further valuation or differentiation of value by virtue of the form of life to which they belong. Does it count that what we are confronted with is plant life, as distinct from animal or human life? Or that the organism before us is an insect rather than a bird? Or that it is *eucalyptus macrocarpa* rather than *hibbertia scandens*? Is there, in other words, any basis for a form of species discrimination?

These questions have been posed to encourage us to look for specific characteristics of different forms of life, and to determine whether there is anything in those characteristics that we might see as constituting a value. But we need not frame them in quite that way, and before I consider the various life forms I want to suggest that there is another way in which we may affirmatively value their variety.

The fact that a *diversity* of life forms exists may be seen as a good thing, and, with certain caveats, we may consider that the more diversity the better. Why should a diversity of life-forms be affirmatively valued?

There are of course some fairly obvious instrumental values to such diversity. Humans utilize the organic world in the pursuit of their own good. Whether for sustenance, health, or entertainment, humans find in the organic world a great resource. There is some reason to think that the greater the variety of organic life, the greater the resource, and the greater the possibilities for human enjoyment and benefit.

If we associate with this argument the further claim—made by a number of environmentalists, that diminution of diversity begets diminution of diversity, and does so, furthermore, progressively,[9] the implications become quite sobering. As our capacity to appreciate the richness of our environment, and to benefit from it, increases, it is increasingly depleted of its profusion.

But we can also note some noninstrumental values in diversity. Ecologically, diversity is generally associated with complexity, and with complexity there is the matrix for a richness of experience. This we may view as intrinsically good.[10] One of the things that makes human life the affirmatively valuable thing it is—one of the things, indeed, that makes us the valuers we are, is the capacity we have for richness of experience, experience marked by complexity, depth, and creative potential. The human experience is not one of simple reactivity, but of reflective integration, creative intervention, of empathetic identification, and of imaginative transcendence. The greater the diversity available to us, the greater the stimulus to our distinctive capacities.[11]

To some extent this capacity for richness of experience is a function of our rationality, or at least our capacity for thought and reflection.[12] But it is also a function of the environment in which we live. Human development, unlike that of a tree, is not an inwardly fixed process, whose outcome is relatively independent of a diversified environmental experience. Human development is distinctively a function of learning, and an impoverished environment will encourage the development of an impoverished human life.

It might be complained that this account of the value of diverse forms of life attaches that value too much to anthropocentric concerns. For it is the way in which they contribute to the richness of human experience that gives the diverse forms of life their value, and not some properties they have in themselves. But this complaint misses the central point. The point is that the diversity of organic life and the complexity associated with it give rise to the possibility of a richness of experience which valuers value. And they value that richness of experience not just because of the instrumental value it may have but also because of the kind of experience it is. To ask: "Is richness of experience a good thing?" is like asking whether honesty is a good character trait. The very conceptualization of the experience as rich or the character trait as one of honesty already reflects the perspective of a valuer.

We have, then, an argument for a world of diverse living things. It is not an argument for plant life as such or for animal life as such or for plant life as against animal life or vice versa. It is, however, an argument that might be advanced in favor of species, and particularly endangered species. And if we are to accept the argument that the disappearance of a species from an ecological system tends to lead to a weakening of that system, with a consequent threat to other species within the system, then we may have a fairly strong argument for the diversity of species.

We must, however, say something about a possible counterargument. If the diversity of species is important because of the way in which it provides the context for richness of experience, might we not produce that richness of experience artificially—by means of an "experience machine"? Might we not, with the assistance of advanced technology, create "nature-paks"—audio-videos that would reproduce for our pleasure all the wonderful diversity of a nature that once was. Why is the real thing—or the persistence of the real thing—so important?[13] The argument reveals a misunderstanding of the nature of the experience that is valued. What is affirmatively valued is not the experience as a mere psychological

175

or audio-visual phenomenon—not an experience *as of* diversity—but the experience of actual, ongoing diversity. We may be glad of the record, or the re-creation, but if the real thing is no longer there to engage us and to impress its vitality on the world, we will regret its passing as loss. True, some of us would rather watch nature documentaries than engage with nature firsthand, but if documentaries were all that we had, we would almost surely consider the world a poorer place.

Once again, it must be insisted that this argument for the preservation of diversity, and hence for diverse species of living things, is not an argument for diversity come what may. It does not claim that every species is equally important or rule out the propriety of seeking to eliminate some species. All it claims is that there is an affirmative value to the diversity of species that needs to be taken into account when we make decisions that will affect them.

The forms of life revisited

Let us return then to our earlier question and ask whether—apart from their constituting part of the diversity of life—there is anything specific to be said about the intrinsic goodness of the different forms of life.

That there might be something to be said is suggested by the ancient distinction between plant, animal, and human life. This distinction, which predates scientific inquiry as we know it, almost certainly reflects a deeply held, though elastic and culturally mediated, conviction that they are ordered hierarchically—animal life taking precedence over plant life and human life over animal life. Such beliefs are not necessarily rendered obsolete by the contemporary view that one life form has developed out of another—animal out of plant, human out of animal—although it must then acknowledge a radical transformation that is to be accorded evaluative significance.

What lies behind this distinction? Can we point to distinguishing features that ground some differentiation in the value accorded to them? Although I believe that some of the features possessed by particular species of plants, animals, and humans do provide grounds for our according them special value, I want to suggest that the broad, ancient distinction between plants, animals, and humans relates not only or even primarily to value narrowly understood—to affirmative value—but rather to the normative constraints that apply to choosers. We are under greater constraint with respect to our dealings with animals than with respect to our dealings with plants, and we are under greater constraint with respect to our dealings with humans than we are with respect to our dealings with animals.

The ancient plant-animal-human distinction is a rough-and-ready one. It may not exactly correspond to the more finely tuned accounts that modern scientific inquiry is able to offer. Nevertheless, the distinction has its usefulness. As living organisms, plants lack motility relative to animals and humans. Their sources of sustenance must be spatially proximate, and their capacity to survive and flourish is almost wholly independent of what we would call "learning." A seedling is more vulnerable to environmental conditions than a mature plant or tree, but its capacity to realize its developmental *telos* is a function of its internal programming rather than of a learning process.

Animals, on the other hand, must exercise some form of perception and possess some degree of sentience if they are to flourish. They are motile, and may have to seek out their sources of nourishment. Many animals, particularly the higher ones, and those that depend on "parental" support during infancy, may need to pass through a learning process before they are able to deal successfully with their environment.

These are, of course, sweeping generalizations. The animal world in particular, ranging as it does from sponges to chimpanzees (or, if you like, human beings), lends itself to no easy characterization, and I have focused on factors that tend to apply more particularly to those animals that most directly exercise our moral sensitivities.

Human life and flourishing is much more centrally characterized by learning and reflective thought. Our imaginative, linguistic, and reflective capacities do not emerge out of a genetic blueprint like pubic hair—as the (mostly) natural outcome of physiological maturation—but only as the result of a long process of learning. Even though some human beings are able to survive outside a "parental" environment at a remarkably early age,[14] one of the things that generally characterizes human life is the long period of social and psychological dependence that is required if humans are to flourish as the distinctive choosers we believe them to be. It is our status as choosers that makes human good, unlike animal good, such a diverse and open-ended thing. The "good for Man" is almost more procedural than substantive. Our individual goods or *telē* may show only broad convergences.

177

As this brief account of the plant-animal-human distinction makes clear, the different orders tend to be accompanied by or associated with factors that bear on the way in which choosers—valuers—interact with them. Plants are not seen as sentient, animals are not seen as rational, or reflective and imaginative, and for valuers—at least human valuers—both sentience and thought are given normative significance. The point is not that animals value things differently or value different things, but that animals are (broadly speaking) not valuers.

Nevertheless, each of the factors that distinguish plants from animals from humans in its own way grounds some limitations on the ways in which we might reasonably act on its possessor. The experience of pain, especially when it has the duration, intensity, and effects that constitute it as suffering, is, I believe, prototypically an evil. True, there are extraordinary physiological circumstances under which the experience of what is characterized as pain is not minded; but these cases aside, it is natural and appropriate to see pain as an experience whose imposition needs to be justified. Even though we might reasonably argue that a person who cannot feel pain or is not bothered by it lacks a valuable capacity—since pain is an important register of danger—we may consider its infliction as an evil. People may be warned by it, they may even be elevated through the experience of it; but these and other goods that may come from the experience of pain would show only that despite the evil it is, good may sometimes come of it or its infliction can sometimes be justified.

Not all, apparently, agree with these assertions. J. Baird Callicott, for example, declares "with all soberness that [he sees] nothing wrong with pain. It is a marvelous method, honed by the evolutionary process, of conveying important organic information."[15] But without for the moment calling Callicott's evolutionary analysis of pain into question, it does not seem to me that his conclusion follows from his premise. For even if it can be argued that without the capacity to experience pain human life would be gravely imperiled, such pain, even when seen as instrumentally good, may still be intrinsically bad. Whether or not pain serves a purpose—evolutionary or otherwise—its infliction calls for justification.

Whether it is experienced by humans or animals, pain (or the suffering in which it often manifests itself) is an evil. That is why its gratuitous—and sometimes purposeful—infliction on animals can constitute cruelty. This is not to deny that the infliction of gratuitous pain on humans and animals can be morally differentiated. In the case of humans, the experience of pain can interfere with so much else of normative significance—e.g., the ability to exercise one's distinctively human capacities. It is partly because of these additional factors that we do not generally have the qualms about "putting an animal out of its misery" that we do in the case of human beings. Putting an animal out of its misery will not generally foreclose a future—however meager—it may have wished for the opportunity to realize; whereas humans are often replete with aspirations that give them reason to endure interminable pain.

Thus, so far as human life is concerned, the capacity to experience pain is only one of the factors having normative bearing. There is in addition the human capacity for self-reflection and self-determination—the capacity for transcending the bounds of immediate experience, the ability to project and to choose between possible futures. For human beings, the frustration of that capacity is counted an intrinsic evil. Indeed, so important is this capacity to characteristically human life that it has become the main focus of a distinctive normative vocabulary. The ideas of human dignity, of respect for persons, and even, according to some writers, of rights, are closely bound up with the fact that humans are able to be the agents of their own tomorrow.

Although I have suggested that the foregoing features of animal and human life may provide a basis for differentiating them—for seeing progressive constraints being placed on our intervention—I do not want to exclude the possibility that they might also provide a basis for a differential affirmative valuing of them. There is a sense in which our limited—but not total lack of—capacity to empathize with animals draws us to them more than to plants. It is not so much a form of kinship that we have with them, but the way in which their additional capacities offer us the prospect of a richness of experience that we would not otherwise have. Both through their lives in the wild, and in their relations to us, animals may display a complex diversity of lifeways and sensitivities. Thus animal and human life, by providing us with increasing opportunities for rich and fulfilling experience, may be accorded greater intrinsic value than plants.

In addition, there are of course reasons why particular kinds of plants or animals or even particular individuals of such may be affirmatively valued more highly than others. Some of these reasons may be instrumental, e.g., the benefits they might make possible.

But there may be aesthetic values that some possess—the song of the nightingale, the grace of an eagle—that constitute an added value for us. And domesticated animals and pets will provide a different source of affirmative value.

Hierarchy and the discourse of value

In chapters 1 and 2, I tried to indicate some of the complexities involved in appeals to "the value of life." Not only are there diverse forms and dimensions of life, but there is great variety in the valuational terminology employed in such appeals. It will be useful at this point to return to some of that terminology, to gauge its appropriateness in the light of my discussion in this chapter.

The broad activity of valuing has, I suggested, a fundamentally practical point. Were we not choosers, faced with options, there would be no raison d'être for valuing. Even if it is not exclusive to human beings, valuing is certainly most characteristic of them. Not only is this so, but, because of the importance of this form of activity to human life, we have also developed a rich vocabulary of valuational terms.

I suggested that some of this vocabulary could be differentiated by virtue of its choice-relevant, choice-constraining, or choice-determining function. The language of affirmative value, worth, sanctity, and dignity are primarily choice-relevant. The language of rights, respect, reverence, and inviolability, on the other hand, have a primarily choice-constraining function. I suggested that some of the factors that were choice-relevant would also provide a ground for choice-constraint, though the relation is not simply one in which choice-constraint depends on the presence of (enough) choice-relevant features.

1. Choice-relevant features of life. In chapter 1, I distinguished a number of senses in which we might speak of something having value. But of these, only one—what I spoke of as the affirmative sense of value—concerns me here. In affirmatively valuing something we indicate that it possesses a choiceworthiness. And it may do so, either because its features that we consider make it choiceworthy for its own sake or because it is instrumental to ends that we regard as inherently choiceworthy.

I have suggested that at this level, there are several grounds on which we might value "life." We may affirmatively value organismic life in both its unity and diversity. And we may value it both for itself as well as for its instrumental value. As life in general, we may identify with and admire the independence manifested by organic life, the way in which, like ourselves, particularly in our embodiment, the various life forms engage and succeed in their struggle for existence. Also, we may possess a certain admiration for the way in which this "achievement" of life or "overcoming of non-being" takes the form of a telic development. Even though we are unlikely to value the accomplishments of plants as highly as those of humans, there are, if we attend to them, enough affinities between the character and cycle of plant life and human biological life to make it appropriate to value plants for what they are. Even though there is much, much more to human than plant life, we do well not to forget that what we understand as distinctively human is embedded in and emerges out of a physiology to which plants are linked. We share life. The person who fails to appreciate the "triumph" that life is has failed to appreciate part of his or her own achievement.

But we may also value life in its diversity. The myriad manifestations of life, their variety and complexity, the wonder of an ecological system, may provide for us an enriching experience that we value for its own sake. It was something like this abundant profusion and "vitality" of life that captivated Schweitzer in his trip down the African river.

The diversity of life forms may also be valued instrumentally for the way they may contribute to our own ends. Whether as food, medicine, as an economic or aesthetic resource, or as providing opportunities for recreation, living things have much to offer us. I think we may sometimes undervalue the instrumental worth of living things. The "contingency" of instrumental value makes it a fragile basis for defending organismic life. Nevertheless, such values are not inconsiderable, and should not be forgotten while we search for something more enduring.

The language of dignity, I have suggested, tends to be restricted to human life, and is generally thought to belong to that life by virtue of its self-determining abilities. As I earlier indicated, there is some dispute as to whether dignity is possessed by human life only by virtue of its being under rational or deliberative control, or whether dignity may belong to any human life by association.

The former understanding probably best captures our sense of the idea. The fact that humans are autonomous or free beings is seen as something affirmatively valuable about them. It gives them a certain nobility of aspect. It is also seen as something that can constrain us in our dealings with them. It requires that in our dealings with them we do not objectify them, treat them as though they are not choosers in their own right, with a right to some say in how we treat them. May we treat animals or plants with indignity? We may treat them cruelly, we may exploit them, but I am not sure that we can treat them with indignity. We cannot humiliate or shame them: or, to hedge my bets, to the extent that we can shame or humiliate them, they can be possessors of dignity.

Human life may also be accorded a certain sanctity. The language of sanctity has a double role.[16] By virtue of its common associations with a religious perspective, life's sanctity is seen, on the one hand, as a special affirmative value, and on the other hand, as having a special status. The view that human life is fashioned in God's image and likeness is believed, by those who share that view, to give it a certain elevated character, spirituality, or significance. God, for believers, is no mere demiurge or first cause, but the source and manifestation of good. At the same time, however, this distinctiveness is believed to set human life apart in a special way—as inviolable or an object of respect. The language of sanctity tends to be choice-constraining as well as choice-relevant. Attributing sanctity to life functions not only to accord it certain special valuable qualities that elevate it or render it awe-inspiring, but also to check our conduct with respect to it.

Again, it is usually human life that is accorded sanctity. Human life alone possesses those qualities or the divinely ordained elevation or standing that makes the language of sanctity appropriate. True, some writers, seeing in livingness a *mysterium tremendum*, and wishing to accord it a quasi-religious grandeur, have used the language more generally. But for the most part that language—to the extent that it has credibility—applies most comfortably to human life. Whether it has credibility will to a large degree depend on the credibility we wish to give to the religious categories that it reflects.

2.   Choice-constraining features of life. Some of our normative discourse is relational in the sense of spelling out for us certain conduct we should observe. There are reasons for requiring or desisting from conduct that affects the interests of the bearers of those interests. As I noted above, the language of sanctity is sometimes used in this manner, at the same time as it is also used to signify the presence of certain choice-relevant features. But other parts of our valuational vocabulary often make this much more explicit. Talk of reverence for life or of the inviolability of life, or of respect for life

or the right to life are most often used relationally—as indicators of a stance that we must adopt toward (some) life.

The language of reverence for life, popularized by Schweitzer, seems to have its origins in a religious framework, wherein life is given a quasi-divine or divinely ordained status. Although Schweitzer presents the idea of reverence as a secularized one, it is secularized only marginally. Basically, it attributes to life a moral status such that its processes should—ceteris paribus—be deferred to. The person who willfully or negligently destroys life does not merely fail to take into account an affirmative value that life possesses, but violates a constraint that life imposes on choosers.

How appropriate is it to see life as something to be revered? Outside human life, it is not clear that the religious tradition from which Schweitzer drew most of his inspiration provides grounds for reverence. For value, yes, but nothing quite so strong as reverence. Plants are given to Man and the animals for food, and animals are placed under the dominion of Man. True, there is every reason to think that the rape and wanton destruction of plant and animal life were not contemplated in this initial "ordering." Nevertheless, nothing so strong as reverence for all life was intended. Indeed, perhaps only God—and not even Man—was to be revered. The response to the Psalmist's question, "What is Man, that you should spare a thought for him?" accords a dignity to Man—an alien dignity that manifests itself in an inherent dignity—but makes it clear that reverence is appropriately reserved for God.[17] Outside a specifically religious framework, the language of reverence has relatively little to commend it.

To some extent, the language of respect provides a secularized alternative to the language of reverence. However, as we saw in chapter 1, respect is a complicated notion. In some of its historical uses, it is closely associated with the idea of reverence—at least in its more "awesome" and high-status dimensions. Our contemporary appeals to respect tend to focus not on life so much as persons. The reason is not too difficult to see. As a choice-constraining notion, respect is the appropriate stance to have towards what Kant called a rational will—a being who is his/her own center of reasons for action.

Nevertheless, there are senses in which people still speak of respect for life. Sometimes, of course, this is just an elliptical way of referring to respect for persons—a respect for the lives of rational agents. But there are other uses. On one account, to have respect for life is to see it as morally considerable, i.e., as having a claim to the consideration of moral agents. This is a fairly weak notion, in which respect seems to have more of a choice-relevant than choice-constraining function. A stronger view interprets respect for life as the ascription to it of a status that warrants our deference. This is the secularized version of reverence. It is not clear that life in general demands our respect in this sense. Only when thought of as a respect for human life does it have much going for it. An even stronger interpretation sees respect for life as indicating a certain inviolability. Unless this is spelled out against the background of some religious tradition, it is not clear how such a strong position can be maintained, even with respect to human life.

Finally, there is the now-dominant appeal to the right to life, an appeal that is heard not only in relation to human life but also in regard to plant and animal life. Because the language of rights has become so fashionable, especially as a political catchcry, it has been pressed into service on behalf of almost every normative claim. In consequence it has acquired a certain amorphous, catchall quality.

To some extent, the reasons for the proliferation of rights-talk lie in its history. As we have already observed, rights originally constituted legally enforceable claims. When the language of rights was initially taken over into moral discourse, rights were considered to be moral claims of sufficient weight to warrant, if necessary, the enforced recognition of others. Those claims, in the minds of early rights theorists, were socio-moral demands (usually to forms of noninterference) that humans could make on their behalf by virtue of their status as reasoning beings. The language of natural rights became the language of civil disobedience and revolution. It morally secured for the individual a sphere of action over which the state—and others—had no legitimate jurisdiction, and in protection of which force could be used.

In subsequent developments, different elements in this complex came to the fore in the appeal to rights. For some writers, the fact that moral/human/natural rights-talk began as the language of human liberation—a liberation grounded in the capacity for individual choice—provided a basis for their claim that qualification as a right-holder presupposed a capacity for choice. On this view, rights were seen as discretionary powers. Other writers, however, focused on the political significance of rights-talk. The fact that rights warranted the use of force in their securement encouraged them to employ the language of rights whenever it was thought a moral claim should be enforced. Whether the claim was made on behalf of a rational being was not important. A further development came from the reflection that any moral consideration that could justify the use of force to secure it would have to relate to important factors like basic needs. And so rights evolved from being essentially protective to positive, contribution-demanding considerations. A person might be seen to have a right not only to negative goods such as the right not to be killed or interfered with, but positive goods such as the right to education or health care. On this view rights were seen as advantages constituted by welfare interests.

Choosing between "discretionary power" and the "enforceable claim" approaches is no easy matter, and I doubt whether the arguments for accepting one are much stronger than those for accepting the other. Here there is something of an indeterminacy in our conceptual structure, reflective of an ambivalence in our moral intuitions. Nevertheless, I am inclined to press more strongly for some version of the broader view, in which rights are thought of as enforceable welfare interests.

According to H.L.A. Hart, who champions the more restrictive view, the possession of a right puts one morally in a position to determine by one's choice how another will act, and in this way to limit the other's freedom of choice.[18] Rights so conceived are discretionary powers (where powers are thought of as competences), capacities to tighten or loosen a moral grip. As Hart expresses it, "The precise figure is not that of two persons bound by a chain, but of *one* person bound, the other end of the chain lying in the hand of another to use if he chooses."[19] If this is so, rights will be the exclusive possession of beings having a developed capacity for choice (or preferences). And the right to life will accordingly be restricted to those whose self-understanding enables them to determine whether to further or relinquish their life.

The broader view, in which rights are viewed as advantages constituted by welfare interests, starts from a recognition that those things to which we wish to lay claim as rights are generally considered beneficial or advantageous to us: life, liberty, the pursuit of happiness, etc. But not any old benefits are in view, nor benefits that might be considered idiosyncratic, only those that are fundamental to the pursuit of our varied ends. These are what Rawls refers to as "primary goods,"[20] or as I would term them, "welfare interests," interests that are distinguished not primarily as those in which we have some conscious stake (as the discretionary view supposes), but as those basic prerequisites for the pursuit of whatever it is that we may have or come to have a stake in.[21] Welfare interests predate any choice behavior or preferences on the right-holder's part. It is largely on the basis of this view that rights, including the right to life, are extended or proposed for extension, to infants, fetuses, animals, and even plants and ecosystems.

A case for choosing the beneficiary view (albeit with its expansionist possibilities) can be made by considering Hart's chain metaphor more closely. Call the two persons A and B, and take A as having a right against B. What, then, does Hart mean when he writes that "the precise figure" is of B bound, the other end of the chain lying in A's hand, to be used at the latter's discretion? There is an unfortunate ambiguity in the metaphor, for in saying that B is bound, it is not clear whether B is simply bound, or bound *to A*. Yet the figure of the chain simply "lying" in A's hand, to be used only "if he chooses," suggests that B is not bound to A *unless A* grips the chain. Put more schematically, the statement form, "A has a right to x against B" may be thought to entail either "B has a duty to give x to A unless A chooses otherwise" or "B has a duty to give x to A only if A chooses." It may of course be questioned whether either of these is entailed, but if we are to choose the one that most nearly captures the discretionary element in rights-talk, the first formulation seems to be best suited. B's duty to respect A's rights does not have to wait for A's assertion of them, and if A waives them, he releases B from what is already due to him. If A has a right against B, the chain that binds B does not merely *lie* in A's hand. A has a firm grip on it, though he may release it. However, advocates of the discretionary position (such as Hart), tend to adopt the second formulation, and this explains the exclusion of infants, animals, etc. from the company of right-holders. For the second, though not the first, formulation presupposes the right-holder's actual ability to choose.[22] It would seem, therefore, that in order to capture the discretionary element in rights-talk, we do not need to tie it directly to interests which only actual choosers can have.

Although I have expressed this argument in favor of the beneficiary view somewhat formally, it is important to recognize that the issue is not a *merely* formal one. It is a choice about the role that rights-talk is to play in our moral discourse. My own view is that what Hart and others have seen as the "specific force" of rights-talk can be preserved on the beneficiary view if we recognize that for some right-holders a measure of liberty constitutes a welfare interest.

What then of the right to life? Who possesses it? Do plants, animals, only humans, all humans? It does not seem to me that our investigation has uncovered any general right to life.

On the view that plants and animals have a good which their welfare interests subserve, then there is some reason to extend to them certain rights—those that will help to secure their welfare interests against predations that are under the control of moral agents. Such rights would be possessed primarily by individual plants and animals, though some would want to extend them to ecological systems, and to speak more generally of environmental rights.

But granted that it does make sense to speak of the welfare interests of plants and animals, are they such as to warrant the coercive protection (or vindication) that rights-talk is first and foremost designed to secure? That is a harder question. Clearly some of those who press for the rights of plants, animals, and the environment think so, for that is precisely the point of their appeal to rights. Yet it may not do simply to point out that plants and animals have welfare interests, unless some case is made for *our* thinking that these welfare interests are so important that they should have the backing of force. It is true that the welfare interests of particular plants and animals are very important to their survival and flourishing, but is there a case for our believing that their survival and flourishing is of such importance that we should grace those welfare interests with the language of rights?

My suspicion here is that it will be very difficult to speak generally about the rights of plants or animals. As I indicated earlier, a case can be made for valuing plant and animal life both in itself and for its instrumental significance. But I doubt whether these instrumental values could be appealed to as a basis for ascribing rights to the plants or animals themselves, even though they may sometimes be considered important enough to justify their coercive protection. Any rights here will be human rights, and not plant or animal rights. Might our intrinsic valuing of them make rights-talk appropriate? Will such values be substantial enough to warrant coercive protection? But here again the values, though significant, are not obviously or in all cases of such importance that their coercive securement would be justified. The person who does not value plants and animals for the kinds of reasons I have mentioned may reveal a certain atrophy of spirit or a meanness of imagination, but it is not clear that we should fight this by coercive means.

187

Or, if we do, it should be in the indirect way that J. S. Mill supported, when he argued for the public sponsorship of culture. He claimed that there should remain available to the human spirit works of imagination, even though a culture became so barbarized that its members individually preferred pushpin to poetry.[23] In a profiteering society, dedicated to private accumulation and reared on the glitter of artifice, it might be a good thing to support the preservation of wild nature and its values, even though it is not possible to argue that it, or its inhabitants have a right to our protection. It is, perhaps, we ourselves who have some right to the intrinsic values of nature.

If we take the more restrictive view of rights, in which rights are seen as the exclusive possession of choosers, then it is much more difficult to press the view that plants and animals have rights. Indeed, it will follow from such a view that only some human beings will have rights. Infants, the severely retarded, and the permanently comatose might well be seen as lacking rights. And that, as we know too well from the existing debates, might be taken either as a confirmation or as a reductio ad absurdum of the discretionary position.

Review

It would have been gratifying had this "constructive" chapter yielded a comprehensive and systematic *Lebensphilosophie* in which the various questions that initially engaged us, and that were subsequently added to, could be seen in their relation to each other, and answered with some assurance. But that has not been the way in which this inquiry has developed. The vocabulary of value is diverse, responsive to the varied practical concerns of choosers, but not patterned in any tightly systematic way. The sources of value have likewise proven diverse and controversial, wider-ranging than the classical theories would have us believe, and apparently less secure. Even with the wisdom of centuries as our heritage, we are in no strong position to speak for today or tomorrow.

Nevertheless, I have attempted to draw on that deposit of past reflection and discussion to offer a number of considerations that should incline us to accord some practical significance to livingness, both generally and in its varied representations. As valuers ourselves, given to normative discrimination because of our capacity to choose how we may live, it is hardly surprising that we should accord a special status to other choosers, and that our relations to them should generally be mediated by reason rather than force.

But our choices can be only as rich as our physical and social environment allow, and the medium for such choice is organic embodiment. To a considerable extent the richness of our world is given through the plenitude of living things—in their diversity, their complex interactions, their utility. And in the struggle of life, in the capacity of organisms to survive the "forces of nature" and to perpetuate their success through succeeding generations, we see a replay or at least hear an echo of our own embodied existence. To value such life should not be difficult for the beings we are.

True, we are not at all clear about what value to place upon the phenomenon of life in general, or on its varied forms, or on particular instantiations of it. And so we find that in the inevitable competition that is given in our earthly condition, our choices are difficult and controversial, and we are called upon to use what our history has shown to be the limited and wayward resources of our deliberative capacities. There is no alternative to this, and I do not think that we should seek some Cartesian solution. Our cause is best served by recognizing the limitations of our condition and remaining as open as we can to the voices around us.

In the next chapter I shall attempt to respond to some of those voices as they bear on several of the practical controversies surrounding the value of life.

E I G H T

SOME APPLICATIONS

> The proposition that life is sacred is no more than a guiding principle. The forms of human life that are sacred, however, are so variegated, so often in tension with each other, and so resistant to being placed on a clear-cut scale of degrees of sacredness, that infinitely difficult problems remain in deciding what is permissible or intolerable.   —Edward Shils[1]

Over the past several chapters I have offered an analysis and appraisal of appeals to "the value of life." To some extent this discussion has been abstracted from both the particular controversies in which such appeals are heard and the competing considerations against which the varied values of life are ranged. The destruction of flora and killing of animals for food, abortion, and embryo experimentation, the treatment of anencephalic and severely retarded newborns, organ and tissue "harvesting" and genetic manipulation, capital punishment and war, suicide, euthanasia and the maintenance of those in persistent vegetative states, have all been opposed on the ground that they undervalue or violate "life." In this final chapter I shall turn to some of these controversial issues, and endeavor to provide a clearer picture of the way in which the varied appeals to life's "value" may function in the ongoing moral debate.

To investigate all the foregoing issues, at the depth each deserves, would require several volumes, and not a single chapter. So I shall not attempt to discuss them all, and those that I do discuss will not be exhaustively pursued. Indeed, my purpose is much more limited. I am interested in showing how the broad issue of life's value manifests itself in these applied contexts, and in determining the weight that it should be given. In other words, although I am concerned to indicate the normative force of broad appeals to the value of life, this is not the place to attempt to resolve the particular controversies to which such appeals are relevant.

Vegetarianism

Vegetarianism is not a single position, but a cluster of positions generally unified by opposition to the killing of animals for food. Some of its more extreme proponents (vegans) oppose even the eating of animal products, but most vegetarians limit their opposition to the eating of animal flesh. There are, however, still considerable differences. Some oppose the killing only of "higher" animals—here thought of as those animals possessing either a sufficiently developed awareness or a nervous system of sufficient complexity to enable them to experience suffering or pain. Others extend their opposition to all animals. Those taking the former position generally ground their opposition on the fact of animal suffering and/or pain rather than on any inherent value attributable to animal life. Those taking the latter position frequently appeal in addition to the inherent value and other claims of conscious or animal life. Here I shall be concerned with vegetarianism only to the extent that it involves a broad appeal to the value of animal life.

The two approaches I have just outlined may be linked as follows. Even though it is (sometimes) possible to kill animals without causing them or other animals pain and suffering, killing them will nevertheless deprive the world of a repository of pleasurable experiences and satisfactions, a repository whose pleasures may well have exceeded its sufferings. Pleasure and satisfaction are seen as intrinsic goods or ends-in-themselves, and on this argument the killing of animals is seen as the disvaluable termination (albeit not overridingly so) of a source of pleasurable experiences or satisfactions.

The background to this view is usually—though it need not be—some form of classical utilitarianism. Pleasure/satisfaction is taken to be the ultimate good, and right conduct is determined as the course of action conducive to the maximization of that ultimate good. Adoption of this view would not automatically rule out the painless killing of animals for food, since the disvalue involved in destroying such repositories of pleasurable experience would have to be offset against the pleasures gained in killing and consuming them. Nevertheless, many utilitarian vegetarians would want to argue that the significant pleasures of meat consumption could be achieved at less cost in aggregate pleasure or satisfaction.

The difficulties confronting this way of defending vegetarianism occur at a number of levels. Most generally, the adequacy of its utilitarian underpinnings can be challenged. But since I do not believe that doctrinal utilitarianism necessarily underlies the view that the (one) affirmative value associated with animal life is the capacity for pleasure, and since utilitarian-based vegetarianism is most often and most plausibly defended by reference to the *actual* pain and/or suffering caused to animals reared and killed for food, I shall not pursue that line of attack.

A more telling difficulty concerns replaceability. If what is wrong with the painless killing of animals is the destruction of sources of pleasure, then, other things being equal, their killing poses a problem only so long as they are not replaced. If for every animal killed another (with similar prospects for pleasurable experiences) is bred to replace it, then it is difficult to see how there has been any reduction of repositories for pleasurable experiences. An affirmative valuing of animal life that allows such replaceability provides weak support for vegetarianism.

We should note that this response will work only to the extent that animal lives lack individuality, and therefore the kind of non-replaceability that human lives are able to possess. However, it is generally much easier to replace a dead pet than a dead child. And because of the individuality of children the attempt (by bereaved parents) to replace one with another is fraught with problems. It is true that domestic animals are frequently accorded something approaching individuality, and where that is so it will be difficult to use the replaceability argument. And in general, the richer—more individualized—our descriptions of animal life and animal society become, the more problematic it becomes to appeal to replaceability. For the most part, though, such individuality may be difficult to attribute to animals used for food.

An argument that focuses on the intrinsic value of pleasure and satisfaction as the basis for affirmatively valuing animal life values animal life only contingently. It is not animal life that is viewed as an end-in-itself, but only the pleasure and/or satisfaction that animal life makes possible. It is only if particular animal lives are valued for their own sake that vegetarianism is able to gain much support from the affirmative value of animal life.

Support for a broad valuing of animal life would be much stronger were it to be argued—as it is in the case of humans—that the life in question possessed capacities that would make its destruction a violation. Human beings—for the most part—are choosers, and a key presumption of *morality* as a norm of action is that choices are to be respected. But since it is not clear that animals are choosers, it is not clear that animal life can claim this standing, and the protection that goes with it.

Nevertheless, it might be claimed that insofar as animals have *preferences*, their individual lives have the appropriate kind of moral standing and should be respected. But for this argument to take us further than the one concerning pleasure, we must presume that the preferences in question are individual and self-conscious in a way that pleasures are not. And it is not at all clear that animals are capable of such reflexive preferences. As Hegel puts it, "an animal can intuit, but the soul of an animal has for its object not its soul, itself, but something external."[2] Such preferences as animals have seem to be what Harry Frankfurt calls first-order desires; they do not show the animal to be aware of itself as desiring what it desires.[3]

A further difficulty that must be dealt with, should this view about animal life be tied closely to some form of utilitarianism, concerns an apparent obligation to breed as many animals as possible—consistent with the maximization of pleasurable experiences in the world. If it lies within our power to breed more animals—or other sources of pleasurable experience—and if our dominant duty is to maximize the totality or average level (or whatever) of pleasure, then there is a prima facie obligation to breed as many animals as would be consistent with this maximizing requirement. And that would seem to be counterintuitive.

I believe, however, that this problem is mainly a problem for some forms of utilitarianism, and it may well be that a carefully drafted or suitably limited utilitarianism will be able to avoid such counterintuitive demands. Some versions of average utilitarianism, for example, will avoid this difficulty.

Nevertheless, I think these and the other problems I have referred to indicate that defenses of vegetarianism focusing on the broad value of animal life, where that value is grounded in the capacity of animals for pleasurable experiences or satisfactions, cannot play a strong justificatory role. Vegetarians are much better served if they argue from the actual sufferings of animals killed for food.

In suggesting that the vegetarian position—unlike opposition to animal cruelty—is better served by other arguments than those relying on the capacity of animals for pleasurable experiences, I am not wanting to suggest that there is nothing at all to be said for animal life—that animals may be killed and eaten with impunity so long as no pain or suffering is caused. Quite the contrary. Animals

193

are participants in the mystery of life which holds such vast possibilities for ourselves, and although their claims to noninterference cannot be established in the way they are for us, we should nevertheless acknowledge the teleological quality of their lives, and weigh our own interests against theirs.

Fetal life

Arguments for attributing some sort of value to human life, and for condemning the killing of a human being, generally suppose that the human life in question is self-conscious and capable of choice. The—or at least a—problem posed by fetal life is that it is neither self-conscious nor capable of choice. Perhaps the same could be said for neonatal life. Indeed, where a certain quality of self-consciousness and capacity for choice is made the decisive consideration, abortion and infanticide are sometimes considered to be almost equally open options.

For many, however, there are various finer distinctions to be drawn, and even the category of "fetal life" is considered too broad for any moral generalizations. There are significant biological differences between the zygote, embryo, and the viable prenatal fetus, and some of those biological differences and their manifestations are often said to be associated with differences in status. Nidation or individuation, the development of brain function or the central nervous system, the assumption of a human *morphē* or the phenomenon of quickening, viability or birth, have all figured individually or severally in attempts to accord a morally significant status to fetal life. In some cases the particular characteristic is said to be constitutive of the "fully human" status of the fetus. In other cases, the characteristics referred to are simply grounds for attributing an increasing affirmative value or standing to the fetus as it develops towards adult personhood.

Recourse to these diverse features of fetal life is often confused by the ends to which they are directed. Frequently the question is not: "Do these characteristics of fetal life provide us with grounds for affirmatively valuing it and for responding to it in some positive way?" but, more narrowly: "Are these characteristics of fetal life sufficient to constitute it the bearer of rights?" The qualifications for being a possessor of rights need not be identified with those essential to being an object of value. It is a common confusion to think that if the fetus does not qualify as a right-holder it does not qualify as an object of affirmative value—and therefore, absent the interests of third parties, may be treated or disposed of however one may wish.

I do not want to be diverted into a detailed discussion of these various stages or experiences of fetal development, though some of them have been impressively defended as grounding a special fetal claim to protection. At bottom, what they all attempt to do is provide a basis for incorporating the "fetus"—at some stage of its developmental history—into the community of persons. Some characteristic or capacity is taken to show that fetuses are in some respect similar enough to those of us who are indubitably members of the morally significant community to warrant (at least) some of the protections that are due to members of such a community.

I propose instead to dwell briefly on two other arguments for according fetal life moral significance—its symbolism and potentiality.

The first of these arguments has been developed at some length by Stanley Benn. In *A Theory of Freedom*[4] Benn offers an account of moral reasoning and behavior in which two distinctive kinds of moral reason are distinguished and contrasted. Benn speaks of them as *reasons of concern* and *reasons of respect*. The distinction is similar to the one I have made between choice-relevant and choice-constraining considerations. Reasons of concern are value-centered—that is, they have regard to the consequences of conduct, to its value for *axiotima*—things having affirmative value. *Axiotima* may include human beings, works of art, environmental objects, and scientific research. Reasons of respect, however, are person-centered, for it is only in relation to persons that they can be invoked. Reasons of respect are constituted by principles, such as those of freedom, justice, equal respect for persons' rights, and fidelity to truth. To qualify as a "person" a being must be a chooser—it must have the capacity to plan and pursue a future for itself on the basis of its assessment of the appropriateness of whatever paths it takes.

Reasons of respect entitle persons to a consideration not appropriate to mere *axiotima*. For such reasons recognize that persons, as choosers, are themselves centers of choice and consciousness with exactly the same claims to pursue their own projects as other choosers have to pursue theirs. That those persons might be better off pursuing ends I or others might set for them is not a sufficient reason for interfering with them. Only where others employ their powers of choice to interfere with the projects of others might we legitimately intervene, though here, too, we may do so only out of consideration for the standing of those interfered with rather than from some conception of the good or of what will be good for them. Reasons of concern may be given priority only where the *axiotima* are not persons.

From his account of persons as choosers, it would appear to follow—and Benn accepts this implication—that not all human beings qualify as persons.[5] More particularly, human fetuses, neonates, those in permanent vegetative states, and corpses do not qualify for the consideration that is due to persons. They do not possess *rights*—the normative resources exclusive to choosers. Yet Benn is uneasy about seeing them as—at very best—mere *axiotima*, about whose treatment we may make optimizing decisions. We feel, and Benn does, too, that there is something deeply problematic about eating baby flesh or using infants as sources of replacement organs or experimental objects, about making blood and bone out of human corpses or binding books with human skin. But what we acknowledge as deeply troubling here many of us, along with Benn, do not find troubling in the case of (most) animals. We breed animals for food, harvest some of their organs and tissues, use them in experiments, convert their remains into blood and bone, and use leather and pigskin for bookbinding.

How do we account for this? Of course we might question the moral commonplaces that give rise to the problem. There are substantial numbers of people who accord greater status to (many) animals and less consideration to those who fall at one or other end of human life. But this is not Benn's strategy. He accepts—more or less as given—the moral viewpoints underlying the dilemma. And he endeavors to account for these viewpoints in a way that maintains the force and coherence of his initial distinction of reasons. To do this he proposes a third category of reasons for action.

It is Benn's contention that value-centered and person-centered reasons need not and do not exhaust the domain of morally significant reasons for action. Although he does not seek to provide a complete list of practical reasons, or even to spell out what the character of such reasons must be, Benn indicates that both value-centered and person-centered reasons may be "shadowed" by what he speaks of as *symbolic reasons*. If an *axiotimon* is defective or damaged so that it is no longer the valuable object it was, it does not necessarily lose all practical significance, but may continue to possess a shadow affirmative value by virtue of *what it was*. For example, if a valuable work of art is irreparably damaged, someone who thought that it might just as well be used to wrap up the garbage would show him- or herself to be insensitive or to have never affirmatively valued the work of art for what it was.

Benn believes that the same kind of "shadowing" may operate in relation to damaged, defective, or not-yet-formed persons. Such "qualified persons" may or may not be affirmatively valued as *axiotima*. But independent of their valuation as *axiotima*, they may be accorded a shadow-respect. It is because fetuses, infants, the permanently comatose, and corpses will (in the normal course of events) become or have been *persons*, that to treat them—at most— as mere *axiotima* (that is, only as more or less valuable resources for our varied projects) is to deny them a dignity or standing for which their links to personhood qualify them. Someone who treats the human corpse simply as flesh/meat to be disposed of manifestly fails to appreciate the "humanity" that gives this body its particular character.

But it is not altogether clear how Benn conceptualizes this additional category of reasons. Although he speaks of "symbolic reasons" and of the corpse or dead fetus as "a sad symbol of human fears and aspirations, frustrated and cut short,"[6] it is not clear how he understands the idea of a symbol. It does not seem that fetuses and corpses are to be understood as symbols in the way that, say, the national flag is. It is not simply by convention that we accord the fetus or corpse the status it has. There is a continuity between the fetus or corpse and the persons they supposedly "symbolize" that calls forth our recognition of their standing.

Benn's (alternative?) characterization of the fetus and corpse as "shadows" or "reminiscences" of humanity (personhood?)[7] is no less troubling. The link between fetuses and corpses, on the one hand, and "persons," on the other, is much more substantial (in more ways than one) than that between objects and their shadows. Shadows, I take it (*pace* Peter Pan), have no status; however, as Benn acknowledges, there are things that, if we do them to fetuses and corpses, properly attract criticism. In some cases at least, forcible intervention might even be justified.

Though these slightly carping criticisms leave the exact character of Benn's third category of reasons unclear, they do not undermine the essential force of his claims. There is no doubt that—in our culture at least—"we" do conceptualize the pig carcass differently from a human corpse, and that we give the pig carcass an instrumental value that we are not (yet?) ready to accord the human corpse. The pig carcass is "meat" and a "resource" in a way that the human carcass is not:

197

Because we breed animals for food, and use their skins and other parts for a variety of purposes of our own, we have in our culture ready-made ways of conceptualizing dead beasts that ascribe to them a nature more or less independent of the living animal. The idea of a pig bristle hairbrush, for instance, is fully intelligible without our having to consider the function of the bristles as parts of total pig. The reference to its porcine origin is little more than a way of setting this sort of bristle in a context of nylon and other stiff-fibred hairbrushes, from which it is thus differentiated. A human corpse, however, is nothing but a dead human person; *that* description nominates the form which gives it significance.[8]

It is on the basis of our conceptualization of a corpse essentially and exclusively as a *human* corpse that Benn finds fault in the way in which cadavers are sometimes treated in medical schools. Although the corpse as such has no claim on our respect, yet it was once a living, feeling person, with projects and aspirations, hopes, wishes and achievements, and it is under the form of that humanity/personhood that it exists for us. Those who treat it simply as a specimen, or as mere flesh, perhaps to be joked about, demean the humanity/personhood that it in some sense represents. In similar vein, we might consider the revulsion that some feel toward fetal experimentation or abortion or at the way in which (intentionally or naturally) aborted fetuses are sometimes disposed of.[9]

One of the attractions of Benn's category of symbolic reasons is that it appears to offer something of a passage between the Scylla of according to these human *marginalia* the same consideration (rights) as full-fledged persons, and the Charybdis of denying them any claims to our consideration whatsoever. What is more, it may provide us with the tools we need to explain why human infants are usually believed to warrant more consideration than mature animals. For it requires us to look not at capacities *simpliciter*, but to those capacities in their "specific" embodiment. This is not a "speciesist" position, since it does not restrict personhood to human beings. Nevertheless, it does take into account the fact that the human infant is (usually) connected to personhood in a way that the mature animal (usually) is not.

But I still find something troubling about the characterization of this category of reasons as "symbolic," and about their recognition of some shadow-value or shadow-respect. In part that reflects my own uneasiness with Benn's view about the kind of consideration

that is appropriate to fetuses, neonates, the permanently comatose, and human corpses. But it also expresses my puzzlement
about the precise character of these symbolic reasons. Let me try to
articulate my response more clearly.

In chapter 13 of *A Theory of Freedom*, Benn asks us to consider the
case of an infant whose parents deprive him of basic welfare needs,
with the result that he grows up stunted and plagued by poor
health.[10] Were his *rights* as an infant violated? Benn believes not,
because, as he puts it, it would allow us to accord rights to fetuses
and zygotes, and that would not only be uncongenial to those
wishing to support abortion on demand, but also would result in
absurd claims for a "piece of jelly" (a newly fertilized ovum).[11] It is
much better that we limit the ascription of rights to those with "capacities for projects and rational choice,"[12] and instead see in the
infant so badly treated a basis for later complaint grounded in his
not being accorded the recognition that his status as a *human* infant
warranted: "Later on in life when he has become a person, he can
claim that his treatment in his early months or years had not been
appropriate to an entity which should have been grasped in the
light of what, in normal circumstances, it would become."[13]

Can we say the same for the zygote? Suppose the mother-to-be,
knowing that she suffers from an enzyme deficiency, chooses not
to go on a special diet during pregnancy, and the child that is subsequently born to her is retarded.[14] May the child, at a later date,
have as strong a ground for complaint as the maltreated infant?
Benn thinks not:

> The child which is yet to become a person can be understood in
> the light of that potentiality. Because this kind of reason . . .
> depends on a kind of projection, forward . . . to a different
> state of being, to what the infant will be . . . the extent to
> which the subject of the quasi-right actually approximates to
> the fully personal nature or essence in terms of which its pre-
> sent nature is grasped, is going to qualify the extent to which
> respect is accorded. The zygote is so remote from actual per-
> sonhood that it is hard to see it even in the light of this rather
> attenuated principle as a proper subject for respect. The neo-
> nate is much more like a person, though it is certainly not an
> actual one; but if he is neglected and grows up stunted in con-
> sequence, he has genuine grounds for complaint that the treat-
> ment early accorded to him had ignored his nature as a person-
> to-be.[15]

I find this differentiation hard to accept, even on the basis of Benn's own arguments.[16] On the one hand, he appeals to the way in which we conceptualize human *marginalia*, and considers whether the conception of them as *human* is so central that to maltreat them would be to denigrate their nature as persons-to-be. On the other hand, he appeals to their potentiality—a potentiality frustrated by the treatment they receive. The first of these might be taken to provide some basis for differentiation; the second, with which it is run together, does not really distinguish between them.

It is probably true that we find it more difficult to "identify" with a zygote than with a young child. But that is in part because, morphologically, we can characterize a zygote—but not an infant—as "a piece of jelly." Our inability to identify with a zygote, however, may show a lack of imagination as much as any morally significant difference. Were fertilization to be registered by a transformation of the conceptus into a being having a minute humanlike *morphē*, we would find this differentiation much more difficult to make.[17] No doubt the further fact that an infant can suffer, whereas a zygote cannot, also bears on our sense of "identification." But this difference need not be taken to show more than that an infant can be harmed in ways that a fetus cannot. Someone who is comatose and incapable of experiencing pain does not thereby lose his/her humanity.

Most of the moral weight of Benn's argument seems to be borne, not by the symbolic character of fetuses, infants, the comatose, and corpses, but by their potentiality and residuality. Shortly I will discuss potentiality and residuality in more detail. But it may be appropriate at this point to preview that discussion by noting that in *A Theory of Freedom*, unlike some of his earlier work, where potentiality seemed to be interpreted as mere possibility,[18] Benn works with a much stronger—and, I believe, more plausible approach to potentiality. Perhaps the same could be said for residuality, which is not understood here *merely* as past. However, to the extent that this is so, I think Benn's differentiations become much harder to make. The potentiality of the zygote is not, in general, significantly different from that of the neonate. For what we are talking about here is not a matter of statistics but of what I call a developmental trajectory. The zygote and the neonate are on the same developmental trajectory, albeit at different points. And the same might be said for the irreversibly comatose, who are situated on its decline.

What I am suggesting, then, is that human potentiality and residuality are best seen as part of a developmental or downward trajectory of which "full-fledged" personhood is the zenith or *telos*. Human beings are continuants, organisms with a history that extends beyond their immediate present, usually forward and backward. What has come to be seen as "personhood," a selected segment of that organismic trajectory, is connected to its earlier and later phases by a complex of factors—physical, social, psychological—that constitute part of a single history. The earlier and later phases of that history are not related to full-fledged personhood as mere "symbol" or "shadow," but as integral parts.

At one point in his discussion, Benn comes close to recognizing this. Speaking of the "kind of dignity" appropriate to a corpse, he writes: "We see it, as it were, under the aspect of humanity, not under the aspect of meat, or garbage, suitably food for pigs. The form of humanity still provides the corpse with human significance, albeit defectively. To see it as a dead human being is to characterize it not merely in terms of what it is, as if it had no history, but also in terms of what it was."[19] The notion of a human corpse is not fully accounted for by its material features. It is not just a piece of meat having a certain shape and mass. It is the residuum of some particular individual, and its fate as a corpse will be part of that individual's history. We fail to appreciate a significant event in Queen Jezebel's history if we leave out of it the fact that Jezebel's body was left in the street, to be eaten by the city dogs. It is a central part of her judgment, her humiliation.[20] Karen Ann Quinlan's biography did not end in 1975, when she became permanently comatose. It continued for another ten years. That was part of the tragedy of her life.

What is true of the end of life is also true of its beginning, though here we are dealing with a history that generally has had little as yet to distinguish or individualize it. Even here, however, we may wish to draw attention to its features, and to include them within the history of the person whose life is in question. The biblical accounts of the lives of John the Baptist and Jesus draw attention to features of its uterine episode.[21] So too may we want to draw attention to aspects of the short history of the son of Pamela Rae Stewart. His mother continued to use drugs during pregnancy, and he died of brain hemorrhage a few hours after birth.[22]

What I am claiming here is that the distinction between persons and (mere) human beings is, as Benn's own language so often suggests, less easily made than his arguments claim, and that the reasons we may have for according to fetuses, neonates, the comatose, and corpses some special moral consideration is not that they are mere "symbols" or "shadows" of persons but stages in their history.

I am not suggesting that our moral responsibilities to what I would prefer to call "full-fledged persons" are the same as those to fetuses, infants, or the comatose. Clearly, the capacities of persons differ, depending on whether they are at a fetal, neonatal, adolescent, or senescent stage, and on their normality or state of health. And these differences of capacity are relevant to our responsibilities. Where people are able to make decisions of their own, we have a responsibility to acknowledge that in our dealings with them. That responsibility may be more or less demanding. A parent should no doubt take seriously a child's wishes with respect to the subjects it wants to study in school. But we may not see the child's wishes as overriding. If, however, a child wants to go to school but is prevented from doing so by a parent, we may be reluctant to allow the parent to prevail. Where we are dealing with the self-regarding wishes of a mature adult, however, we may be very reluctant to interfere.

In sum, the promise of symbolic reasons, when pressed, collapses into an appeal to potentiality and residuality. Though Benn may have wished to avoid this appeal, because of what he saw as its serious defects, his argument gravitates in that direction. That this was an appropriate direction in which to move, I shall now attempt to show.

This second argument, also parasitic on the qualities of adult humans, does not base the affirmative value of fetal life, and/or any claim it may have to special consideration, on its symbolic significance or in any actualized or realized qualities it manifests, but instead on its *potentialities*—on its capacity, given developmental opportunities, for manifesting the richness of human life.

The general form taken by this argument is as follows: Because the fetus is genetically endowed with the potential for the self-reflective, deliberative life that characterizes personhood, it should be accorded respect and given the protections normally afforded to human beings.

Of course, the argument need not have practical implications as strong as those indicated; nevertheless, it is generally invoked to further some such protective or practical end.

The usual reply to this argument goes roughly as follows: Potentiality is much too broad a characteristic to figure usefully in moral argument. For, given an appropriate set of conditions, almost anything is potentially anything else. And even if this *reductio* is ignored, it cannot mint any moral coinage. For, at very best, the fetus's potential for self-reflective, deliberative life shows only that it has the potential for a life that would qualify it for the protections normally afforded to human beings. The potential for such a life is not the possession of such a life, however, and so the fetus does not actually qualify but at most only potentially qualifies for the protections claimed for it.

Is this response decisive, or may potentiality possess a moral importance in its own right?

To answer this question, we need to attend to several issues. Some concern the nature of the potentiality at issue. Others concern the moral relevance of that potentiality. I shall consider them in order.

The nature of potentiality. Joel Feinberg articulates "the paradoxes of potentiality" as follows:

> Dehydrated orange powder is potentially orange juice, since if we add water to it, it will be orange juice. More remotely, however, it is also potentially lemonade, since it will become lemonade if we add a large quantity of lemon juice, sugar, and water. It is also a potentially poisonous brew (add water and arsenic), a potential orange cake (add flour, etc., and bake), a potential orange-colored building block (add cement and harden), and so on *ad infinitum.*[23]

In other words, "anything at all can be potentially anything else at all." Clearly this reduces to absurdity the appeal to potentiality as a basis for moral assertions. But, as Feinberg recognizes, this conclusion is not the end of the matter. It is hardly likely that those who appeal to potentiality have in mind anything so embracing. So he distinguishes between what he calls "direct or proximate" potentialities and "indirect or remote" ones, and suggests how a line may be drawn between them.[24] One basis for differentiating them may be the causal importance of the X that is said to be a potential Y. Of course, the notion of causal importance is itself none too precise, and Feinberg argues that—as with other causal conditions—it can be established only relative to our purposes and interests.[25] In relation to these, one such factor may be the ease or difficulty involved in transforming the X into a Y. A second basis for differentiating proximate from remote potentialities may have regard to the extent to which the X will, "in the normal course of events," become a Y. But this, too, like the first criterion, can be articulated only against a particular background of human purposes and understandings.

Feinberg is right to see that the appeal to potentiality is not as unstructured as "the paradoxes of potentiality" suggest. I am not persuaded, however, that what is needed is some criterion for distinguishing between "direct or proximate" and "indirect or remote" potentialities. I think this puts the emphasis in the wrong place. What he characterizes as "indirect or remote" potentialities are better seen as potentialities only in a very attenuated sense. Although the term "potentiality" can be used in this way, it is not a use that generates any great philosophical interest. It is preferable, I think to distinguish between "weak" and "strong" senses of "potentiality."[26]

We may say that X is a potential Y in a weak sense if all we mean is that X may feature causally and substantively in the production of Y. Or, to put it in other words, X is part of a causal complex whose outcome is Y, and X is a material element in Y.[27] A mere catalyst for the transformation of X into Y is not a potential Y. Although it is part of the causal process, the catalyst does not become a constituent element in Y. In this weak sense of "potential" a particular piece of wood may be a potential statue: that is, a statue may be fashioned out of it. And, science-fictionally, a cat may be a potential person: we may discover a substance that, when injected into cats, transforms them into persons. Potentiality in this sense need not bespeak a particular outcome. The same block of wood may be a potential toy or box or piece of firewood. The cat may be a potential experimental animal or pet or ratcatcher or food or person.

It is not in this weak sense that we speak of a kitten being a potential adult cat or of the human fetus being a potential adult person. True, the kitten and fetus feature causally and substantively in the production of their respective adults. But more than that, the kitten and human fetus are set on developmental trajectories that, given normal conditions, will result in their becoming, respectively, an adult cat and an adult person. In this strong sense of "potential," potentiality will be almost exclusively a property of organisms.[28]

No doubt there can be some dispute over the boundaries of "normal conditions." And, as Feinberg rightly recognizes, our judgments about normal conditions will reflect a background of interests and expectations. The human fetus is not like an oak seedling that, if watered by nature, will eventually grow into an oak tree.[29] Nor is the human fetus like a kitten that, if given sustenance, will develop into a relatively functional adult cat. The human fetus is not fully or partially programmed for human personhood in the way an oak seedling and kitten are programmed to become a mature oak and adult cat. Human maturity is as much a matter of social learning as of simple biological development. The natural history of human development is communal. Because, and to the extent that, a social environment is considered as part of the normal or natural conditions of human life, its growth into adult human personhood will be considered part of its normal developmental trajectory. Human beings who survive outside those conditions and do not develop in that way present a significant moral challenge.

We have, then, a strong sense of "potentiality" that must be distinguished from its paradoxical weak relative. It is this strong sense that allows us to say that a human fetus is potentially an adult human being in a way that a particular sperm and ovum are singly not. The human sperm and ovum as such do not have a strong potentiality for human personhood. Only with the fertilization of the ovum, and the consequent formation of a new genetic being, do we have a potential human adult in the strong sense. Only with this kind of potentiality do we focus on what is claimed to have moral weight.[30]

The moral relevance of potentiality. Why should strong potentiality be of moral relevance? And what kind of moral relevance might it have?

Consider a situation in which a human being is conceived, born, and raised as a pet or physiological specimen. It is well fed, but its parents/keepers do not teach it a language or educate it or attend to any of its social needs. Do they do anything wrong? My intuition here is that something very wrong is being done, and it is being done precisely because this human's potential is being ignored and frustrated. It is being diverted from or prevented from following its normal developmental trajectory.

Here I think we have a case in which potentiality creates certain positive duties—duties having to do with the realization of the child's potential. And I believe the same might be said of the fetus. In just the same sense it has certain potentialities that may, because of the treatment it receives, be frustrated. These potentialities may be frustrated by physical injury, social deprivation, or death.

Before this can be said with any confidence, however, I need to consider some countervailing arguments. Michael Lockwood, for example, has argued that the embryo's potential for developing into an adult human person does not confer on it any special claim to protection because at that stage of its development it does not qualify as a human being.[31] It is a human organism, certainly, but until it has developed those structures that mark out its potential as a human individual, it does not qualify for the special consideration that is due to human beings. For Lockwood, this status is acquired only with the development of those brain structures that will subsequently support mental life, and this does not occur until at least eight weeks after conception.

Without wanting to deny the significance of brain development in the natural history of the human organism, I am at something of a loss to understand why its actual development should have such importance. After all, given its particular stage of development in the human fetus, it is as yet unable to support the mental life that one day will be so important to its moral standing. And given that it cannot yet support that mental life, why should we not accord as much moral weight to the genetic code carried by the embryo, and that will, in due course, result in the formation of brain that has the potential for mental activity? Why support one potentiality over another?[32]

There is some reason to think that Lockwood is impressed by the prospect of a symmetry between brain death as a criterion for the death of a human individual and brain formation as a criterion for the coming into being of a human individual. But whether or not brain death is itself a suitable criterion for the death of a human individual, there is no particular reason to think that an individual's coming into being should be symmetrically conceived. The same applies to those arguments that focus on a symmetry of loss and gain of heart function.

Stephen Buckle suggests a cut-off point that more or less corresponds with nidation or implantation. Drawing on physiological accounts of post-fertilization development, he argues that since an embryo proper does not come into being until approximately two weeks after fertilization, the cell cluster that precedes that development cannot be termed a potential person. From that cluster of cells there develops not only the embryo, but also the placenta and other tissues that surround the embryo and fetus during gestation. This leads Buckle to claim that the human conceptus prior to implantation has only the (weak) potential *to produce* a person and not the (strong) potential *to become* a person.[33]

Buckle's physiological observations certainly provide some basis for our reconceptualizing the conceptus prior to implantation. But I am not sure that it establishes his claim that what exists prior to implantation possesses only weak potential (the potential *to produce*). True, what will develop from the fertilized ovum will not only be a person, but also a number of other tissue structures. The fertilized ovum does not yet constitute a distinct organism. But it does contain the distinctive genetic code that will later be a particular person, and it contains it as part of an active developmental complex with an internally guided trajectory.[34] This seems to me to indicate a strong rather than weak form of potential, even if there would be difficulties in saying *simply* that the newly fertilized ovum was "a potential person."

But these questions aside, is my argument able to avoid the objection that potentiality can at best sustain a potentiality for some kind of value? I believe so, because the argument I am presenting takes a significantly different form. I am not saying that because the fetus is potentially a possessor of characteristics that would, if possessed, give it certain claims on others, it therefore has those claims on others. Rather, I am saying that its potentiality for those characteristics gives it certain claims on others. In other words, it is its potentiality for certain characteristics that is the source of the claims, not simply characteristics which it potentially has. The (strong) potential for developing certain characteristics is itself a characteristic that may ground certain claims.[35]

These claims are not, so far as I can see, contingent on the particular human being's subsequently *minding* what is done to it. For all I know, the child reared as a pet or specimen may have little appreciation of its deprivation. It is for the same reason that we sometimes recoil at childrearing practices that confine—albeit contentedly—children to narrow traditions that stifle the development of some of their distinctively and acceptably human potential.

But what claims may strong potentiality ground, and how strong are they? My belief is that at its broadest, we have a duty to allow organisms—the primary possessors of strong potentiality—to realize their potential. They have a good, and their realization of that good is itself a good—the kind of good that is choice-constraining.

The realization of that good is not incumbent on us simply because they have a good, but their good provides a structure for our recognition of the duty to allow them to realize their good. Such realization is not an overriding duty, but it is at least a duty whose frustration needs to be justified. It is most easily justified where we are dealing with plants; it is least easily justified where we are dealing with humans.

Is the duty to allow organisms to realize their potential compatible with human abortion or fetal experimentation? The answer—or answers—we give will depend in part on the strength of the duty in question. Is it a correlative of some right possessed by fetuses? Or does it rest on some less demanding considerations? And of course there will also be competing considerations to take into account—the claims of the mother or parents, wider social factors, and so on. All I wish to argue here is that there is a substantial claim grounded in the fetus's potentiality. The fact that a fetus is not yet a full-fledged person does not exclude it from the domain of moral considerability or render its moral standing merely prospective. By virtue of its potentiality, its life should be accorded moral significance.

Capital punishment

The factors that make the affirmative value and status of fetal life so problematic are not generally at issue in capital punishment. With the exception of certain kinds of sociopaths who might be thought to lack some essential human abilities or capacities and who might, therefore, be considered on a moral par with animals,[36] capital punishment is generally reserved for human beings whose status as persons is acknowledged, but whose conduct is said to warrant their death. May their claim to continued life be overridden or forfeited by conduct in which they have engaged?

Significantly and interestingly, both defenders and opponents of capital punishment frequently make some sort of appeal to human life's value as a basis for their respective positions. Defenders have argued that human life is so important that those who take it either forfeit their own claim to it or may have that claim overridden. Opponents have argued that human life is so important that not even the most heinous crime can justify taking it. In part—though not wholly—the difference can be explained as a difference in focus. Defenders focus on the lives of "innocents," maintaining that the willful destruction of such lives is so repugnant that only the death penalty can appropriately express our moral revulsion. Opponents focus on the lives of the guilty, claiming that "even the vilest criminal remains a human being possessed of common human dignity."[37]

Those who defend capital punishment by means of some appeal to life's value generally do it in one of two ways. Either—as consequentialists—they point to what they see as a deterrent function of capital punishment, or—as deontologists—they claim that certain crimes deserve the death penalty. The consequentialist argument focuses on the number of lives saved, the assumption being that the more lives saved the better. The deontological argument compares the claims of the life lost to the claims of the life responsible for that loss.

The consequentialist argument for capital punishment relies heavily on the sustainability of the proposition that execution deters more efficiently than less severe forms of punishment. It is a proposition that has been strongly challenged by opponents of the death penalty. Either—at their most cautious—they have claimed that the data is inconclusive, or—at their boldest—they have claimed that use of the death penalty may even precipitate further killings. No doubt—given what may appear to be its intuitive psychological implausibility—the force of this consequentialist argument against the death penalty depends significantly on the fact that the risk of suffering the death penalty actually faced by, say, murderers, is quite small. In the United States, at least, the likelihood of being executed for murder in a jurisdiction that upholds the death penalty is not that much greater than in a jurisdiction that eschews it. One is more likely to be shot by pursuing police.

What is more problematic about the consequentialist position, however, is its aggregative rather than distributive focus. The issue, ultimately, is one of numbers of lives and not—except contingently—the relative moral claims of those lives. Although defenders of capital punishment who make some kind of appeal to life's value in support of their position undoubtedly believe that, other things being equal, the more lives saved the better, the plausibility of their position generally rests on the assumption that other things are not equal—that the murderer has acted in a manner that undermines *his* claim to life. Without some such additional assumption the case for capital punishment looks very anemic.

In fact, the classic defense of capital punishment focuses primarily on considerations of justice or desert, and the appeal to deterrence is probably best understood as a possible basis for the *state's* authority to employ the death penalty rather than as that penalty's underlying rationale. It is asserted that the claim to life is such that the person who takes the life of another forfeits his own claim to it.[38] Few have stated this deontological or retributive position with as much rhetorical force as Kant:

> What kind and what degree of punishment does legal justice adopt as its principle and standard? None other than the principle of equality . . . the principle of not treating one side more favorably than the other. Accordingly, any undeserved evil that you inflict on someone else among the people is one that you do to yourself. If you vilify, you vilify yourself; if you steal from him, you steal from yourself; if you kill him, you kill yourself. Only the law of retribution (*jus talionis*) can determine exactly the kind and degree of punishment. . . . If [the offender] has committed a murder, he must die. In this case, there is no substitute that will satisfy the requirements of legal justice. There is no sameness of kind between death and remaining alive even under the most miserable conditions, and consequently there is also no equality between the crime and the retribution unless the criminal is judicially condemned and put to death. But the death of the criminal must be kept entirely free of any maltreatment that would make an abomination of the humanity residing in the person suffering it. Even if a civil society were to dissolve itself by common agreement of all its members (for example, if the people inhabiting an island decided to separate and disperse themselves around the world), the last murderer remaining in prison must first be executed, so that everyone will duly receive what his actions are worth and so that the bloodguilt thereof will not be fixed on the people because they failed to insist on carrying out the punishment; for if they fail to do so, they may be regarded as accomplices in this public violation of legal justice.[39]

The Kantian argument is grounded in the retributive view that wrongdoing justly requires a commensurate requiting infliction. And for Kant that retributivism is itself grounded on a "high" view of human life. The legal system is seen as the creation of rational individuals—as an expression of their recognition of each other as rational choosers, possessing an equality of status. Justice, the chief virtue of a system so construed, is realized in equality of treatment. And so a community that fails to carry out the death penalty for murder violates its own character as a community of moral beings. It is also in recognition of this mutual respect that the offender himself is not to be subjected to a degrading death. Although the murderer has forfeited his claim to continued life, it is as a rational being that he killed and it is as a rational being that he is to be put to death. His death should uphold both the dignity of human life as well as his own dignity as a human being.

The Kantian argument draws on some deep human moral dispositions and something like it has wide popular support. Yet the dispositions that feed it are themselves structured by controversial assumptions in need of detailed justification. Retributivism, for example, is a controversial theory of punishment, and Kant's version a controversial retributivist position. Does retributivism require punishment or does it simply render it permissible? Does respect for the lives of victims require retributive punishment? Does retributive punishment imply equality or only proportionality? Is that equality or proportionality when imposed on murderers only or even best expressed in the death penalty? Do real-life convicted murderers qualify for death on Kantian theory? Is it really possible to execute a murderer without indignity, or is the very process of condemnation to death and execution necessarily attended by a denial of the dignity of human life? If murder warrants the death, is it appropriate for the state to inflict that penalty? These are hard questions, and though I believe that some of them can probably be answered affirmatively, the answers are not obvious, and convincing arguments are difficult to provide. Here I shall canvass just a few that are of particular relevance to the present project.

Take first the issue of respect for the lives of victims, and what that requires vis-à-vis their victimizers. We might argue that respect for the life of the *murdered* person is shown primarily by the treatment accorded to that person after his or her death—mourning, speaking well of the deceased, a decent burial, and so on—and that although it may show a lack of respect not to pursue the offender's punishment, nevertheless, a due regard for the life lost need not require anything as strong as capital punishment.[40]

There is a certain kind of respect that will be most appropriately shown in the activities indicated. We referred to it earlier as "appraisal respect." But this is not the kind of respect to which Kant calls us. For even if the person who is killed evokes no positive regard from us, respect for his life (in the Kantian sense) demands that his killer be commensurately punished. Kantian respect for life is shown not only or especially in some positive regard for the victim of crime, but in requital for wrongdoing: in subjecting the wrongdoer to an imposition that registers the victim's equality of

211

standing as a person. For Kant a *rational* response to wrongdoing is to inflict on the wrongdoer an "equivalent" evil. Not to do so is to belie the victim's equality of standing (as a person) with both the wrongdoer and other members of the community.

It is for this same reason that Kant resists the idea that an "equivalent" punishment may include the wrongdoer's degradation. The wrongdoer is a person—a moral agent—and punishment must be inflicted in a manner that does not demean. There is, however, a very grave practical difficulty in Kant's prescription, since it can be argued that the processes involved in confirming and executing the death penalty will inevitably result in the criminal's degradation. This indeed has been a common complaint from Beccaria to Camus and Koestler.[41] Not only do the gallows excite public sentiments of a debased and inhumane kind—as Beccaria complained—but, as Koestler suggests, they also express a form of moral barbarism. Were we to set aside our psychological defenses and overcome our emotional detachment, we would, he claims, see the gallows as "the oldest and most obscene symbol of that tendency in mankind which drives it towards moral self-destruction."[42]

To some extent these criticisms attach to particular forms of capital punishment—the guillotine in Camus' case, the gallows in Koestler's. No doubt others could be added. But in many communities that retain the death penalty there has been an attempt to replace them by methods that are less "ugly"—gassing, injection, and so on. However, even if these methods were less problematic, this recourse would probably not assuage the concerns of those who believe the penalty barbaric. For the barbarism is thought to reside as much in the drawn-out anticipations of death necessitated by our legal processes, and in the very fact that we so "give up" on a human being (and hence on the regenerative power of the human spirit) that our response is to do away with him.

These complaints strike me as serious, though not decisive. The "due process" requirements of our legal system, which allow for a succession of drawn-out appeals against the death penalty, are at one level a witness to our respect for persons and their lives—our concern that capital punishment not be lightly imposed. Yet it is clear that the reality is frequently otherwise. The adversarial system, supposedly committed to the values of truth and justice, too often degenerates into a gladiatorial display, a contest of lawyers, in which the dignity and humanity of both victim and defendant are at best instrumental. It may be that capital punishment, however much deserved, cannot be cleansed sufficiently from cultural barbarism and the egos of the criminal justice system's principals, to satisfy Kant's requirement.[43]

Just as the argument for capital punishment based on respect for life may take a number of forms, so the respect-for-life opposition to capital punishment may also take a number of forms. On one view, human life is so important—so sacred—that it may never be taken. Thus Abe Fortas, in his critique of capital punishment, speaks of a "pervasive, unqualified respect for life" as "the basis of our civilization." So central is this commitment that we are forbidden to take anyone's life, even the murderer's.[44] This extreme pacifist commitment to life is not to be confused with passivism, a refusal to defend life and its liberties. The point is rather that there are limits to what may be done to secure these goods, and killing—even to save a life—is outside those limits.

The argument from pacifism is so radical and raises so many issues of its own that it really deserves separate treatment. But since it only rarely constitutes the basis for opposition to capital punishment I shall confine myself to one observation. If what is at issue in the pacifist position is respect for life, then it needs to be explained why, where one person's life is being threatened by another, and defense or self-defense would require killing the criminal aggressor, killing would not be justified. If the argument is that regrettable as such a situation would be one must nonetheless never personally be the agent of death, then the charge of moral self-indulgence must be faced.[45] Perhaps it is sometimes understandable that one would not defend one's own life by killing another, but if the threatened life is another's, and one resists the opportunity to kill the aggressor, some justification is needed. A mere invocation of the "sanctity of life" is not enough. No doubt it could be argued that refraining from saving the threatened third party is not the same as killing the aggressor, but in a case such as this a moral preference for the former as against the latter would be much harder to sustain.

This of course is not sufficient to dispose of the extreme pacifist position. However, it does present it with a challenge, and in so doing it raises the problem of line-drawing. If we do allow that killing may occasionally be justified, how do we distinguish—in a morally satisfactory manner—those cases in which it is justified from those in which it is not?

That indeed is the problem faced by the less extreme position that allows some killing but rejects capital punishment as a violation of life. Why is it justifiable to kill in defense of life but not as punishment? The question of course is not rhetorical, and there are many other possible reasons for rejecting capital punishment besides this one: "the inevitability of caprice and mistake," the other goals that a state has besides the administration of justice, and so on. But here I am concerned only with the argument based broadly on "the value of life," and it is not easy to see how that can differentiate the cases.

Can we produce an argument to show that although the affirmative value or normative status of human life is not absolute, murderers do not deserve to die? The usual argument here is that the Kantian position outlined earlier works with an unrealistic understanding of murderers—that many of those who kill do so in circumstances that call into question their rationality, and that therefore the *lex talionis* is too crude a measure of desert. This may or may not be so. And to the extent that murderers are not in control of what they do, then a strict *lex talionis* principle will be too crude.[46] But I don't think that this should trouble the Kantian too much. Kant does not argue for a *lex talionis* divorced from an assessment of the responsibility of the murderer. Quite the contrary. It is a principle that presupposes the offender's responsibility. The problem it faces is in fact the very problem it seeks to overcome—of providing a principle for distributing punishment in circumstances where mitigating circumstances operate. Because it seeks to impose on the offender suffering of *equal value*—and not simply *identical*—to the suffering caused, it is difficult to know how this is to be assessed.

Comatose life

We have looked at the possibility that humans may *forfeit* an existing claim to life by acting badly. It is sometimes argued that this claim to life—or to a life of affirmative value—can also be *lost*. If a person loses some of the capacities that play a central role in the regard to which, as a human being, he is entitled, does there remain any basis for according affirmative value or rights to his life? Does a person who slips into a persistent vegetative state retain any of the rights of a person, or is he left only with whatever—if any— value may attach to some general "livingness"?

Why should we maintain those who can no longer participate in the world of persons, whose organic structures no longer support any identifiable or distinctive self-awareness or sentience? The debate that surrounds this question has often focused on an alleged distinction between "quality" and "quantity" of life, and I shall consider some of the ramifications of this debate in the present section.

In broad outline, we are asked to confront the following: Modern medical technology has enabled us to detach human biological or organic life from the possibility of biographical life—or at least from biographical life of any significant richness. Put in other words, "quantity" and "quality" of life may now be brought into some sort of conflict, and we may need to choose between them. This has forced us to decide what it is about human life that is of importance, so far as our protective or preservative interventions are concerned. Is it the biological fact of life itself? Or the fact that it is the life of a member of the species *homo sapiens*? Or the fact that the life in question will be able to achieve a certain level of satisfactoriness (variously articulated)? Although the distinction is too crude, much of the debate has been presented as a choice between what I shall call "vitalism" and "realizationism," where vitalists are said to focus on the preeminence of quantity of life and realizationists are said to focus on the preeminence of quality of life. Though much of this debate has concerned the end of life, and the plight of those experiencing extreme and unrelieved pain or alienation, or who are in some form of persistent vegetative state, it is also actively heard at the beginnings of life, where our growing ability to engage in prenatal diagnosis and postnatal prognosis sometimes enables us to predict major life prospects with some accuracy.

The broad contrast between the two positions is brought out—albeit somewhat tendentiously—by Leonard Weber:

> The quality of life ethic puts the emphasis on the type of life being lived, not upon the fact of life. . . . What the life means to someone is what is important. Keeping this in mind, it is not inappropriate to say that some lives are of *greater value than others*, that the condition or meaning of life does have much to do with the justification for terminating that life. The sanctity of life ethic defends two propositions: 1. That human life is sacred by the very fact of its existence; its value does not depend upon a certain condition or perfection of that life. 2. That, therefore, all human lives are of *equal value*: all have the same right to life. The quality of life ethic finds neither of these two propositions acceptable.[47]

Weber, a vitalist, takes the view that the choice between vitalism and realizationism is an exclusive one—for, on the one hand, only vitalism is committed to the sacredness and equal affirmative value of all human life, and, on the other hand, allowing considerations of quality to play a part in decisions to preserve and/or treat places us on a slippery slope of graded life.

It is the slippery slope of graded life that appears to bother vitalists most of all—the apparent commitment to a utilitarianism of life, in which the value of a life is measured by its worth or usefulness to others, or its ability to attain a certain standard of excellence. The specter of graded life, of *lebensunwertes Leben*, life unworthy of life, is raised. At the same time, vitalists believe their own commitment to the sacredness and equal affirmative value of life is both intuitively appealing and unproblematic.

For their part, realizationists claim that slopes are only as slippery as you make them, that skilled and sensitive skiers can stop even on steep slopes, and that vitalists are committed to the cruel, pointless, and degrading prolongation of intolerably painful or merely vegetative life.

I do not think that there is much benefit to be obtained from a simple opposition of vitalism and realizationism. It lends itself too easily to a caricaturing of the alternative. True, the two views are often taken to instance the wider clash between deontological and utilitarian positions in ethics, but even those latter two positions need not be assessed in a purely oppositional fashion. What we have instead is a variety of considerations—some more commonly associated with one position than the other—which bear, sometimes competitively, on our decision-making.

Let us consider in more detail some of the factors that are said to weigh in favor of and against these contending perspectives.

1.   One major vitalistic argument has been that the human organism, even when it no longer sustains a "subjective" life, nevertheless has an affirmative value of its own, and, moreover, warrants our respect. We have already encountered a version of this in the writing of Holmes Rolston. Human bodily life, he claims, has an integrity and intelligibility of its own, a *telos*, and "ought to be given moral respect, although at a level which is reduced from our respect for the full human personality."[48] This bodily ("objective") life is not something alien to or "other" than the personal ("subjective") life with which it was previously associated, for it was out of this bodily life that the personal developed, and it was the bodily life that sustained the personal life. More than that, "the comatose individual provides occasion for recalling the very ancient succession in which he or she stands"[49]—a succession that is not only personal, but familial and evolutionary. He writes:

Life is a question of an information flow which maintains a cybernetic countercurrent to entropy and decay. In humans, this occurs most dramatically at the subjective level, where it is conscious and deliberate, but it continues from ancient origins at the objective level, somatically and spontaneously. From this perspective, we can now ask: Does it not seem parochial to restrict dignity in life to the personality, finding no respect for this subtending biochemistry still vigilant in the half-dead?[50]

The question is not quite rhetorical. The fact that *a* "subtends" *b* does not establish that if *b* is to be respected *a* is also to be respected. That surely depends on the kind of subtension involved. The hard-nosed realizationist would probably find in Rolston's rhetoric an unsustainable sentimentalism. Thus Joseph Fletcher: "Are we not allowing ourselves to be deceived by our self-preservative tendency to rationalize a merely instinctive urge and to attribute spiritual and ethical significance to phenomena appertaining to the realm of crude, biological utility?"[51] For Fletcher, respect is not an appropriate stance to have toward merely bodily life, since merely bodily life is without interests (of the appropriate kind), and it is the having of interests that qualifies an organism as an object of respect. Bodily activity is at best a necessary, but not a sufficient condition for respect.[52]

Rolston would not disagree with the view that the case for respect is closely bound up with the possession of interests. But, unlike Fletcher, he does not believe that those interests have to be conscious or self-aware: "True, the patient can subjectively take no interest in his welfare, yet the patient objectively takes an interest in his life, as is proved by what the body does in the presence of benefit (nourishment, water) or harm (infection, injury)."[53] This returns us to an earlier discussion about the character of the interests that need to be possessed if the choice-constraining terminology or "respect," "rights," and (sometimes) "sanctity" is to be used.

2.   Rolston has a further reason for according respect to the continuing bodily life of the irreversibly comatose. It draws on what he presumes to have been the view of the person whose bodily functions are now all that remain. That person would have affirmatively valued and respected his or her bodily life as such; so, therefore, should we also respect it:

When the patient was yet self-aware, he counted these biological processes among his goods and interests, roughly summed up as his "life and health," for which (if he was religious) he praised God, for which (if he was ethical) he felt entitled by natural right, for which (at the very minimum) he considered himself fortunate. Now exactly the same kind of natural good here continues, diminished in degree in his debilitated condition. Somatically, objectively, he still fights for life and health. From the patient's perspective, if we can still judge such a thing on the basis of his continuing life efforts, the former goodness has not been neutralized by no longer having a subjective owner. So then we who care for him have to ask ourselves what duty is still owed to this objective side of life.[54]

This is not an argument for equivalence of respect for "objective" and "subjective" life. The claim is only that some measure of respect is due: "Some of the 'quality of life' is protohuman. Much of the wondrous 'essence of life' is still to be found here, even though the still more wondrous essence of personality is missing."[55]

Even as a claim for reduced respect, however, Rolston's argument is problematic. For when the patient regarded his life and health as a good, it may have been only because that bodily life and health sustained personality, or personality of a sufficiently satisfactory kind. Would the patient have felt the same about a bodily organism no longer capable of sustaining or expressing a—or his—personality? The desire to avoid certain kinds of end-of-life bodily invasions and the growing interest in "living wills" suggests that for many people the goodness of bodily life is to a significant extent contingent on its capacity to support personality.

3. There is, however, a further, less ambitious vitalistic argument. Realizationists, it may be claimed, operate with an attenuated view of human individuals as here-and-now beings without histories, their beings constituted by what they are at a particular point of time. It is the sort of view that has to puzzle over whether persons exist when they are asleep or unconscious, a view that sees anything other than active capacities as a problem (albeit a soluble one). But if instead we see persons as historical beings, as continuants with a past and future as well as a present, then we will not divorce the person who has entered into a persistent vegetative state from what he was. We will see what he now is as part—albeit a dark and sad part—of *his* history. And we will see our duties with respect to him as duties to *him*, and not (problematically) to some biological organism with no personality, no desires or preferences of its own. True, such a person is but a shadow of his former self, but we are still dealing with the same person. That is why we may regret what he has become.

If Albert Grimes becomes irreversibly comatose at age forty-five, and remains in this state until his death at age fifty, those last five years are as surely part of Albert Grimes' history as the first forty-five. True, they constitute a tragic dimension of his history, and in this case a sad ending to it. But they are just as much part of his biography (though not autobiography) as they would be if, at age fifty, Albert Grimes emerged from his coma and began to re-establish his old relationships. So long as Albert Grimes is a biologically functional being, and the biological organism he has become is the biological organism that at an earlier point sustained an interactive human life, we owe him the basic regard we owe our fellows, recognizing of course, that his present condition permits certain paternalistic invasions that we would in other circumstances eschew.[56]

Although vitalism sometimes takes the form of "preservation-of-life-at-any-cost," it need not be so interpreted. It may be understood as a call to recognize the narrative character of human life—a reaction against certain atomistic tendencies to abstract that life from its ongoing and communal nature, and to see only in certain acts of will a manifestation of the person. While we may agree that self-assertion represents a distinctive and in some ways admirable expression of personality, this manifestation of human being by no means exhausts the meaning of personhood, and in any case is undergirded by a supporting web of communal responsibility. The vitalist might well fear a disintegration of that support should the integrity of human biological life not be respected.

The point here is not that life as such is to be reverenced (as in Schweitzer) or that we cannot know whether the irreversibly comatose will miraculously recover, but rather that placing the irreversibly comatose outside the bounds of respect betrays an attitude towards human life in general that is corrupting. For it sees human worth in terms of achievement, and not sui generis; it encourages us to look at each other functionally rather than historically, as time-slices and not as continuants. It undermines some of the very factors that make human life the rich and wondrous thing that it is.

With this form of vitalism we need find no conflict between a vigorous maintenance of comatose life and a withdrawal of various forms of life support should this reflect the values of the comatose person. Just as—within some limits—we respect the expressed wishes of the conscious patient who desires to discontinue some form of medical intervention, so too we must have regard for those wishes when the person is no longer able to give them voice.

Nevertheless, the view that a particular person's life extends beyond the point of self-assertion into the shadowy realm of a persistent vegetative state does give vitalists the opportunity to engage in unseemly interventions. One reason for this is a vitalistic failure to distinguish adequately between *sustaining life* and *prolonging dying*.

At some point death comes to us all, and it comes not because someone did not intervene zealously or vigorously enough on our behalf, but because our body can no longer support itself as an integrated, self-sustaining organism. That process of dying may be prolonged if certain vital functions are taken over by artificial devices. In such cases these devices do not act as temporary supports while the body recovers its functions, but they become permanent substitutes for those bodily functions.

Where vitalism results in the endless use of technology to stave off death, it fails in respect for the natural person to whom it is theoretically committed. Instead a fetishistic commitment to life takes over, with little regard for the integrity of the organism whose life it is. Certainly it may sometimes be difficult in practice—as it was in the case of Karen Quinlan—to determine whether a particular form of support is sustaining life or simply prolonging dying;[57] and it is one of the hazards of vitalism that this determination will frequently have to be made. That, however, provides no basis for either an extreme vitalistic or a realizationist position.

4. One final impetus to the vitalist position is the assumption that it does not involve physicians—or others—in "playing god." *Hubris*—human arrogance—is a common contaminant of medical judgment. Professional expertise often assumes a more general competence. Vitalists sometimes claim that life-and-death decisions, in which quality of life factors must play a part, are too sensitive for such risks to be taken: it should not be left to physicians to determine the end of life.

The charge that realizationists will be committed to "playing god"—and will not play it very well—has most plausibility where one person decides that the quality of another person's life does not justify its maintenance. Where the decision reflects the patient's own perception (as detailed in a living will) the charge is more difficult to make. In that context, the charge is more likely to be literal than metaphorical: it may be seen as an act of theological insubordination, in which a person decides for himself what some believe to be for God alone to decide.

But need the appeal to "quality of life" considerations in other-regarding contexts constitute—in some bad sense—"playing god"? Granted, there may be contexts in which quality-of-life judgments will involve an appeal to factors about which significant and reasoned differences will exist. But should this be a problem in the case of a person who is irreversibly comatose? It may not be, though if we cast our net a bit wider to include all those in a persistent vegetative state, controversial borderlines start to appear.

The charge that realizationism leads to a utilitarianism of life is serious but not necessarily unanswerable. Talk of a utilitarianism of life conjures up the idea of a social evaluation of life—of the usefulness of a life to various social ends. And of course to the extent that this is so, the concern about slippery slopes and social control is appropriate. But realizationism need not be based on anything so crude. For what may lie behind it is a teleological rather than a utilitarian conception of life.

Interpreting realizationism teleologically, we may claim that each kind of life has a natural *telos*—an end toward which its capacities and inner structure dispose it—and in terms of which its particular instantiations can be judged good or poor. By reference to such an understanding, it is reasonable to think that there is a threshold below which the quality of a particular life may fall, and by reference to which it no longer has any moral claim upon us as *a life of that kind*.

In the case of plants and animals, this teleological understanding and the positing of a threshold need not present too many problems. In the case of human beings it is much more difficult. Do humans have a natural *telos,* or is it one of the distinctive features of human existence that our *telos* is self-prescribed? And if it is self-prescribed, does not this expose the realizationist to some of the slippery slope problems that confront a utilitarianism of life?

It is the desire to avoid some of the problems engendered by such judgments that helps sustain a vitalistic commitment to human life that is no longer able to manifest the abilities and powers that gave it its distinctive character. Even though there are good reasons for thinking that the permanently comatose individual can no longer claim from us the full regard that belongs to a normal adult, concern about the social consequences of a teleological approach may lead us to refrain from withdrawing support in cases where the human organism is still capable of spontaneous functioning.

Some vitalists, however, will believe that the issue is not simply one of controversial borderlines. They see the issue as one of authority—of our right to decide, on whatever criteria, that a particular life is no longer worth living. We are not in a position to be judges of life and death, they claim, and we should have the humility to recognize it.

This stronger stance, however, may reflect back on the vitalist. For if the decision not to continue certain forms of treatment places one in the role of god, does not one equally play that role in deciding to intervene—to maintain biological life in the face of the "natural" tendencies of disease or injury? A decision is required to commence or continue treatment, just as much as it is required to cease it.

5. The major thrust behind realizationism is humanitarian. Taking quality of life considerations into account is said to reflect the values of benevolence, sympathy, and compassion, a regard for the dignity of human life—or the particular human life in question. Even if—as is the case with the permanently comatose—no suffering is involved, the preservation of a human being's biological functions, without some reasonable prospect of a recovery of those distinctive qualities that make for human dignity, is felt to be debasing to the person concerned.

The appeal to benevolence needs to be qualified if it is not itself to express a demeaning paternalism. For even though the permanently comatose individual is not in a position to state a view on the continuation of treatment, respiration, nutrition, or hydration, there may have been a time in which his/her views on these things were expressed. And if the desire was expressed for continued treatment, etc., its withdrawal on account of the substandard quality of life involved, even though benevolently motivated, would itself manifest a disrespect for the individual in question. If realizationists wish to argue that their position is humanitarian, they must also allow that judgments about the quality of life need to be modified or moderated by a consideration of the values and desires of its possessor.

Realizationists need not be greatly troubled by this concession, for it will often be the case that judgments about the substandard quality of a life will have primary regard—so far as it is possible—for the tolerability of that kind of life to its bearer. Nevertheless, to the extent that such judgments do not reflect the determinations of the person whose quality of life is being judged, realizationists will have to confront the fears frequently expressed by vitalists.[58]

Genetic engineering

In *The Foundations of Bioethics*, H. Tristram Engelhardt, Jr., argues that as products of "the blind forces of mutation and natural selection" we are not fashioned according to some divine blueprint to which we are obligated to conform.[59] Our destiny is in our own hands. Not only may we manipulate our environment so that it is shaped more closely to our purposes and goals, but we may also manipulate our bodies so that they too may serve us better. Indeed, he claims, we may go even further—to manipulate the human germ line itself, "to shape and fashion our human nature in the image and likeness of goals chosen by persons."[60] To such radical genetic engineering, provided it is engaged in "with proper reasons and proper caution," he sees no significant objections.

Those who work within a framework of traditional Judeo-Christian belief may not find Engelhardt's more radical possibilities so congenial. It may be considered that for Man made in God's image and likeness, and moreover, made "good," such tampering would constitute an act of supreme *hubris*—Man playing God, the creature playing Creator. Within this framework, if there is any room at all for genetic manipulation, it may be thought to be limited to medical interventions designed to remedy defects that now afflict the natural order.

Quite apart from the general questions that might be asked about the Judeo-Christian tradition—and the further questions that might be raised about enshrining it in regulation—we might wonder whether it is as inimical to Engelhardt's general project as it initially appears. For the "imaging" of God might well be interpreted to refer, not to some barren conformity, but instead to the possibility of the creative and beneficial application of a God-given autonomy. The issue, then, will be not "whether" but "how."

One need not possess conservative religious commitments, however, to wonder whether Engelhardt has crossed the bounds of human propriety. There are several possible reasons for this. One, to which Engelhardt may not give sufficient weight, is what we might call the Invisible Frankenstein Factor.[61] Intended acts may combine to have unintended—and unwelcome—consequences. Even if Nature is blind, she has, to continue the metaphor, been around a long time, and makes her inexorable way with measured tread. Man, on the other hand, is short-sighted and impatient, and—if history is any guide—cannot really be trusted with his powers.

Engelhardt sees this as a reason for caution rather than abstention. He has sufficient confidence in human ability to believe that we are likely to be able to make informed and far-sighted decisions in this connection. And he notes that not intervening may have unintended repercussions too.[62] But Engelhardt's confidence may—at this point of history—be unwarranted. As humans have extended their domain, they have not shown a corresponding ability to improve their judgment, and—it might be argued—the repercussions of bad decisions are becoming increasingly serious. In addition, although a conservative attitude toward intervention may have unexpected outcomes, the risks are not likely to be as critical as those created by intervention.

As well as the Invisible Frankenstein Factor there is the Jekyll-and-Hyde Factor—the possibility that such powers will be abused. The development of our powers of manipulation may indeed, like nuclear energy, be put to beneficial uses. Yet such powers may also be put to evil use, as the nuclear cloud under which we inhabit the earth makes all too clear. It will of course be responded that the possibility of misuse has attended every human invention, and, in advance of some argument to the effect that this particular knowledge will almost certainly be put to bad rather than good use, or more bad than good use, it is difficult to see the risks of abuse as a decisive objection. What makes nuclear power so specially problematic is our actual knowledge of the havoc it could cause. With genetic manipulation, massive abuses still belong exclusively to the realm of science fiction.

Some of these objections are linked more specifically to questions about the sanctity of life raised by Edward Shils. Speaking of our "unprecedented knowledge and capacities to intervene purposefully and effectively in the course of the life of individuals and in the reproduction of generations," Shils asks: "How is the human race as we have known it, with all its deficiencies, to be protected from the murderous and manipulative wickedness of some of its members and from the passionate curiosity and scientific and technological genius of others?"[63] It is the latter, in particular, that will fuel the thrust toward genetic engineering, a development that we face with apprehension. "These apprehensions," he says, "are not just vestiges of archaic theological beliefs; they are not just 'learned cultural responses.' They are also direct responses to sacrilege."[64] We possess, Shils claims, a deep, proto-religious commitment to the sanctity of life, and genetic engineering challenges that commitment.

When Shils speaks of the sanctity of life, he has in mind what he speaks of as human life's "normal" and "natural" forms. Such sanctity involves a commitment to "the individual human organism, which experiences and appreciates its vitality, . . . [to] the continuity of the vitality of one's own breed and progeny, unborn and unknown, the vitality of the territorial and civil community of which one is a member and the vitality of the species."[65] It is to this complex conception that genetic engineering constitutes a challenge. For, along with A.I.D. and artificial inovulation, it

> intrude[s] into and disrupt[s] the lineage; they provide a "descendant" who is not in a direct genetic line with his ancestors. . . . The new or prospective forms of intervention penetrate into the center of the process and they therewith confront the primordial sentiment of the sacredness of the stream of life passed down through membership in a common physiological substance. They create a human being who lacks the genetic continuity with the line of descent of those who take him (or her) as a child.[66]

But despite this challenge to life's sanctity, Shils does not believe that genetic engineering need attract "extreme and unqualified condemnation." He has two major reasons for this. The first relates to the way in which our understanding of the doctrine of life's sanctity tends to be colored by cultural idiosyncrasies—a moral chauvinism that associates the "normal" and "natural" with the culturally familiar. Since that is so, let us be cautious about enforcing what may only be cultural prejudices.

The second, related reason arises out of the complexity of the commitment to life's sanctity. Because this doctrine embraces not only "the life of the lineage," but also "the life of the human organism" and "the life of the individual human being, as an individuality located in a discrete organism,"[67] a particular human being may satisfy some elements better than others. And if we choose to give greater weight to those that are satisfied, then the fact that an intervention into "nature" is disruptive of a less important element may not count decisively against it. Indeed, that is what Shils believes may be the case in genetic engineering. One of the advances in civilization, he believes, is to be found in "the diminution of the weight attributed to lineage as a criterion by which to estimate the value of a human being. . . . We are living in an epoch in which the center of gravity of the sanctity of life has been displaced from the sanctity of the lineage of genetically linked individual lives to the individuality of discrete human organisms."[68] To the extent, then, that genetic engineering "unambiguously entails the vitality and individuality of the living," Shils believes it to be "quite acceptable." Such interventions will "probably not involve a complete break with the line." And in most present cases, they "do not di-

225

minish life, [but] improve it. . . . Apart from the disruption of line-age, they do nothing other than increase and enlarge the vitality of oncoming generations."[69]

Like Engelhardt, Shils believes that genetic engineering need pose no deep threat to human sanctity and dignity. Yet both authors, and particularly Engelhardt, fail to come to terms with a deeper worry about genetic engineering. As they both recognize, "we"—and we must recognize the cultural character of this "we"[70]—accord to human individuality a special significance. We see in self-determination a distinct moral value. Yet it is just such self-determination that may be threatened by genetic engineering, especially if, as Engelhardt envisages, we may one day intervene in the human germ line to reconstruct elements of our nature.

Although human personality emerges out of a social environment, in which we are deeply indebted to communal forces, its individuality comes into sharper focus only as those social influences become themselves the object of reflective attention and creative engagement. To the extent that we have been channeled into firm molds of others' making, our individuality is diminished. Now one of the virtues of Shils' linking of human sanctity to the "normal" and "natural" is the way it accords a special value to Nature's endowment. It involves a recognition that our sanctity consists in part of what we are individually able to make of what is impersonally "given," and not simply in what traits we possess. The inhabitants of Huxley's *Brave New World* may be happier and more rational than those of our present world, but they are also less "human"—less able to take credit for what they are and do. Unlike most of the inhabitants, John the Savage, who has escaped test-tube shaping of the architects of Brave New World, forms goals, experiences emotions, and pursues courses of action that reflect on *him*. Most of the other inhabitants, on the other hand, act out of reasons and desires that have been implanted or at least so structured by others, that there is little room for thought, feeling, and conduct that is humanly *their own*.

The danger of reconstructive interventions into human nature is that they will diminish our autonomy. For what we will be able to become will not be something over which we have individual control, but will instead reflect the manipulative efforts of genetic engineers. Impersonal "Nature" poses no threat to human autonomy; humans may do so. If the reason I cannot jump three hundred feet into the air is that I have not been physiologically endowed with that capacity, that is no constraint on my autonomy. But if the only reason I cannot jump that high is that somebody intervened in my genetic makeup to prevent it, then my freedom will have been impaired. The same would hold were I not able to jump three feet into the air. What most threatens individuality is human intervention, not Nature.

Engelhardt sees in the development of our capacity to intervene in the human germ line and, perhaps, to diminish our capacity for aggression, a triumph of human creativity.[71] On the part of those who intervene it may well be. That is how the architects of *Brave New World* saw it. But on the part of those who result from such interventions, it will be dehumanizing. The control that they are able to have over their emotions will no longer be something for which they can take credit, as an achievement of their own. It will possess only the appearance of virtue.

Of course not all genetic interventions will pose a threat of this kind. Some—particularly those that relieve people of physiological defects from which they would otherwise suffer—may even enhance the possibilities for autonomy. But where we are dealing with changes to what Engelhardt calls "human nature" we are penetrating a dimension of human experience that is integral to our character as autonomous beings.

Review

Although "life's value" is frequently invoked as a moral *terminus a quo*, it does not represent a single or simple starting point, but an appeal that is shaped by its context. Although it is very often limited to or at least focused on human life, in some recent debates it has encompassed or been directed to animal or plant life or livingness in general. Vegetarians, for example, have often wished to maintain that animal life has an integrity and directedness that warrants our noninterference. Although I have not accepted that the claims of animal life are strong enough in themselves to justify a vegetarian conclusion, I have not wished to deny that the disregard of their lives that has often characterized our treatment of animals has little to be said for it.

In the human context, appeals to life's value vary greatly in their thrust and character. Abortion, capital punishment, and genetic manipulation generate very different appeals to life's value. Frequently, those who make such appeals expect them to carry a decisive weight in practical argument. However, as I have suggested in this chapter, these appeals, though significant, are not on their

227

own sufficient to determine the issue. In part, of course, this is because what is called the issue is itself very complex—often one in which morality, law, and politics are involved. But as well the very appeal to life's "value" does not have a single focus in these cases, and different understandings need to be articulated and to confront each other. In abortion, the claims of fetal life (survival) need to be ranged against the claims of maternal life (frequently, autonomy); in debates about capital punishment, the claims of "innocent" life have to be ranged against the claims of human life (here, the life of the offender); in debates about those who are irreversibly comatose, the claims of biological life must be considered in relation to the claims of biographical life; and in genetic engineering, the claims of individual life may come into tension with the claims of lineage.

It has not been my purpose to attempt some resolution of these longstanding problems. It would be foolish to attempt that in this brief compass. But what I hope to have done is to have brought some illumination to that oft-heard appeal, and, by focusing, not on the question, "What justifies our killing?" but rather, "What may be said for life?", to have helped to articulate what in many minds is simply the intuitive feeling that "there must be something to be said for it."

NOTES

Introduction

1. Justice Robert Muir, Jr., "Opinion in the Matter of Karen Quinlan", Superior Court of New Jersey, Chancery Division, Morris County, N.J. (10 November 1975), reprinted in Thomas Mappes and Jane Zembaty (eds.), *Social Ethics: Morality and Social Policy* (New York: McGraw Hill, 1976), 41–42. For a full transcript, see *In the Matter of Karen Quinlan: The Complete Legal Briefs, Court Proceedings, and Decision in the Superior Court of New Jersey* (Frederick, Md.: University Publications of America, Inc., 1975–76), 2 vols.
2. Edward Shils, "The Sanctity of Life," in Edward Shils et al., *Life or Death: Ethics and Options* (Seattle: University of Washington Press, 1968).
3. James V. Schall, "Surgical Death," *Linacre Quarterly* 49 (November 1982): 307.
4. Albert Schweitzer, *The Philosophy of Civilization*, trans. C. T. Campion (New York: Macmillan, 1949), 310.
5. Something like this is suggested in R. M. Hare, *The Language of Morals* (Oxford: Clarendon Press, 1952), 69. See also Hare's elaboration in Douglas Seanor and N. Fotion (eds.), *Hare and Critics* (Oxford: Clarendon Press, 1988), 202.

Chapter I

1. Ludwig Wittgenstein, *Tractatus Logico-Philosophicus* (1921), trans. D. F. Pears and B. F. McGuinness (London: Routledge & Kegan Paul, 1961), para. 6.41.
2. Steve F. Sapontzis, "Must We Value Life to Have a Right to It?" *Ethics and Animals* 3 (March 1982): 2–11.
3. Richard Stith, "Toward Freedom from Value," *The Jurist* 38 (1978): 48–81.
4. X need not be a material object. We may affirmatively value events, conditions, processes, acts, practices, and so on. For convenience, however, I shall generally speak of the object of affirmative value as a "thing."
5. P. H. Nowell-Smith, *Ethics* (Harmondsworth: Penguin, 1954), 112–21. In fairness to Nowell-Smith, his use of the term is rather different from the one I am making.
6. David Hume, "On Suicide." Cf. his later remark, in the same essay: "It would be no crime in me to divert the Nile or Danube from its course

were I able to effect such purpose. Where then is the crime of turning a few ounces of blood from their natural channel?" Hume's point, of course, is not that value requires a valuer, but that valuing is a function of sentiment, and not of reason—a point and contrast with which I would take issue.

7. For an extended development of these views, see Julius Kovesi, *Moral Notions* (London: Routledge & Kegan Paul, 1967); id., "Valuing and Evaluating," in B. Y. Khanbhai, R. S. Katz, and R. A. Pineau (eds.), *Jowett Papers 1968–1969* (Oxford: Blackwell, 1970), 53–64.

8. Karl Binding and Alfred Hoche, *Die Freigabe der Vernichtung lebensunwerten Lebens: Ihr Mass und ihre Form*, (Leipzig: F. Meiner, 1920). For the translation of this idea into the Nazi "euthanasia" program, see Helmut Ehrhardt, *Euthanasie und Vernichtung "Lebensunwerten Lebens"* (Stuttgart: F. Enke, 1965).

9. Albert Schweitzer, *The Philosophy of Civilization*, third edition, trans. C. T. Campion (New York: Macmillan, 1949). See, particularly, the Preface to pt. 2: "Civilization and Ethics, " and chap. 26.

10. Michael Davis, "The Moral Status of Dogs, Forests and Other Persons," *Social Theory and Practice* 12 (Spring 1986): 55.

11. J. Robert Nelson, "On Life and Living: The Semitic Insight," *Journal of Medicine and Philosophy* 3 (June 1978): 137.

12. Lawrence Davis, "Reverence," paper read at the APA Pacific Division Meeting (March 1985).

13. Herbert W. Richardson, "What is the Value of Life?" in Donald R. Cutler (ed.), *Updating Life and Death: Essays in Ethics and Medicine* (Boston: Beacon Press, 1968), 171.

14. Deut. 1:17; II Chron. 19:7.

15. Joel Feinberg, "Some Conjectures about the Concept of Respect," *Journal of Social Philosophy* 3 (April 1973): 1–3.

16. Ibid., 2.

17. Ibid.

18. Stephen L. Darwall, "Two Kinds of Respect," *Ethics* 88 (October 1977): 38.

19. Ibid.

20. Ibid., 45.

21. Ibid., 38.

22. Ibid., 42–43.

23. Ibid., 44.

24. I think the phrase "moral considerability" was introduced into the literature by Kenneth Goodpaster. See his "On Being Morally Considerable," *Journal of Philosophy* 75 (1978): 308–25.

25. Edward Shils, "The Sanctity of Life," in Edward Shils et al. (eds.), *Life or Death: Ethics and Options* (Seattle: University of Washington Press, 1968), 12.

26. William K. Frankena, "The Ethics of Respect for Life," reprinted in John Howie (ed.), *Ethical Principles for Social Policy* (Carbondale: Southern Illinois University Press, 1983), 1–2.

27. Elizabeth A. Maclaren, "Dignity," *Journal of Medical Ethics* 3 (1977): 40.

28. Richard C. Dales, "A Medieval View of Human Dignity," *Journal of the History of Ideas* 38 (October–December 1979): 557–59.

29. Maclaren, "Dignity," 40.

30. See Daniel Callahan, "The Sanctity of Life," in Cutler (ed.), 190. See also Paul Ramsey, "The Morality of Abortion," in James Rachels (ed.), *Moral Problems* (New York: Harper & Row, 1971), 11ff.

31. See, e.g., Axel Stern, "On Value and Human Dignity," *Listening* (Spring 1975), 78; Willard Gaylin, "What's So Special About Being Human?" in Robert Esbjornson (ed.), *The Manipulation of Life* (San Francisco: Harper & Row, 1984), 55–57.

32. Marvin Kohl, "Voluntary Beneficent Euthanasia," in Marvin Kohl (ed.), *Beneficent Euthanasia* (Buffalo, N.Y.: Prometheus Books, 1975), 133.

33. Ibid.

34. Robert S. Morison, "The Last Poem: The Dignity of the Inevitable and Necessary," *Hastings Center Studies* 2 (May 1974): 64.

35. This phrasing is from Maclaren, "Dignity," 41.

36. Immanuel Kant, *The Doctrine of Virtue*, trans. Mary J. Gregor (New York: Harper Torchbooks, 1964), 99.

37. Maclaren, "Dignity," 41.

38. Ibid.

39. This distinction is critical to Stith in "Toward Freedom from Value," and is central to the moral theory developed by Stanley Benn in *A Theory of Freedom* (Cambridge: Cambridge University Press, 1988).

40. A more detailed discussion of this development can be found in my "Human Rights, Legal Rights and Social Change," in Eugene Kamenka and Alice Erh-Soon Tay (eds.), *Human Rights* (London: Edward Arnold, 1978), 36–47.

41. H.L.A. Hart, "Are There Any Natural Rights?" *Philosophical Review* 64 (April 1955): 175–91.

42. A. Delafield Smith, *The Right to Life* (New Haven, Conn.: College & University Press, 1955), 12.

43. Quoted in Hugo Adam Bedau "The Right to Life," *The Monist* 52 (October 1968): 551.

44. Joel Feinberg, *Social Philosophy* (Englewood Cliffs, N.J.: Prentice-Hall, 1973), 70–71.

45. See Stuart M. Brown, Jr., "Inalienable Rights," *Philosophical Review* 64 (April 1955): 192–211; William K. Frankena, "Natural and Inalienable Rights," *Philosophical Review* 64 (April 1955): 221–32.

46. See the discussion in Joel Feinberg, "Voluntary Euthanasia and the Inalienable Right to Life," *Philosophy & Public Affairs* 7 (Winter 1978): 114–18. Even the notion of nonwaivability is complex. Waivers may be temporary or permanent, and the assertion of nonwaivability can be interpreted as a logical, legal, moral, or psychological thesis. For some of these alternative understandings, see David Braybrooke, *Three Tests for Democracy: Per-*

sonal Rights, Human Welfare, Collective Preference (New York: Random House, 1968), 21, 23; John Locke, *Second Treatise of Civil Government* (1690), chap. 4, para. 23; cf. chap. 11, para. 135.

47. See Braybrooke, *Three Tests for Democracy*, 23.

Chapter II

1. Norman W. Pirie, "Concepts out of Context: The Pied Pipers of Science," *British Journal for the Philosophy of Science* 2 (February 1952): 280.

2. See, e.g., Paul Edwards, s.v. "Panpsychism," in Paul Edwards (ed.), *The Encyclopedia of Philosophy* (New York: Macmillan & The Free Press, 1967), 6:22–31. For a recent discussion, see Thomas Nagel, "Panpsychism," in *Mortal Questions* (Cambridge: Cambridge University Press, 1979), chap. 13.

3. See Goblet D'Alviella, s.v. "Animism," in James Hastings (ed.), *Encyclopedia of Religion and Ethics* (New York: Charles Scribner's Sons, 1908–1926), 1:535–37.

4. See T. G. Kalghati, *Jaina View of Life* (Sholapur: Jaina Samskriti Samrakshaka Sangha, 1969); S. Gopalan, *Outlines of Jainism* (New Delhi: Wiley Eastern Ltd., 1973), pts. 4 & 5.

5. Carl Sagan, s.v. "Life," *Encyclopaedia Britannica*, 15th ed. (Chicago: Encyclopaedia Britannica Inc., 1974), *Macropaedia*, 22:987.

6. Edward Shils, "The Sanctity of Life," in Edward Shils et al. (eds.), *Life or Death: Ethics and Options* (Seattle: University of Washington Press, 1968), 12.

7. Hans Jonas, *The Phenomenon of Life: Toward a Philosophical Biology* (New York: Harper & Row, 1966; reissued by University of Chicago Press, 1982).

8. Ibid., 89–90.

9. Ibid., 84, 100.

10. Ibid.

11. Ibid., 83–85.

12. Ibid., 6.

13. Ibid., essay 4.

14. Ibid., essay 7.

15. Ibid., 3. Here Jonas seems to depart significantly from Heidegger. The latter sees Man's ontological distinctiveness in his possession of freedom. Where Heidegger sees a radical break, Jonas sees the endpoint of a continuum.

16. Ibid.

17. This account of the naturalistic fallacy is developed in Julius Kovesi, *Moral Notions* (London: Routledge & Kegan Paul, 1967).

18. G. T. Fechner, *Zend-Avesta; oder, über die Dinge des Himmels und des Jenseits, vom Standpunkt der Naturbetrachtung*, 2d ed. (Hamburg: L. Voss, 1906), 1:179.

19. James Lovelock and Sidney Epton, "The Quest for Gaia," *New Scien-*

tist 65 (6 February 1975): 304. See also James Lovelock, *Gaia: A New Look at the Earth* (London: Oxford University Press, 1974).

20. Sir Harold Himsworth, "The Human Right to Life: its Nature and Origin," in Bruce Hilton, Daniel Callahan, Maureen Harris, Peter Condliffe, and Burton Berkley (eds.), *Ethical Issues in Human Genetics Counseling & the Use of Genetic Knowledge* (New York: Plenum Press, 1973), 172.

21. Daniel C. Dennett, *Content and Consciousness* (London: Routledge & Kegan Paul, 1969), chap. 6.

22. Ibid., 121, 131.

23. Michael Tooley, *Abortion and Infanticide* (Oxford: Clarendon Press, 1983), 121.

24. Jeremy Bentham, *Introduction to the Principles of Morals and Legislation*, ed. Wilfrid Harrison (Oxford: Blackwell, 1948), 412.

25. Hans-Walter Wolff, *The Anthropology of the Old Testament* (Philadelphia: Fortress Press, 1974), 62.

26. I discuss this further in chap. 6. See also Gregory Vlastos, "The Individual as Object of Love in Plato's Dialogues," in *Platonic Studies*, 2d ed. (Princeton: Princeton University Press, 1981), 3–42.

27. James Rachels, "The Sanctity of Life," in James M. Humber and Robert F. Almeder (eds.), *Biomedical Ethics Reviews 1983* (Clifton, N.J.: Humana Press, 1983), 33.

28. Richard Wollheim, *The Thread of Life* (Cambridge, Mass.: Harvard University Press, 1984), 1.

29. Rachels, "Sanctity of Life," 34.

30. Ibid., 26.

31. See, e.g., Alastair S. Gunn, "Why Should we Care about Rare Species?" *Environmental Ethics* 2 (Spring 1980): 17–37; J. Baird Callicott, "On the Intrinsic Value of Nonhuman Species," in Bryan G. Norton (ed.), *The Preservation of Species: The Value of Biological Diversity* (Princeton: Princeton University Press, 1986), 138–72.

32. The sanctity of tribal life may be maintained by killing off defective newborns.

33. Shils, "Sanctity of Life," 29.

Chapter III

1. Albert Schweitzer, "The Ethics of Reverence for Life," *Christendom* 1 (Winter 1936): 239. This essay is reprinted as an Appendix to Henry Clark, *The Ethical Mysticism of Albert Schweitzer* (Boston: Beacon Press, 1962), 180–94.

2. Schweitzer published the first two parts of a projected four-part work, *The Philosophy of Civilization*, in 1923. Work on the first part, *The Decay and Restoration of Civilization* was begun at the turn of the century, but its distinctive thrust did not emerge until the period of his internment. That is developed in the second part, titled *Civilization and Ethics*. An English

translation of the third edition by C. T. Campion was published in 1949 (London: A & C Black; New York: Macmillan). All references are to the American edition, which has different pagination.

3. Schweitzer, *Philosophy of Civilization*, 95; cf. xiii.

4. The ideas of world- and life-affirmation are not altogether clear, though the general notion is of an outlook which actively affirms both the world and the life which is found within it. It is not fatalistic or escapist.

5. Schweitzer, *Philosophy of Civilization*, esp. chaps. 22–24. In this connection, it is interesting to note how Schweitzer describes the circumstances that led to his fundamental "insight":

> Slowly we crept upstream, laboriously feeling—it was the dry season—for the channels between the sandbanks. Lost in thought I sat on the deck of the barge, struggling to find the elementary and universal conception of the ethical which I had not discovered in any philosophy. Sheet after sheet I covered with disconnected sentences, merely to keep myself concentrated on the problem. Late on the third day, at the very moment when, at sunset, we were making our way through a herd of hippopotamuses, there flashed upon my mind, unforeseen and unsought, the phrase "Reverence for Life." The iron door had yielded: the path in the thicket had become visible. Now I had found my way to the idea in which affirmation of the world and ethics are contained side by side! Now I knew the ethical acceptance of the world and of life together with the ideals of civilization contained in this concept, has a foundation in thought.

[Albert Schweitzer, *Out of My Life and Thought: An Autobiography*, trans. C. T. Campion, with Postscript 1932–49 by Everett Skilling (New York: New American Library, 1955), 124.]

6. Schweitzer, *Philosophy of Civilization*, 76. Despite their differences in expression, there are significant similarities between Schweitzer's position and that of Wittgenstein in the *Tractatus*.

7. Ibid., 107.

8. Ibid., 78.

9. See Schweitzer, *Civilization and Ethics*, chap. 17.

10. Schweitzer's survey, though immensely erudite, has much of the quirkiness of Russell's *History of Western Philosophy*.

11. Schweitzer, *Philosophy of Civilization*, 246.

12. Discussed in Schweitzer, *Civilization and Ethics*, chap. 11.

13. Schweitzer, "Ethics of Reverence for Life," in Clark, *Ethical Mysticism*, 182–3.

14. Ibid., 185.

15. Ibid.

16. See Schweitzer, *Reverence for Life*, trans. Reginald H. Fuller (New York: Harper & Row, 1969), 115: "a lacy snowflake glistens in your hand. you can't help looking at it. See how it sparkles in a wonderfully intricate

pattern. Then it quivers, and the delicate needles of which it consists contract. It melts and lies dead in your hand. It is no more."

17. Ibid.

18. Schweitzer, "Ethics of Reverence for Life," in Clark, *Ethical Mysticism*, 185. In the same essay, he goes on to argue that geese, monkeys, and sparrows "are compelled by ethics," i.e., the will-to-live externalized (192–93).

19. Schweitzer, *Out of My Life*, 158.

20. Schweitzer, *Philosophy of Civilization*, 282.

21. Ibid., 230. Cf. Schweitzer, "Ethics of Reverence for Life," in Clark, *Ethical Mysticism*, 187.

22. Schweitzer, "Ethics of Reverence for Life," in Clark, *Ethical Mysticism*, 184.

23. Albert Schweitzer, *Indian Thought and its Development* (1935), trans. C.E.B. Russell (Boston: Beacon Press, 1936), 83–84.

24. F. Nietzsche, *Twilight of the Idols* trans. R. J. Hollingdale (Harmondsworth: Penguin, 1969), 88.

25. Ibid.

26. Schweitzer, *Philosophy of Civilization*, 290.

27. Cf.: "Nature knows no . . . reverence for life. It produces life a thousandfold in the most meaningful way and it destroys it a thousandfold in the most meaningless way" (Schweitzer, "The Ethics of Compassion," in *Reverence for Life*, 120).

28. Schweitzer, *Philosophy of Civilization*, 317.

29. Ibid., 318.

30. Ibid. Here Schweitzer's thought seems to extend beyond organismic life to mere livingness. The wanton destruction of the flower is not ipso facto the wanton destruction of the plant.

31. Schweitzer, *Out of My Life*, 181.

32. Schweitzer, *Philosophy of Civilization*, 317.

33. Herbert Spencer, *Social Statics* (New York: Robert Schalkenbach Foundation, 1970), 391.

34. He speaks of morality as "a species of transcendental physiology" (ibid.).

35. Ibid.

36. Hans Jonas, *The Phenomenon of Life: Toward a Philosophical Biology* (New York: Harper & Row, 1966; reissued by University of Chicago Press, 1982), 3.

37. Ibid., 83.

38. Ibid., 3.

39. Ibid., 4.

40. S. I. Benn, "Freedom, Autonomy and the Concept of a Person," *Proceedings of the Aristotelian Society*, N.S. 76 (1975–76), 116. In an elaborated form, autarchic freedom constitutes personal autonomy.

41. See, for example, Bryan G. Norton, "On the Inherent Danger of Un-

dervaluing Species," in Norton (ed.), *The Preservation of Species: The Value of Biological Diversity* (Princeton: Princeton University Press, 1986), 110–37.

42. Robert Nozick, *Anarchy, State, and Utopia* (New York: Basic Books, 1974), 42–45. For an application of this argument to environmental ethics, see Richard Routley and Val Routley, "Human Chauvinism and Environmental Philosophy," in D. S. Mannison, M. A. McRobbie and R. Routley (eds.), *Environmental Philosophy* (Canberra: Philosophy Department, Australian National University, 1980), 154.

43. Jonas is more successful in avoiding theological assumptions than Schweitzer, though the latter has the following revealing remarks in a letter he wrote in 1923, in response to the suggestion that his position could be seen as pantheistic rather than theistic:

> It has always been my practice not to say anything when speaking as a philosopher that goes beyond the absolutely logical exercise of thought. Therefore I do not speak of "God" in philosophy, but of the "universal Will-to-Live," which meets me in a twofold guise: a creative will outside me; as ethical will within me. To be sure, the tentative conclusion which you speak of may be readily drawn, but I am very doubtful as to whether drawing this conclusion is a matter for philosophy, or whether to do so would be advantageous for one's worldview. Consequently I prefer to limit myself to a description of the process of thought and to let pantheism and theism remain in undecided conflict within me. For that is the bare fact of experience I keep coming back to.
>
> But if I am speaking the traditional religious speech, then I make use of the word "God" in its historical preciseness and lack of preciseness, just as I also in such cases say "love" instead of "reverence for life." For here the idea is to convey the familiar thought in its direct vitality and in its relation to traditional piety. In following this custom I am not making any concession either to nature philosophy or to religion. For in both cases the content remains the same: abandonment of knowledge concerning the world and establishment of the primacy of the universal will-to-live which is experienced within me.

[Letter to Oskar Kraus, in Oskar Kraus, *Albert Schweitzer: His Work and His Philosophy* (London: A & C Black, 1944), 38–39.]

44. Traditional sources (within the Judeo-Christian tradition) for the view that life is a gift of God include Gen. 1:21; 2:7; Job 1:21; etc. I leave it open whether these texts can be configured into an argument-form of the kind under consideration. See also Thomas Aquinas, *Summa Theologiae*, II, ii, q. 64, art. 5.

45. See Rom. 6:23.

46. C. L. Stevenson, "Persuasive Definitions," *Mind* 47 (1938): 331–50.

47. A. Schopenhauer, *The World as Will and Idea* (1819), trans. R. B. Haldane and J. Kemp (London: Trubner & Co., 1886) 3:390.

48. See Ps. 50:10–11. Insofar as life, and God's property generally, is

valuable, there is no implication that it is equally valuable (see Matt. 10:31; Lk. 12:7). See further Thomas Aquinas, *Summa Theologiae*, II, ii, q. 64, art. 5.

49. J. Locke, *Second Treatise of Civil Government* (1690), II.ii.6.

50. Ibid., II.v.25–26.

51. Plato, *Phaedo*, 62d.

52. Locke, II.v.27.

53. (1) Does Locke see God's creative labor as sufficiently analogous to human labor for this argument to hold? I think so. Although Locke may have seen God's creative work as ex nihilo, the relevant feature for his argument to go through is present—God's personality is "impressed" on his labors. (2) Locke's position is more complicated (and problematic) than I have indicated. The day laborer does not come to own the product of his labor; rather he is compensated by the landowner for whom he works.

Chapter IV

1. *The Jerusalem Bible* (Garden City, N.Y.: Doubleday, 1966).

2. Aristotle, *Politics*, trans. T. A Sinclair (Harmondsworth: Penguin Books, 1962), bk. 1, chap. 8 (1256b). However, this passage oversimplifies both Aristotle and the traditional view. The latter always acknowledged the direct as well as indirect value that plants have for Man. And Aristotle's position on plants becomes less anthropocentric when we turn from the *Politics* to the *Metaphysics* and his writings on natural history. See John Rodman, "The Other Side of Ecology in Ancient Greece: Comments on Hughes," *Inquiry* 19 (1976): 110–11.

3. Eric Katz offers a suggestive argument to the effect that writers who construe ecosystems on the model of an *organism* are pushed into resolving the affirmative value of plant life into its ecological role, whereas those who favor a community model can preserve an independent value for plant life alongside the value it acquires by virtue of its place in an ecosystem. See "Organism, Community, and the 'Substitution Problem,'" *Environmental Ethics* 7 (Fall 1985): 241–56.

4. See Evelyn B. Pluhar, "Two Conceptions of an Environmental Ethic and Their Implications," *Ethics and Animals* 4 (1983): 110–27.

5. J. Donald Hughes, "Ecology in Ancient Greece," *Inquiry* 8 (Summer 1975): 115–25.

6. Ibid., 117.

7. Ibid., 124.

8. Rodman cites John Evelyn's (1664) complaint that his contemporaries no longer revered trees as sacred, and John Muir's (1912) opposition to the radical alteration of a wilderness area because it profaned a sacred place where the holy could be encountered (in Rodman, "The Other Side," 109).

9. Ibid., 110.

10. Empedocles, Fragment 8, in Hermann Diels, *Die Fragmente der Vor-*

sokratiker, 4th ed. (Berlin: Weidmannische Buchhandlung, 1922), vol. 1; trans. by Philip Wheelwright, *The Presocratics* (New York: Odessey Press, 1966), 127.

11. Rodman, "The Other Side," 111.

12. Empedocles, Fragment 117, in Diels; trans. Wheelwright, *The Presocratics*, 141.

13. See Isaiah 40:6–7.

14. See Carl Sagan, s.v. "Life," *Encyclopaedia Britannica*, 15th ed. (Chicago: Encyclopaedia Britannica Inc., 1974), *Macropaedia*, 22:985–1002.

15. Arne Naess, "The Shallow and the Deep, Long-Range Ecology Movement: A Summary," *Inquiry* 16 (1973): 95.

16. J. Baird Callicott, "Intrinsic Value, Quantum Theory, and Environmental Ethics," *Environmental Ethics* 7 (Fall 1985): 257–75; Alan Watts, *The Book on the Taboo Against Knowing Who You Are* (New York: Pantheon, 1966). Fritjof Capra, in *The Tao of Physics* (Boulder: Shambala Publications, 1975), attempts to integrate Eastern and modern scientific approaches.

17. Callicott, "Intrinsic Value," 275.

18. Ibid., 274.

19. See James Lovelock, *Gaia: A New Look at Life on Earth* (London: Oxford University Press, 1974); James Lovelock and Sidney Epton, "The Quest for Gaia," *New Scientist* 65 (6 February 1975): 304–6; James E. Lovelock, "Gaia: The World as Living Organism," *New Scientist* 112 (1986): 25–28; James E. Lovelock, "Geophysiology: A New Look at Earth Science," in R. Dickenson (ed.), *Geophysiology in Amazonia: Vegetation and Climatic Interactions* (New York: John Wiley, 1987). In "Noosphere, Gaia, and the Science of the Biosphere," *Environmental Ethics* 10 (Summer 1988): 121–37, Rafal Serafin points out that the Gaia hypothesis has a number of historical antecedents.

20. Lovelock, *Gaia*, 9.

21. Ibid., 148.

22. See, e.g., S. H. Schneider, "A Goddess of the Earth? The Debate on the Gaia Hypothesis—An Editorial," *Climatic Change* 8 (1986): 1–4.

23. For further discussion of Gaian ethics, see Anthony Weston, "Forms of Gaian Ethics," *Environmental Ethics* 9 (Fall 1987): 217–30.

24. May nonliving things also be said to have a good of their own? This is disputed. Most environmentalists allow that inanimate objects may have a good, but argue that their good is not a good "of their own," independent of functions and roles which we have given to them. See Robin Attfield, *The Ethics of Environmental Concern* (New York: Columbia University Press, 1983); Paul W. Taylor, "Are Humans Superior to Animals and Plants?" *Environmental Ethics* 6 (Summer 1984): 152; also Joel Feinberg, "The Rights of Animals and Unborn Generations," in William T. Blackstone (ed.), *Philosophy and Environmental Crisis* (Athens, Ga.: University of Georgia Press, 1974), 51. For an opposing view see L. W. Sumner's review of Attfield in *Environmental Ethics* 8 (Spring 1986): 80–81; also Robert Elliot's critical no-

tice of the same book in *Australasian Journal of Philosophy* 63 (December 1985): 507.

25. Paul W. Taylor, *Respect for Nature: A Theory of Environmental Ethics* (Princeton: Princeton University Press, 1986), 75. Taylor distinguishes "inherent worth" from "intrinsic value," "inherent value," and "merit." An object is accorded intrinsic value when valuers value it because of its enjoyableness to them "in and of itself." It is accorded inherent value when "we believe [it] should be preserved, not because of its usefulness or its commercial value, but simply because it has beauty, historical importance, or cultural significance" (p. 73). Unlike intrinsic value and inherent value, inherent worth is—according to Taylor—independent of valuers. Such objects as have inherent worth have it independent of the satisfactions or regard of valuers. Merit applies to individuals in virtue of various properties that differentiate them. Worth is something they have by virtue of their possessing a good.

26. Ibid., 99. At an earlier point (p. 60n), Taylor indicates that by "respect for nature" he has in mind what Stephen Darwall calls "recognition respect" (see sup., p. 16).

27. Taylor, *Respect for Nature*, chap. 3.

28. Ibid., 117.

29. Taylor, "The Ethics of Respect for Nature," *Environmental Ethics* 3 (Fall 1981): 209.

30. Taylor, *Respect for Nature*, 122. I find this way of talking very problematic. For similar misgivings, see Gerald H. Paske, "The Life Principle: A (Metaethical) Rejection," *Journal of Applied Philosophy* 6 (October 1989): 219–25.

31. Ibid., 152.

32. Ibid., 154.

33. Ibid., 121.

34. See Eric R. Pianka, "On r- and K-Selection," *American Naturalist*, 104 (1970), 592–97. Members of species possessing r-selection traits tend to be short-lived, reproduction-oriented, highly fertile, and opportunistic. Many desert flowers and small birds fall into this category. The members of species with K-selection traits, on the other hand, are long-lived, they produce few offspring, with a relatively low mortality rate, and are well adapted to their particular habitat. Larger trees and animals tend to fall into this category. We are, of course, speaking here of a continuum rather than a rigid division.

35. See Gene Spitler, "Justifying a Respect for Nature," *Environmental Ethics* 4 (Fall 1982): 259.

36. Taylor, *Respect for Nature*, 133. As he states his point, it looks as though Taylor is falling into the non sequitur of arguing from "X has a good" to "X is a good." However, he explicitly denies that this inference is intended.

37. Ibid., 148.

38. Ibid., 149.

39. Ibid., 130.

40. See, e.g., Richard Routley and Val Routley, "Human Chauvinism and Environmental Ethics," in D. S. Mannison, M. A. McRobbie, and R. Routley (eds.), *Environmental Philosophy* (Canberra: Research School of Social Sciences, Australian National University, 1980), for its most detailed statement. For other and similar versions of the argument, see Robert Elliot, "Environmental Degradation, Vandalism and the Aesthetic Object Argument," *Australasian Journal of Philosophy* 67 (June 1989): 191–204.

41. Attfield, *Ethics of Environmental Concern*, 155.

42. See Stanley Benn, "Personal Freedom and Environmental Ethics: The Moral Inequality of Species," in G. Dorsey (ed.), *Equality and Freedom: International and Comparative Jurisprudence* (Leiden: Sijtof, 1977) 17–19; Elliott Sober, "Philosophical Problems for Environmentalism," in Bryan G. Norton (ed.), *The Preservation of Species: The Value of Biological Diversity* (Princeton, N.J.: Princeton University Press, 1986), 190–91.

43. Donald H. Regan, "Duties of Preservation," in Norton (ed.), *Preservation of Species*, 205–8.

44. Elliot believes that shifting the disvalue to the vandalizer's "attitude" makes sense only if nature itself is seen as having inherent worth ("Environmental Degradation," 199). But this strong presumption is not required. It is enough that nature be intrinsically valued.

45. Robert Elliot, "Faking Nature," *Inquiry* 25 (1982): 81–93.

46. For an attempt to construct such an argument, see A. Carlson, "Nature and Positive Aesthetics," *Environmental Ethics* 6 (1984): 5–34.

47. Stuart Hampshire, after Proust, persuasively develops a similar argument against "false aestheticism":

> The deliberate loss of human lives in preserving for posterity a single work, for instance, Vermeer's *View of Delft*, could not be justified, because the value of this most beautiful painting, of the actual physical object, resides in the lifelong work and thought, and solitary dedication, of Vermeer; it resides in the imagination of that unique person, elaborating his own singular vision of what painting might be as a representation of reality. If the physical object had been destroyed, the spiritual value residing in that individual's dedicated labour and vision would not have been destroyed; but posterity would forever have lost direct access to this extraordinary human being and to his unique discoveries in painting.

(*Innocence and Experience* [Cambridge, Mass.: Harvard University Press, 1989], 130.)

48. See the illustrated edition of Leopold's *A Sand County Almanac* (Tamarack Press, in association with Oxford University Press, 1977).

49. Katz, "Organism, Community," 254.

50. Ibid., 253.

51. In some cases, the preservation of plant life may be justified by refer-

ence to the needs of future generations. On the problems raised by this, see R. Sikora and Brian Barry (eds.), *Obligations to Future Generations* (Philadelphia: Temple University Press, 1978).

52. See John Rawls, *A Theory of Justice* (Cambridge: Harvard University Press, 1971); Nicholas Rescher, *Welfare: The Social Issues in Philosophical Perspective* (Pittsburgh: University of Pittsburgh Press, 1972).

53. See Lilly-Marlene Russow, "Why Do Species Matter?" *Environmental Ethics* 3 (1981): 101–12.

Chapter V

1. George Orwell, *Animal Farm* (New York: Harcourt, Brace, 1946), chap. 10.

2. The occasion was an article "Animal Liberation," published in the *New York Review of Books* 20 (5 April 1973): 17–21. It was later expanded into a book-length study under the same title (New York: New York Review, 1975). For Singer's reflections on a decade of debate, see "Ten Years of Animal Liberation," *New York Review of Books* 31 (17 January 1985): 46–52. An entree to the historical debate on animals can be gained via Charles R. Magel's *A Bibliography on Animal Rights and Related Matters* (Washington, D.C.: University Press of America, 1981).

3. Although most of Singer's attention is given to animal pain as the basis for restructuring our treatment of animals, it is at least arguable that there are other sources of suffering to which (many) animals are susceptible and that provide a broader base for our moral consideration. Thus, Hans Jonas writes that "the suffering intrinsic in animal existence is . . . primarily not that of pain (which is occasional and a concomitant) but that of want and fear, i.e., an aspect of appetitive nature as such" (*The Phenomenon of Life: Toward a Philosophical Biology* [Chicago: University of Chicago Press], 105).

4. See J. Baird Callicott, "Animal Liberation: A Triangular Affair," *Environmental Ethics* 2 (1980): 311–38; Mark Sagoff, "Animal Liberation and Environmental Ethics: Bad Marriage, Quick Divorce," *Osgoode Hall Law Review*, 22 (1984); Robert W. Loftin, "The Morality of Hunting," *Environmental Ethics* 6 (Fall 1984): 241–50.

5. Michael W. Fox, *Returning to Eden: Animal Rights and Human Responsibility* (New York: Viking Press, 1980). I have not included all the affinities that Fox adduces, but those I have fairly represent his position.

6. Willard Gaylin, "What's So Special About Being Human?" in Robert Esbjornson (ed.), *The Manipulation of Life* (San Francisco: Harper & Row, 1984), 61. For a sober review of the evidence, see Jonathan Bennett, "Thoughtful Brutes," *Proceedings and Addresses of the American Philosophical Association* 62 (Supp.) (September 1988): 197–210.

7. For a good discussion of sympathy and its role in ethics, see Philip Mercer, *Sympathy and Ethics* (London: Oxford University Press, 1972). John

A. Fischer, in "Taking Sympathy Seriously," *Environmental Ethics* 9 (Fall 1987): 197–215, appeals to sympathy to establish our responsibilities to animals. He does not, however, have a very clearly articulated understanding of sympathy.

8. The magnitude of that exercise in sympathetic understanding is well brought out by Thomas Nagel in "What is it like to be a Bat?" reprinted in *Mortal Questions* (Cambridge: Cambridge University Press, 1979), chap. 12.

9. I don't think that Rachels intends these terms to be used interchangeably, though he appears to believe that in each case their use requires the subject to "have a life." His views are developed in "Do Animals Have a Right to Life?" in Harland B. Miller and William H. Williams (eds.), *Ethics and Animals* (Clifton, N.J.: Humana Press, 1983), 275–84; "The Sanctity of Life," in James M. Humber and Robert F. Almeder (eds.), *Biomedical Ethics Reviews 1983* (Clifton, N.J.: Humana Press, 1983); and *The End of Life*, Oxford University Press, 1986), chaps. 2 & 3.

10. Rachels, "Do Animals Have a Right to Life?" 282–83.

11. Ibid., 283.

12. Rachels, *The End of Life*, 26.

13. Sup., pp. 41–42.

14. Rachels, *The End of Life*, 5.

15. Rachels, "Do Animals Have a Right to Life?" 283.

16. Ibid.

17. Henry Johnstone, Jr., makes this point generally about inanimate objects and animals to distinguish them from persons:

> The being of a person is reflexive in a way in which the being of an inert thing is not. One cannot be a person without knowing what it is like *to oneself* to be a person. It is entirely by virtue of this knowledge that persons place whatever value or disvalue they do on life. . . . An animal does not know what it is like *to itself*—from its own piscine, avian, feline, or canine point of view—to be a fish, bird, cat, or dog. While it enacts the behavior of its species, it does so without taking a point of view. The fish behaves like a fish—not to itself, but to us.

("On Being a Person," in E. G. Baught [ed.], *Essays in Metaphysics* [University Park, Pa.: Pennsylvania State University Press, 1970], 138.)

18. Edward Johnson, "Life, Death, and Animals," in Miller and Williams (eds.), *Ethics and Animals*, 128.

19. Ibid., 129.

20. Ibid.

21. Regan's arguments have changed over time. The arguments he appeals to in "The Moral Basis of Vegetarianism," reprinted in *All That Dwell Therein* (Berkeley: University of California Press, 1982), 1–39, an earlier defense of the animal right to life, are abandoned in *The Case for Animal Rights* (Berkeley: University of California Press, 1983). My discussion focuses on the latter.

22. Regan, *The Case for Animal Rights*, 243.

23. Ibid., 247, 248, 280.

24. Ibid., chaps. 7.6, 7.8, 8.4, 8.5.

25. Ibid., 245.

26. J. S. Mill, *Utilitarianism* (1861), ed. George Sher (Indianapolis: Hackett, 1979), 52. We should note, though, that Mill (quite properly, I believe) does not restrict such social interventions to those that are coercive: "When we call anything a person's right, we mean that he has a valid claim on society to protect him in the possession of it, either by the force of law or by that of education and opinion" (ibid.).

27. See Donald VanDeVeer, "Of Beasts, Persons and the Original Position," *The Monist* 62 (1979): 368–77; id., "Interspecific Justice and Animal Slaughter," in Miller and Williams (eds.), *Ethics and Animals*, 147–62; Michael S. Pritchard and Wade L. Robison, "Justice and the Treatment of Animals: A Critique of Rawls," *Environmental Ethics* 3 (1981): 55–61; Russ Manning, "Environmental Ethics and Rawls' Theory of Justice," *Environmental Ethics* 3 (1981): 155–66; Tom Regan, "Duties to Animals: Rawls' Dilemma," *Ethics and Animals* 2 (1981): 76–81; Alan E. Fuchs, "Duties to Animals: Rawls' Alleged Dilemma," *Ethics and Animals* 2 (1981): 83–87; Robert Elliot, "Rawlsian Justice and Non-Human Animals," *Journal of Applied Philosophy* 1 (1984): 95–106; Brent A. Singer, "An Extension of Rawls' Theory of Justice to Environmental Ethics," *Environmental Ethics* 10 (Fall 1988): 217–31.

28. John Rawls, *A Theory of Justice* (Cambridge, Mass.: Harvard University Press, 1971), esp. 136–42.

29. VanDeVeer, "Interspecific Justice," 154.

30. Ibid., 159.

Chapter VI

1. *The Jerusalem Bible* (Garden City, N.Y.: Doubleday, 1966).

2. See J. M. Rist, *Human Value: A Study in Ancient Philosophical Ethics* (Leiden: E. J. Brill, 1982). This section has benefited considerably from Rist's suggestive work.

3. Plato, *Euthyphro* 10D-E; *Phaedrus* 249C.

4. As quoted in Helga Kuhse, *The Sanctity-of-Life Doctrine in Medicine* (Oxford: Clarendon Press, 1987), 18.

5. Plato, *Republic*.

6. Rist, *Human Value*, 39.

7. G.M.A. Grube, *Plato's Thought* (Boston: Beacon Press, 1958), 148.

8. Plato, *Republic* 460C1–5.

9. Ibid., 406E.

10. Plato, *Laws* 854DE, 855Cff.

11. See Rist, *Human Value*, 81.

12. Whereas Plato's gods are worthy of imitation because they are to the greatest degree possible characterized by the Forms (*Phaedrus* 249C),

Aristotle's god exemplifies *theoria*—contemplation (*Nicomachean Ethics* 1177B30ff).

13. Aristotle, *Politics*, 1253A29; *Nicomachean Ethics*, 1145A31, 1148B17, 1150A.

14. *Nicomachean Ethics*, 1100A2.

15. Ibid., 1103A.

16. I appreciate that my interpretation of Aristotle's highest good is controversial. Many would argue that he sees *sophia* (theoretical wisdom) and *phronesis* (practical wisdom) as coordinate constituents of human good (*Nicomachean Ethics*, book 6). This may offer a better synthesis of Aristotle's position, though there is some heuristic value in maintaining the contrast between Plato and Aristotle.

17. Rist, *Human Value*, 63.

18. Ibid., 71.

19. Ibid., 78–80.

20. Ibid., 82.

21. W.E.H. Lecky, *History of European Morals from Augustus to Charlemagne*, eleventh ed. (London: Longmans, Green & Co., 1894), 2:18, 20, 34.

22. Ibid., 34.

23. The biblical writers do not regard immortality as a structural feature of human existence (e.g., I Timothy 6:16). See, further, Oscar Cullmann, *Immortality of the Soul or Resurrection of the Dead? The Witness of the New Testament* (London: Epworth, 1958).

24. John Locke, *Second Treatise of Civil Government* (1690), 2.ii.6.

25. Paul Ramsey, "The Morality of Abortion," in James Rachels (ed.), *Moral Problems* (New York: Harper & Row, 1971), 13.

26. Daniel Callahan, "The Sanctity of Life," in Donald R. Cutler (ed.), *Updating Life and Death: Essays in Ethics and Medicine* (Boston: Beacon Press, 1968), 190.

27. I can no longer locate the reference to the Thielicke quotation.

28. Genesis 1:26.

29. Ibid., 9:6.

30. Karl Barth, *Church Dogmatics*, trans. Geoffrey W. Bromiley (Edinburgh: T. & T. Clark, 1958), vol. 3, pt. 1, p. 193.

31. Irenaeus, *Adversus Haereseis*, V.6, 16. See Rist, *Human Value*, 157–8.

32. Clement of Alexandria, *Stromateis*, 6. See Rist, *Human Value*, 159–63.

33. Genesis 2:7; 1:24.

34. Ibid., 5:3.

35. There are, in fact, serious difficulties in the way of a morphological interpretation of the image's original meaning. See John Kleinig, "The Value of Life," *Interchange* 28 (1980), 14–16.

36. John Dryden, "Poems from Examen Poeticum: The First Book of *Ovid's* Metamorphoses," ll. 107–10, in James Kinsley (ed.), *The Poems of John Dryden* (Oxford: Clarendon Press, 1958), 2:802.

37. D.J.A. Clines, "The Image of God in Man," *Tyndale Bulletin* 19 (1968): 81, citing K. H. Bernhardt.

38. Ibid., 85. See also Boyo Ockinga, *Die Gottebenbildlichkeit im Alten Ägypten und im Alten Testament* (Wiesbaden: Harrassowitz, 1984). Ockinga observes that in Egyptian texts both "image" and "likeness" are spoken of. The latter, however, is used in relation to some quality or characteristic possessed by (one of) the gods, and those who share that "likeness" need not be kings. Unlike "image" it does not designate a status—though in the case of the king his "likeness" may consist in qualities appropriate to his rulership as God's representative.

39. Genesis 1:28.

40. Ibid., 2:3.

41. Edward Shils, "The Sanctity of Life," in E. Shils et al., *Life or Death: Ethics and Options* (Seattle: University of Washington Press, 1968), 9, 12.

42. Ibid.

43. Ibid., 13, 14.

44. Ibid., 12.

45. Ibid., 15–18.

46. Ibid., 19.

47. Ibid.

48. Ibid., 36–37.

49. Ibid., 19, 26.

50. Ibid., 29.

51. Joseph Butler, *Works*, ed. W. E. Gladstone (Oxford: Oxford University Press, 1896), vol. 2: Sermon 7, 132–33.

52. For an expansion of these remarks, see John Kleinig, *Punishment and Desert* (The Hague: Martinus Nijhoff, 1973), chap. 1: "Moral Justification."

53. See Edward W. Keyserlingk, *Sanctity of Life or Quality of Life in the Context of Ethics, Medicine and Law* (Ottawa: Law Reform Commission of Canada, 1979), 16.

54. William Warren Bartley III, *The Retreat to Commitment* (New York: Knopf, 1962).

55. Friedrich Nietzsche, *Twilight of the Idols*, trans. R. J. Hollingdale (Harmondsworth: Penguin, 1969), 30.

56. Ibid.

57. Ibid.

58. Ibid.

59. Ibid., 45.

60. Ibid.

61. Ibid.

62. Ibid., 88–89.

63. F. Nietzsche, *The Will to Power*, trans. Walter Kaufmann and R. J. Hollingdale (New York: Vintage, 1968), sect. 899.

64. Ibid., sect. 1001.

65. For a detailed exposition of Nietzsche's ideas on the value of life,

see Richard Schacht, *Nietzsche* (London: Routledge & Kegan Paul, 1983), pt. 6.

66. Ibid.

67. Richard McCormick, "The Quality of Life, The Sanctity of Life," *Hastings Center Report* 8 (February 1978): 30.

68. Paul R. Johnson, "Selective Nontreatment of Defective Newborns: An Ethical Analysis," *Linacre Quarterly* 47 (February 1980): 40.

69. Michael D. Bayles, "The Value of Life—By What Standard?" *American Journal of Nursing* 80 (December 1980): 2226.

70. "What is good is not just living, but living well."

71. Holmes Rolston III, "The Irreversibly Comatose: Respect for the Subhuman in Human Life," *Journal of Medicine and Philosophy* 7 (November 1982): 342.

72. Sometimes Rolston appears to espouse an almost Schweitzerian vitalism: "The comatose individual provides occasion for recalling the very ancient succession (evolution) in which he or she stands" (ibid., 340). Why should this matter? He states: "The very experiencing of this precious elemental vitality, and the urgency of its defense, will produce a conservative belief in its sacredness" (ibid., 343).

73. Ibid., 338.

74. Ibid., 339.

75. Stanley Benn, *A Theory of Freedom* (Cambridge: Cambridge University Press, 1988), chap. 1, sect. 5; chap. 13.

76. T. G. Roupas, "The Value of Life," *Philosophy & Public Affairs* 72 (1978): 155.

77. Ibid., 164.

78. Ibid., 168–69. Just *what* is it that the person prefers—"existence" or certain goods that existence makes possible? Roupas is not clear.

79. Ibid., 173–74.

80. Ibid., 177.

81. Ibid., 177–78.

82. Tooley's critique of Roupas is found in *Abortion and Infanticide* (Oxford: Clarendon Press, 1983), 250–54. In that critique he makes use of Parfit's discussion in "On Doing the Best for our Children," in Michael Bayles (ed.), *Ethics and Population* (Cambridge, Mass.: Schenkman, 1976), 100–115.

83. Tooley, *Abortion and Infanticide*, 252.

84. Ibid., 253–54.

85. See Michael Stocker, "Desiring the Bad: An Essay in Moral Psychology," *Journal of Philosophy* 76 (1979): 738–53.

86. Louis I. Dublin and Alfred J. Lotka, *The Money Value of a Man* (1930) (New York: Ronald Press Co., 1946).

87. Quoted in Rich Feeley, Diana Walsh, and Jonathan Fielding, "Structural Codes and Patient Safety: Does Strict Compliance Make Sense?" *American Journal of Law and Medicine* 3 (1977–78): 447–54.

88. One possibility that needs to be considered is that the different models are context-relative. See John G. Cullis and Peter A. West, "Valuing

Human Life," in *The Economics of Health: An Introduction* (Oxford: Martin Robertson, 1979), 209–10.

89. "The basic DFE approach takes the average age at which death of people killed by a certain type of disease or accident occurs and computes what their future income would have been if they had lived a normal term. This future income is discounted, since a dollar received today can be invested and is thus worth more than a dollar received in future years. The 'present value' figure that results is taken as the value of life for the average member of the group in question. Though the procedure is simple enough, the actual figures used recently have ranged from under $100,000 to over $400,000. Significant differences result from the use of different discount rates or from studying different groups. (Air travelers make more money than motorists and the value of their lives is higher.) However, the highest values are explained mainly by a decision by many economists to use the DFE amount only as a base figure to which other values are added. And there are also those who use DFE as a base from which individual consumption is subtracted" (Steven E. Rhoads, *Valuing Life: Public Policy Dilemmas* [Boulder, Colo.: Westview Press, 1980], 12).

90. Highly sophisticated mathematical formulae have been developed to give expression to these various models. My concern will not be with the adequacy of these formulae to the valuational models they are intended to realize, but with the appropriateness of the models to "valuing life." Unless the models have themselves been adequately grounded, the quantification exercise will be pointless. There is some point to E. J. Mishan's caution that "there is more to be said for rough estimates of the precise concept than precise estimates of economically relevant concepts" ("Evaluation of Life and Limb: A Theoretical Approach," *Journal of Political Economy* 79 [July/August 1971]: 705) and his later complaint about the "bright-eyed academic" who creates "a lavish model that serves more to exhibit his technical *legerdemain* than it does to shed light on crucial concepts" ("Recent Contributions to the Literature of Life Valuation: A Critical Assessment," in M. W. Jones-Lee [ed.], *The Value of Life and Safety* [Amsterdam: North-Holland Publishing Co., 1982], 82).

91. Charles Fried, "The Value of Life," *Harvard Law Review* 82 (May 1969): 1415–37.

92. Ibid., 1423.

93. Ibid., 1427.

94. Ibid., 1429.

95. Ibid., 1430.

96. Ibid., 1431.

97. Ibid., 1433–37.

98. Even limited trading, such as the trading of sports stars, sometimes has unpleasant overtones of human commodification.

99. John Broome, "Trying to Value a Life," *Journal of Public Economics* 9 (February 1978): 91–100.

100. Mishan, "Recent Contributions," 83.

101. Mishan, "Evaluation of Life and Limb," 694.

102. Gary Fromm, "Civil Aviation Expenditures," in R. Dorfman (ed.), *Measuring Benefits of Government Investment* (Washington, D.C.: Brookings Inst., 1965), 193–96.

103. See Mishan, "Evaluation of life and Limb," 691; Cullis and West, "Valuing Human Life," 204.

104. Nicholas Rescher, *Risk: A Philosophical Introduction to the Theory of Risk Evaluation and Management* (Lanham, Md.: University Press of America, 1983), 177.

105. Ibid., 173. Perhaps this indicates that insurance policies are not merely devices for burden-spreading but are also intended as agents for social control.

106. Ibid., 179.

Chapter VII

1. Thomas Nagel, Preface to *Mortal Questions* (Cambridge: Cambridge University Press, 1979), x.

2. For an influential but controversial statement of this, see Alasdair MacIntyre, *After Virtue*, 2d ed. (Notre Dame: University of Notre Dame Press, 1981).

3. As quoted in Arthur Schlesinger, Jr., "The Opening of the American Mind," *New York Times Book Review* (7/23/89), 27.

4. R. M. Hare, *The Language of Morals* (Oxford: Clarendon, 1952), where a stronger level of practical commitment is claimed.

5. The existence of such obligations has been recently questioned by Robert E. Goodin, *Protecting the Vulnerable: A Reanalysis of our Social Responsibilities* (Chicago: University of Chicago Press, 1985).

6. Albert Schweitzer, *The Philosophy of Civilization*, trans. C. T. Campion (New York: Macmillan, 1949), 318.

7. Might not the *telē* of some organisms be seen as inherently bad—the smallpox or AIDS viruses? I don't think this follows, even though the devastation they are able to cause to human well-being might justify seeking to eradicate them. It is no more part of their *telē* to invade and disrupt the human body than it is part of the human *telos* to make war or nuclear weapons.

8. Am I denying the possibility that livingness might be accounted for in complex "mechanistic" terms, at least to the extent that we can artificially create objects that have all the character of living organisms? I think not. However, this does not gainsay the fact that the difference in complexity of organization will be so great that we will continue to speak of a difference in kind, and not merely of degree. Reductionism will remain an oversimplification. A hairy man is not simply one who is not very bald.

9. This argument is developed and documented in Bryan G. Norton, "On the Inherent Danger of Undervaluing Species," in Bryan G. Norton

(ed.), *The Preservation of Species: The Value of Biological Diversity* (Princeton: Princeton University Press, 1986), 111–24.

10. Peter Miller, in "Value as Richness: Toward a Value Theory for an Expanded Naturalism in Environmental Ethics," *Environmental Ethics* 4 (Summer 1982): 101–14, gives "richness" a key role in an environmentally sensitive value theory. However, for him the richness is a quality of nature, and not of experience. I have given "complexity" the role that "richness" plays in his paper.

11. It is not my intention to imply that diversity and complexity are always and everywhere to be preferred. Uniformity and simplicity have their virtues too.

12. In *Innocence and Experience* (Cambridge, Mass.: Harvard University Press, 1989), 38ff., Stuart Hampshire draws attention to the "ideological" overtones that "reason" and "rationality" have acquired in philosophical contexts, and of the need to loosen ourselves from the dichotomies with which they have become associated. He opts for "thought" and "reflection" as less theory laden.

13. The device of an experience machine has been given contemporary philosophical prominence by Robert Nozick, in *Anarchy and Utopia* (New York: Basic Books, 1974), 42–45. It has been used in the present context by Richard Routley and Val Routley, "Human Chauvinism and Environmental Ethics," in D. S. Mannison, M. A. McRobbie, and R. Routley (eds.), *Environmental Philosophy* (Canberra: Department of Philosophy, Australian National University, 1980), 154.

14. See, e.g., Colin Turnbull, *The Mountain People*, New York: Simon & Schuster, 1972), where children are expected to fend for themselves once they reach the age of three. What also must be recognized, however, is the impoverishment—in every sense—of those lives. More extreme are socalled feral children, whose distance from recognizably human consciousness is even greater.

15. J. Baird Callicott, "Animal Liberation: A Triangular Affair," *Environmental Ethics* 2 (1980): 333.

16. "Sanctity," and "holiness" (usually seen as being more or less equivalent) derive from terms that originally conveyed the idea of separateness or being set apart (particularly in a religious context). But with this separation there was also associated the idea of purity and exaltedness. Hence the dual character of references to the sanctity of life.

17. Psalm 8:4.

18. H.L.A. Hart, "Are There Any Natural Rights?" *Philosophical Review* 64 (April 1955): 175–91. In this early article, Hart links rights-talk with there being a reason for legal coercion. However, in the later "Natural Rights: Bentham and John Stuart Mill," he claims that any connection between the idea of a moral right and there being a reason for enforcement by law is only a contingent fact: "It cannot be something secured by the meaning of a moral right if we are to regard the existence of moral rights as providing moral reasons why there should be certain legal rights" (in *Essays on Ben-*

tham: Studies in Jurisprudence and Political Theory [Oxford: Clarendon Press, 1982], 92). My own position, however, is not *both* that it is part of the meaning of "moral right" that its legal enforcement would be justified *and also* that something's being a moral right provides a moral reason for enforcing it. On my view, we use the terminology of rights to mark out those moral considerations that are weighty enough to warrant (if necessary) a coercive backing. We do not then appeal to moral rights as independent grounds for coercion.

19. Ibid., 181.

20. John Rawls, *A Theory of Justice* (Cambridge, Mass.: Harvard University Press, 1971), 62, 92.

21. See John Kleinig, "Crime and the Concept of Harm," *American Philosophical Quarterly* 14 (January 1978): 30–32; cf. Nicholas Rescher, *Welfare: the Social Issues in Philosophical Perspective* (Pittsburgh: Pittsburgh University Press, 1972), 4.

22. It is, perhaps, slightly disingenuous to say that the first formulation does not presuppose the right-holder's actual ability to choose: "unless *A* chooses otherwise" at least suggests that *A* might do so. And that is not the case if *A* is not an actual (or even potential) chooser.

23. J. S. Mill, *Principles of Political Economy* in John M. Robson (ed.), *Collected Works of John Stuart Mill*, vols. 2 & 3 (Toronto: University of Toronto Press, 1965): 947–48.

Chapter VIII

1. Edward Shils, "The Sanctity of Life," in E. Shils et al., *Life or Death: Ethics and Options* (Seattle: University of Washington Press, 1968), 19.

2. G.W.F. Hegel, *The Philosophy of Right*, trans. T. M. Knox (Oxford: Oxford University Press, 1952), 236.

3. Harry Frankfurt, "Freedom of the Will and the Concept of a Person," *Journal of Philosophy* 68 (1971): 6–7.

4. S. I. Benn, *A Theory of Freedom* (Cambridge: Cambridge University Press, 1988), chaps. 1 & 13. This category of reasons was prefigured in his article, "Abortion, Infanticide, and Respect for Persons," in Joel Feinberg (ed.), *The Problem of Abortion* (Belmont, Calif.: Wadsworth, 1973). Some of the material from this section is drawn with the kind permission of Chicago University Press from my "Persons, Lines, and Shadows," *Ethics* 100 (October 1989): 108–15.

5. He also allows that to be a person one need not be a human being. But I shall not comment on this here.

6. Benn, *A Theory of Freedom*, 16.

7. Benn speaks regularly of "humanity," when his general thesis suggests that he should be speaking of "personhood." Later I will argue for minimizing the distinction.

8. Benn, *A Theory of Freedom*, 15–16. One might be tempted to say that

human hair wigs and transplanted body parts do not pose the problem that Benn's remarks suggest. but I think he could argue that in these cases the beneficiaries are humans, and that the uses to which they are put cannot be construed as a denigration of their origins. What if human hair could be used for soft-bristled toothbrushes? What if human organs were transplanted into animals? That might strike us as more problematic, though the replaceability of human hair, and the circumstances of its collection, act as a counterpoising consideration. The idea of using wigs made from the hair of Holocaust victims is much more problematic.

9. In some U.S. states, it is required by law that fetal remains be disposed of in a manner that is consistent with the disposal of "other human remains." For references and related discussion, see Jeffrey A. Parness, "Crimes Against the Unborn: Protecting and Respecting the Potentiality of Human Life," *Harvard Journal on Legislation* 22 (Winter 1985): 97–172.

10. Benn, *A Theory of Freedom*, 252–53.

11. Ibid., 253.

12. Ibid.

13. Ibid., 255.

14. See John A. Robertson and Joseph D. Schulman, "Pregnancy and Prenatal Harm to Offspring: The Case of Mothers with PKU," *Hastings Center Report* 17 (August/September 1987): 23–33.

15. Benn, *A Theory of Freedom*, 255.

16. Any differentiation we make here is more likely to be influenced by the character of the interference than the time at which it occurred. The maltreated infant is likely to be "made to suffer" over a prolonged period of time in a way that the neglected zygote is not. But we could change the example to avoid those overtones. Suppose the parents bring up their infant as though it were a pet, not teaching it a language or human social skills, so that it grows up unable to speak a language or participate as an equal in communal activities. The child might not suffer, but I believe we would consider it grossly wronged.

17. Compare Roger Wertheimer, "Understanding the Abortion Argument," *Philosophy & Public Affairs* 1 (1971): 67–95.

18. See Benn, "Abortion and Respect for Persons."

19. Benn, *A Theory of Freedom*, 253–54. However, as Gerald Gaus has pointed out, Benn cannot amend his theory to accommodate these criticisms (see "Practical Reason and Moral Persons," *Ethics* 100 [October 1989]: 141–44).

20. II Kings 9:33–37.

21. Luke 1.

22. The case occurred in 1986. For discussion of its problematic legal history, see Dawn Johnsen, "A New Threat to Pregnant Women's Autonomy," *Hastings Center Report* 17 (August/September 1987): 33–40. Additional discussion can be found in Symposium: "Criminal Liability for Fetal Endangerment," *Criminal Justice Ethics* 9 (Winter/Spring 1990): 11–51.

23. Joel Feinberg, "The Rights of Animals and Unborn Generations,"

reprinted in *Rights, Justice, and the Bounds of Liberty* (Princeton: Princeton University Press, 1980), 183.

24. The same nomenclature, though with a somewhat different intension, is used by Francis C. Wade, "Potentiality in the Abortion Discussion," *Review of Metaphysics* 29 (December 1975): 249.

25. Feinberg, "The Rights of Animals," 184.

26. Cf. the related but not identical Aristotelian/Thomist distinction between passive and active potency/potentiality in Wade, "Potentiality," 239–55.

27. Cf. Jim Stone, "Why Potentiality Matters," *Canadian Journal of Philosophy* 17 (December 1987): 818.

28. Cf. Michael Kottow, "Ethical Problems in Arguments from Potentiality," *Theoretical Medicine* 5 (1984): 294. The element of a developmental trajectory is overlooked by those writers (e.g., Michael Lockwood, R. M. Hare, Mary Anne Warren) who claim that, given suitable conditions—e.g., their joint presence, with nutrients, in a Petri dish—a sperm and ovum have the same potential for human adulthood as a fetus. It may be true that there is as high a *probability* that the sperm and ovum will combine and that an adult human will eventually result as that a particular zygote will develop into an adult human. But potentiality in the strong sense is not a simple matter of probabilities. We are talking, rather, of an organism's developmental trajectory. Human adulthood is not part of the developmental trajectory of either the sperm as such or the ovum as such, and the mixture in the Petri dish does not possess a developmental trajectory.

29. Here I simply note that I have deliberately spoken of an oak seedling rather than an acorn. A fair bit of philosophical ink has been spilled over a supposed analogy between the relation of an acorn to an oak tree and a fetus to an adult human. The analogy is closer—though still not identical— if it is drawn between a germinated seedling and an oak tree. See, among others, Judith Jarvis Thomson, "A Defense of Abortion," *Philosophy & Public Affairs* 1 (Fall 1971): 47, 48; John Finnis, "The Rights and Wrongs of Abortion," *Philosophy & Public Affairs* 2 (Winter 1973): 144, 145; Marvin Kohl, "Abortion and the Argument from Innocence," *Inquiry* 14 (1971): 149.

30. In a recent article, however, Stephen Buckle links the weak/strong potentiality distinction (which he terms a distinction between the "potential *to produce*" and the "potential *to become*") to two different moral theories. The former he associates with consequentialist, and the latter with deontological theories ("Arguing from Potential," *Bioethics* 2 [July 1988]: 227–53). Although I do not think the link is as close as he suggests (he says the distinction "reflects" the two different kinds of moral theory), it is certainly common for consequentialists to interpret "potentiality" in what I called a "weak" sense. And they do so usually to argue that potentiality is of minimal moral relevance. It is also common for deontologists to interpret "potentiality" in a "strong" sense. And there are reasons within consequentialist and deontological theory for gravitating in these directions.

But I think that the strong/weak potentiality distinction lies outside the particular theories.

31. Michael Lockwood, "Warnock Versus Powell (and Harradine); When Does Potentiality Count?" *Bioethics* 2 (July 1988), esp. 197–208; id., "When Does Life Begin?" in Michael Lockwood (ed.), *Moral Dilemmas in Modern Medicine* (Oxford: Oxford University Press, 1986), 9–31. See also Eike-Henne W. Kluge, "The Right to Life of Potential Persons," *Dalhousie Law Journal* 3 (January 1977), esp. 839–43.

32. It seems to me that Lockwood confuses (at least) two stages in brain development—that at which the brain is capable of supporting *some kind of* mental life (e.g., sentience), and that at which it is capable of supporting the mental life that gives human (as against animal) life its distinctive character. The latter may be a much later development.

33. Buckle, "Arguing from Potential," 240.

34. I am of course avoiding the complications engendered by possible twinning. See, e.g., G.E.M. Anscombe, "Were You a Zygote?" in A. Phillips Griffiths (ed.), *Philosophy and Practice* Cambridge: Cambridge University Press, 1985), 111–15; Alan Holland, "A Fortnight of My Life is Missing: A Discussion of the Status of the Human 'Pre-Embryo,'" *Journal of Applied Philosophy* 7 (1990): 25–37.

35. It has been suggested to me that since potentiality is a relation—*aPb*—then, if potentiality is itself a ground for some kind of value, it should make no difference what *b* is. But clearly it does make a difference. Or, if it does not, then it can be accorded no more "value" than that associated with the least valuable living organism. I think these concerns misunderstand the nature of potentiality. We are not dealing with some abstract property or relation, potentiality, but a potentiality *for* certain characteristics, and what those characteristics happen to be is integral to our understanding of the potentiality in question.

36. For the form that such an argument might take, see Jeffrie G. Murphy, "Moral Death: A Kantian Essay in Psychopathy," reprinted in *Retribution, Justice, and Therapy* (Dordrecht: Reidel, 1979), 128–43. Murphy has since abandoned this argument.

37. *Furman v. Georgia*, 408 US 238, 273 (1972) (Justice William Brennan, Jr.).

38. I am aware, of course, that historically other offenses besides murder have been said to warrant the death penalty. And no doubt a full discussion of the topic would require that this be considered. However, since the case for capital punishment has greatest plausibility where murder is the offense, and since the appeal to life's value, affirmative and otherwise, does most work here, I shall limit my discussion to capital punishment for (willful) murder.

39. Kant, *The Metaphysical Elements of Justice* (1797), trans. John Ladd (Indianapolis: Bobbs-Merrill, 1965), 101–2.

40. See, for example, Stephen Nathanson, *An Eye for an Eye?: The Morality of Punishing by Death* (Totowa, N.J.: Rowman & Littlefield, 1987), 10–12.

41. C. Beccaria, *On Crimes and Punishments*, trans. Henry Paolucci (Indianapolis: Bobbs-Merrill, 1963); Albert Camus, "Reflections on the Guillotine," in *Resistance, Rebellion, and Death*, trans. Justin O'Brien (New York: Knopf, 1961); Arthur Koestler, *Reflections on Hanging* (London: Gollancz, 1956).

42. Koestler, *Reflections*, 7–8.

43. For an argument that bears some similarities to this, see Jeffrey Reiman, "Justice, Civilization and the Death Penalty: Answering van den Haag," *Philosophy & Public Affairs* 14 (1985): 115–48.

44. Abe Fortas, "The Case Against Capital Punishment," *New York Times Magazine*, (23 January 1977), 29.

45. For the general form of this argument, see Bernard Williams, "Utilitarianism and Moral Self-Indulgence," in *Moral Luck: Philosophical Papers 1973–1980* (Cambridge: Cambridge University Press, 1981), 40–53.

46. Those who criticize Kant's use of the *lex talionis* for permitting barbaric and inhuman punishments (for barbaric and inhuman offenses) or for providing an impracticable measure for some offenses (embezzlement, rape, airline hijacking, etc.) seem not to have read Kant's own discussion which, for all its inadequacies, at least attempts to address some of these issues.

47. Leonard J. Weber, *Who Shall Live?* (New York: Paulist Press, 1976), 41–42.

48. Holmes Rolston, III, "The Irreversibly Comatose: Respect for the Subhuman in Human Life," *Journal of Medicine & Philosophy* 7 (November 1982): 337.

49. Ibid., 340.

50. Ibid., 341.

51. Joseph Fletcher, *Morals and Medicine* (Boston: Beacon Press, 1972), 211–12.

52. At an earlier point Fletcher writes: "To be a person, to have moral being, is to have the capacity for intelligent causal action. It means to be free of physiology" (p. 194).

53. Rolston, "The Irreversibly Comatose," 341.

54. Ibid., 342.

55. Ibid., 343.

56. But then such paternalistic interventions may be permissible if Albert Grimes temporarily loses control of his faculties.

57. In Karen Quinlan's case, it was believed that the respirator was simply prolonging her dying. That turned out to be incorrect. It was for a time sustaining her life. But her body regained its ability to function as an—albeit limited—integrated whole, and she lived a further ten years. Since that time, similar questions have been raised about artificial hydration and nutrition. Do these—in the case of the permanently comatose—sustain life or simply prolong dying? My own view is that they sustain it. But clearly this needs more argument. See Gilbert Meilaender, "On Removing Food

and Water: Against the Stream," *Hastings Center Report* 14 (December 1984): 11–13.

58. We should note, nevertheless, that vitalistic concerns are not necessarily limited by the desires of the person whose life is in balance. For vitalists frequently argue that even if there is reason to believe that the person concerned would prefer not to go on living, the life in question should be maintained.

59. H. Tristram Engelhardt, Jr., *The Foundations of Bioethics* (New York: Oxford University Press, 1986), 376.

60. Ibid., 377.

61. See Willard Gaylin, "The Frankenstein Factor," *New England Journal of Medicine* 297 (22 September 1977): 665–67.

62. Engelhardt, *The Foundations of Bioethics*, 380–81.

63. Shils, "The Sanctity of Life," 6.

64. Ibid., 10.

65. Ibid., 13.

66. Ibid., 22.

67. Ibid., 29.

68. Ibid., 24.

69. Ibid., 27.

70. For a perceptive discussion, see M. B. Foster, "'We' in Modern Philosophy," in Basil Mitchell (ed.), *Faith and Logic: Oxford Essays in Philosophical Theology* (London: Allen & Unwin, 1957), 194–220.

71. Engelhardt, *The Foundations of Bioethics*, 380–81.

BIBLIOGRAPHY

What follows is not a list of works discussed or cited in the text but an independent research bibliography, confined to books and articles that make substantial reference to the broad topic of valuing life.

Aiken, Henry D. "Life and the Right to Life." In *Ethical Issues in Human Genetics: Genetic Counselling and the Use of Genetic Knowledge*, edited by Bruce Hilton et al., 173–83. New York: Plenum Press, 1973.

Aiken, William. "The Quality of Life." *International Journal of Applied Philosophy* 1 (Spring 1982): 26–36.

Allen, David F. and Victoria S. *Ethical Issues in Mental Retardation*. Nashville: Abingdon, 1979.

Amundsen, Darrel W. "The Physician's Obligation to Prolong Life: A Medical Duty Without Classical Roots." *Hastings Center Report* 8 (August 1978): 23–30.

Anderson, Norman. *Issues of Life and Death*. Chap. 1. London: Hodder & Stoughton, 1976.

André, Shane. "Pro-Life or Pro-Choice: Is There a Credible Alternative?" *Social Theory and Practice* 12 (Summer 1986): 223–40.

Annis, David. "Self-Consciousness and the Right to Life." *Southwestern Journal of Philosophy* 6 (Summer 1975): 123–28.

Anonymous. "The Sanctity of Life." *Tablet* 224 (30 May 1970): 514.

———. *The Principle of Respect for Human Life*. London: Linacre Centre, 1978.

Anscombe, G.E.M. "Were You a Zygote?" In *Philosophy and Practice* (Supplement to *Philosophy*), edited by A. Phillips Griffiths, 111–15. Cambridge University Press, 1985.

Arbor, J. L. "Animal Chauvinism, Plant-Reading Ethics and the Torture of Trees." *Australasian Journal of Philosophy* 64 (September 1986): 335–39.

Armstrong, Robert L. "The Right to Life." *Journal of Social Philosophy* 8 (January 1977): 13–19. Reprinted in *Biomedical Ethics*, edited by T. A. Mappes and Jane S. Zembaty, 432–38. New York: McGraw-Hill, 1981.

Arthur, W. B. "The Economics of Risks to Life." *American Economic Review* 71 (March 1981): 54–64.

Aspinall, John. "Man's Place in Nature." In *Animal Rights—a Symposium*, edited by David Paterson and Richard D. Ryder, 15–21. London: Centaur Press, 1979.

Atkins, Gail M. *The Moral Authority of a Natural Right to Life*. Ph.D. thesis, University of Nebraska, Lincoln, Neb., 1981 (Ann Arbor, Mich.: University Microfilms International, 1986. Publication No. 8118151.)

Attfield, Robin. "The Good of Trees." *The Journal of Value Inquiry* 16 (1981): 35–54.

——. "Multiplication and the Value of Life." Chap. 7, *The Ethics of Environmental Concern*. Oxford: Basil Blackwell; New York: Columbia University Press, 1983.

Baier, Kurt. "The Sanctity of Life." *Journal of Social Philosophy* 5 (April 1974): 1–6.

——. "Technology and the Sanctity of Life." In *Ethics and Problems of the 21st Century*, edited by K. E. Goodpaster and K. M. Sayre, 160–74. Notre Dame, Ind.: University of Notre Dame Press, 1979.

——. "When Does the Right to Life Begin?" In *Nomos XXIII: Human Rights*, edited by J. Roland Pennock and John W. Chapman, 201–29. New York: New York University Press, 1981.

Barry, Robert. "Self-Consciousness and Personhood." *Linacre Quarterly* 46 (May 1979): 141–48.

Barth, Karl. "The Protection of Life." In *Abortion: The Moral Issues*, edited by E. Batchelor, 92–101. New York: Pilgrim Press, 1982.

Battin, Margaret Pabst. *Ethical Issues in Suicide*. Englewood Cliffs, N.J.: Prentice-Hall, 1982.

Bayles, Michael D. "The Price of Life." *Ethics* 89 (October 1978): 20–34.

——. "The Value of Life—By What Standard?" *American Journal of Nursing* 80 (December 1980): 2226–30.

——. "The Value of Life." In *Health-Care Ethics*, edited by Donald VanDeVeer and Tom Regan, 265–89. Philadelphia: Temple University Press, 1987.

Beauchamp, Tom L. "Suicide." In *Matters of Life and Death*, edited by Tom Regan, 67–108. New York: Random House, 1980.

Beauchamp, Tom L.; Blackstone, William T.; and Feinberg, Joel, eds. *Philosophy and the Human Condition*. Englewood Cliffs, N.J.: Prentice-Hall, 1980.

Becker, Lawrence C. "Human Being: the Boundaries of the Concept." *Philosophy & Public Affairs* 4 (Summer 1975): 334–59.

Bedau, Hugo A. "The Right to Life." *The Monist* 52 (October 1968): 550–72.

Bergel, Kurt. "Albert Schweitzer's Reverence for Life." *Humanist* 6 (Spring 1946): 31–34.

Berry, R. J. and Kirby, David. [Letter] "Medical Ethics and the Potentialities of the Living Being." *British Medical Journal* 291 (28 September 1985): 901.

Birch, Charles, and Cobb, John B., Jr. *The Liberation of Life: From the Cell to the Community*. Cambridge: Cambridge University Press, 1981.

Blackstone, William T. "The Search for an Environmental Ethic." In *Matters of Life and Death: Essays in Moral Philosophy*, edited by Tom Regan, 299–335. New York: Random House, 1980.

Bleich, J. David. "The A Priori Component of Bioethics." *Jewish Life* 3 (Summer–Fall, 1978): 71–79.

Blom-Cooper, L., and Drewry, G., eds. "The Sanctity of Human Life." Chap. 6, *Law & Morality: A Reader*. London: Duckworth, 1976.

Blomquist, Glenn. "The Value of Human Life: An Empirical Perspective." *Economic Inquiry* 19 (January 1981): 157–64.

Bloom, Gerald. "Some Thoughts on the Value of Saving Lives." *Theoretical Medicine* 5 (October 1984): 241–51.

Bok, Sissela. "Fetal Research and the Value of Life." In *Appendix: Research on the Fetus* National Commission for the Protection of Human Subjects of Biomedical and Behavioral Research, DHEW (OS) 76–128.

Bollnow, Otto F. "Respect de la vie considere comme principe fondamental de l'ethique." *Revue de l'histoire et de philosophie religieuses* 56 (1976): 118–42 (trans. B. Kaempf).

Bopp, James, Jr., ed. *Restoring the Right to Life: The Human Life Amendment*. Provo, Utah: Brigham Young University Press, 1984.

Boyd, Kenneth M. "The Right to Life." *Journal of Medical Ethics* 7 (September 1981): 132–36.

Braine, David. *Medical Ethics and Human Life*. Old Aberdeen: Palladio Press, 1983.

Brand, P. W. *Is Life Really Sacred?* London: CMF, 1973.

Bridges, H. J. "Why Life is Worth Living." In *Humanity on Trial: A Brief for the Defense*, 266–87. New York: Liveright, 1941.

Brock, Dan W. "Taking Human Life." *Ethics* 95 (July 1985): 851–65.

Brody, Baruch A. "Abortion and the Sanctity of Human Life." *American Philosophical Quarterly* 10 (April 1973): 133–40.

———. *Abortion and the Sanctity of Human Life: A Philosophical View*. Cambridge, Mass.: M.I.T. Press, 1975.

Brook, Richard. "Dischargeability, Optionality & the Duty to Save Lives." *Philosophy & Public Affairs* 8 (Winter 1979): 194–200.

Broome, John. "Trying to Value a Life." *Journal of Public Economics* 9 (February 1978): 91–100.

Brophy, John. *The Meaning of Murder*. London: Whiting & Wheaton, 1966.

Brown, Neil. *The Worth of Persons: A Study in Christian Ethics*. Sydney: Catholic Institute of Sydney, 1983.

Brown, Norman et al. "The Preservation of Life." *Journal of the American Medical Association* 221 (5 January 1970): 76–82.

Brown, Stuart M., Jr. "Inalienable Rights." *Philosophical Review* 64 (April 1955): 212–32.

Buckley, William F.; Muggeridge, Malcolm; and Pilpel, Harriet. "Modern Attitudes Toward Life and Death." *Human Life Review* 5 (Summer 1979): 99–116.

Burtchaell, James. "How Much Should a Child Cost? A Response to Paul Johnson." *Linacre Quarterly* 47 (February 1980): 54–63.

Buss, M. J. "The Beginning of Human Life as an Ethical Problem." *Journal of Religion* 47 (July 1967): 244–55.

Cackowski, Zdzislaw. "Human Life as Goodness and a Measure of Value." *Dialectics & Humanism* 5 (Spring 1978): 163–71.

Callahan, Daniel. "The Sanctity of Life." In *Updating Life and Death: Essays in Ethics and Medicine*, edited by Donald R. Cutler, 181–223. Boston: Beacon Press, 1968. (Comments by Julian R. Pleasants, 223–30; James M.

Gustafson, 230–36; Henry K. Beecher, 236–42; and response by Callahan, 243–50.)

Camenisch, Paul F. "Abortion, Analogies and the Emergence of Value." *Journal of Religious Ethics* 4 (Spring 1976): 131–58.

Cameron, Nigel M. de S. *Embryos and Ethics: The Warnock Report in Debate.* Edinburgh: Rutherford House Books, 1987.

Cantor, Norman L. "A Patient's Decision to Decline Lifesaving Medical Treatment: Bodily Integrity Versus the Preservation of Life." *Rutgers Law Review* 26 (Winter 1973): 228–64.

Carrier, Leonard S. "Abortion and the Right to Life." *Social Theory & Practice* 3 (Fall 1975): 381–401.

Catholic Hospital Association. *Christian Affirmation of Life.* St. Louis: Catholic Hospital Association, 1974.

Cave, George, S. "Animals, Heidegger and the Right to Life." *Environmental Ethics* 4 (Fall 1982): 249–54.

Channer, J. H., ed. *Abortion and the Sanctity of Human Life.* Exeter: Paternoster, 1985.

Clark, Henry. *The Ethical Mysticism of Albert Schweitzer: A Study of the Sources & Significance of Schweitzer's Philosophy of Civilization.* Boston: Beacon Press, 1962.

Clements, Colleen D. " 'Therefore Choose Life': Reconciling Medical and Environmental Ethics." *Perspectives in Biology and Medicine* 28 (Spring 1985): 407–25.

Clouser, K. Danner. " 'The Sanctity of Life': An Analysis of a Concept." *Annals of Internal Medicine* 78 (January 1973): 119–25.

———. "Biomedical Ethics: Some Reflections and Exhortations." *The Monist* 60 (January 1977): 47–61.

Cobb, William Daniel. "Abortion and the Sanctity of Life." *Encounter* 38 (Summer 1977): 273–87.

Cobianu, Elena. "Some Hypotheses for Determining the Moral Quality of Life." *Philosophie et Logique* 20 (October–December 1976): 349–53.

Cohen, Cynthia B. " 'Quality of Life' and the Analogy with the Nazis." *Journal of Medicine and Philosophy* 7 (May 1983): 113–35.

Cohn, H. H. "On the Dichotomy of Divinity and Humanity in Jewish Law." In *Euthanasia,* edited by Amnon Carmi. Berlin: Springer-Verlag, 1984.

Conley, B. C. "The Value of Human Life in the Demand for Safety." *American Economic Review* 66 (March 1976): 45–55.

Connery, John R. "Abortion and the Duty to Preserve Life." *Theological Studies* 40 (June 1979): 318–33.

Cook, P. J. "The Value of Human Life in the Demand for Safety: Comment." *American Economic Review* 68 (September 1978): 710–11.

Crane, Diana. *The Sanctity of Social Life: Physicians' Treatment of Critically Ill Patients.* New York: Russell Sage Foundation, 1975.

———. "The Value of Human Life in the Demand for Safety: Extension and Reply." *American Economic Review* 68 (September 1978): 717–19.

Cullis, John G., and West, Peter A. "Valuing Human Life." In *The Economics of Health: An Introduction*, 197–215. Oxford: Martin Robertson, 1979.

Curran, Charles E. "Human Life: The Fifth Commandment." *Chicago Studies* 13 (Fall 1974): 279–99.

———. "The Fifth Commandment: Thou Shalt Not Kill." In *Ongoing Revision: Studies in Moral Theology*, Notre Dame, Ind.: Fides Publishers, 1975.

———. "Respect for Life: Theoretical and Practical Implications." In *Issues in Sexual and Medical Ethics*. Notre Dame, Ind.: University of Notre Dame Press, 1978.

Dardis, R. "The Value of a Life: New Evidence from the Marketplace." *American Economic Review* 70 (December 1980): 1077–82.

Daube, David. "The Sanctity of Life." *Proceedings of the Royal Society of Medicine* 60 (November 1967): 1235–40.

Davenport, Manuel M. "The Aesthetic Foundation of Schweitzer's Ethics." *Southwestern Journal of Philosophy* 5 (Spring 1974): 39–46.

Davidson, Thomas. "Is Life Worth Living?" *International Journal of Ethics* 6 (1895–96): 231.

Davis, Michael. "The Moral Status of Dogs, Forests and Other Persons." *Social Theory and Practice* 12 (Spring 1986): 27–59.

Dawson, R.F.F. "A Practitioner's Estimate of the Value of Life." In *Health Economics*, edited by M. H. Cooper and A. J. Culyer, 336–56. Harmondsworth: Penguin, 1973.

De Nicola, Daniel R. "Genetics, Justice, and Respect for Life." *Zygon* 11 (June 1976): 115–37.

Den Uyl, Douglas, and Rasmussen, Douglas. "Nozick on the Randian Argument." *Personalist* 49 (April 1978): 184–205.

Derr, Patrick. "Who Shall Live? Who Shall Die? Who Shall Play God? Some Reflections on Euthanasia." *Thought* 57 (December 1982): 422–37.

Diamond, Eugene. "'Quality' vs. 'Sanctity of Life' in the Nursery." *America* 135 (4 December 1976): 396–98.

Diggory, J. C., and Rothman, D. Z. "Values Destroyed by Death." *Journal of Abnormal and Social Psychology* 63, 1 (1961): 205–10.

Dinstein, Yoram. "The Human Right to Life of Physical Integrity and Liberty." In *The International Bill of Rights: The Covenant on Civil and Political Rights*, edited by Louis Henkin. New York: Columbia University Press, 1981.

Donagan, Alan. "Comments on Dan Brock and Terrence Reynolds." *Ethics* 95 (July 1985): 874–86.

Doyle, James F. "Schweitzer's Extension of Ethics to All Life." *Journal of Value Inquiry* 11 (Spring 1977): 43–46.

Duff, R. A. "Intentionally Killing the Innocent." *Analysis* 34 (October 1973): 16–19.

Edwards, Paul. s.v. "Life, Meaning and Value of." In *Encyclopedia of Philosophy*, edited by Paul Edwards, vol. 6: 466–77. New York: Collier-Macmillan, 1967.

Ellington, Preston D. "Right to Life, an Ethical Dilemma: A Physician's

Viewpoint." *Journal of the Medical Association of Georgia* 67 (February 1978): 131–32.

Engelhardt, H. Tristram, Jr. "The Ontology of Abortion." *Ethics* 84 (April 1974): 217–34.

————. "But are they People?" *Hospital Physician* 12 (February 1976): 6–8.

Erdahl, Lowell O. *Pro-Life/Pro-Peace: Life Affirming Alternatives to Abortion, War, Mercy Killing, and the Death Penalty.* Minneapolis, Minn.: Augsburg, 1986.

Ericson, Edward L. "Albert Schweitzer and the Ethical Ecology of Life." *Religious Humanism* 9 (Spring 1975): 50–54.

Ettlinger, Gerard H., S.J. "The Value of Human Life in Judaeo-Christian Perspective." In *Human Life: Problems of Birth, of Living, and of Dying,* edited by William C. Bier, S.J., 3–13. New York: Fordham University Press, 1977.

Ewin, Robert. "What is Wrong with Killing People?" *Philosophical Quarterly* 22 (1972): 126–39.

Farris, W. James S. "Reflections on the Sanctity of Life." In *The Religious Dimension,* edited by John C. Hinchcliff, 91–94. Auckland, N.Z.: Rep. Prep, 1976.

Fearon, John. "States of Life." *Thomist* 12 (January 1949): 1–16.

Feinberg, Joel. "Is there a Right to be Born?" In *Understanding Moral Philosophy,* edited by James Rachels, 346–58. Encino, Calif.: Dickenson, 1976. Reprinted in *Rights Justice, and the Bounds of Liberty,* 207–20. Princeton: Princeton University Press, 1980.

————. "Voluntary Euthanasia and the Inalienable Right to Life." *Philosophy & Public Affairs* 7 (Winter 1978): 93–123.

Ferkiss, Victor. "The Value of Human Life in Technological Society." In *Human Life: Problems of Birth, of Living, and of Dying,* edited by William C. Bier, S.J., 29–42. New York: Fordham University Press, 1977.

Fleck, Leonard M. "Pricing Human Life: The Visibility Issue." Unpublished paper, NASSP Conference, Boulder, Colo., 1985.

Fleming, Lorette. "The Moral Status of the Fetus: A Reappraisal." *Bioethics* 1 (January 1987): 15–34.

Fletcher, George P. "The Right to Life." *Georgia Law Review* 13 (Summer 1979): 1371–94.

————. "The Right to Life." *The Monist* 63 (April 1980): 135–55.

Fletcher, Joseph. "The 'Right' to Live, and the 'Right' to Die." *Humanist* 34 (July–August 1974): 12–15.

Foot, Philippa. "Euthanasia." *Philosophy & Public Affairs* 6 (Winter 1977): 85–112.

Fox, Michael. *Returning to Eden: Animal Rights and Human Responsibility.* New York: Viking, 1980.

Frankel, Yitzhaq Yedidya. "The Sanctity of Human Life." In *The Dying Human,* edited by Andre De Vries and Amnon Carmi, 195–99. Tel Aviv: Turtledove Publishing, 1979.

Frankena, William K. "The Ethics of Respect for Life." In *Ethical Principles* for Social Policy, edited by John Howie, 1–35. Carbondale: Southern Illinois University Press, 1983. Reprinted from *Respect for Life in Medicine, Philosophy & the Law*, edited by Owsei Temkin et al., 24–62. Johns Hopkins University Press, 1976.

Frankl, Victor E. *Man's Search for Meaning*. New York: Washington Square Press, 1985.

Freer, Jack P. "Chronic Vegetative States: Intrinsic Value of Biological Process." *Journal of Medicine and Philosophy* 9 (November 1984): 395–408.

Frey, Raymond. *Rights, Killing and Suffering: Moral Vegetarianism and Applied Ethics*. Oxford: Blackwell, 1983.

———. "Autonomy and the Value of Animal Life." In *New Options, New Dilemmas*, edited by Anne S. Allen, 50–63. Lexington, Mass.: Lexington Heath, 1986.

Fried, Charles. "The Value of Life." *Harvard Law Review* 82 (May 1969): 1415–37. Reprinted in *An Anatomy of Values*, chap. 12. Cambridge, Mass.: Harvard University Press, 1970.

Geddes, Leonard. "On the Intrinsic Wrongness of Killing People." *Analysis* 33 (January 1973): 93–97.

Gellman, Max A. "Philosophical & Religious Implications of the Sanctity of Life Principle in Law and Medicine." *American Journal of Forensic Psychiatry* 1 (May 1978): 28–41.

Gerson, Lloyd. "Abortion and the Right to Life." *Crux* 12, 4 (1974–75): 25–29.

Gillon, Raanan. "To What Do We Have Moral Obligations and Why? I & II." *British Medical Journal* 290 (1 & 8 June 1985): 1646–47, 1734–36.

Glover, Jonathan. *Causing Death and Saving Lives*. Harmondsworth: Penguin, 1977.

———. "Assessing the Value of Saving Lives." In *Human Values*, edited by Godfrey Vesey, N.J.: Humanities Press, 1978.

Goldman, Alan H. "Abortion and the Right to Life." *Personalist* 60 (October 1979): 402–6.

Goodpaster, Kenneth E. "On Being Morally Considerable." *Journal of Philosophy* 75 (June 1978): 308–25.

———. "On Stopping at Everything: A Reply to W. M. Hunt." *Environmental Ethics* 2 (Fall 1980): 281–84.

Goodrich, T. "The Morality of Killing." *Philosophy* 44 (1969): 127–39.

Graham, John, and Vaupel, James. "The Value of a Life: What Difference Does it Make?" *Risk Analysis* 1 (1981): 89–95.

Granberg, Donald. "What Does it Mean to be 'Pro-Life'?" *Christian Century* 99 (12 May 1982): 562–66.

Greene, Theodore M. "Life, Value, Happiness." *Journal of Philosophy* 53 (May 1956): 317–29.

Grene, Marjorie. "On Some Distinctions between Men and Brutes." *Ethics* 57 (January 1947): 121–27.

Grisez, Germain G. "Toward a Consistent Natural Law Ethics of Killing." *American Journal of Jurisprudence* 15 (1970): 64–96.

Grisez, Germain G. "The Value of a Life: a Sketch." *Philosophy in Context* 2 (1973): 7–15.

——. *Life and Death with Liberty and Justice: A Contribution to the Euthanasia Debate*. Notre Dame, Ind.: University of Notre Dame Press, 1979.

Gula, Richard M. *What are they Saying about Euthanasia?* New York: Paulist Press, 1986.

Gustafson, James M. "Mongolism, Parental Desires and the 'Right to Life.'" *Perspectives in Biology and Medicine* 16 (Spring 1973): 529–57.

Hall, Elizabeth, and Cameron, Paul. "Our Failing Reverence for Life." *Psychology Today* 9 (April 1976): 104–6, 108, 113.

Hare, R. M. "Abortion and the Golden Rule." *Philosophy & Public Affairs* 4 (1975): 201–22.

Harrington, Paul V. "Abortion—Part IV." *Linacre Quarterly* 33 (May 1966): 153.

——. "Abortion—Part XVI." *Linacre Quarterly* 37 (November 1970): 270.

Harris, John. "Killing for Food." In *Animals, Men, and Morals: An Enquiry into the Maltreatment of Non-humans*, edited by S. and R. Godlovitch and John Harris, 97–110. London: Victor Gollancz, 1971.

——. *The Value of Life: An Introduction to Medical Ethics*. London: Routledge & Kegan Paul, 1985.

——. "QALYfying the Value of Life." *Journal of Medical Ethics* 13 (September 1987): 117–23.

Hartt, Julian N. "Creation, Creativity & the Sanctity of Life." *Journal of Medicine & Philosophy* 4 (December 1979): 418–34.

Hathout, Hassam M. "The Rights of the Fetus." *Journal of the Kuwait Medical Association* 8 (June 1974): 113–14.

Hauerwas, Stanley, and Bondi, Richard. "Memory, Community and the Reasons for Living. Theological and Ethical Reflections on Suicide and Euthanasia." *Journal of the American Academy of Religion* 44 (September 1976): 439–52.

Hayzelden, J. E. "The Value of Human Life." *Public Administration* 46 (Winter 1968): 427–41.

Held, Virginia. "Abortion and Rights to Life." In *Bioethics and Human Rights: A Reader for Health Professionals*, edited by Bertram and Elsie L. Bandman, 103–8. Boston: Little, Brown & Co., 1978.

Hellegers, André E. "The Beginnings of Personhood: Medical Considerations." *Perkins Journal* 27 (Fall 1973): 11–15.

Henley, Kenneth. "The Value of Individuals." *Philosophy and Phenomenological Research* 37 (March 1977): 345–52.

Henson, Richard G. "Utilitarianism and the Wrongness of Killing." *Philosophical Review* 80 (1971): 320–37.

Himsworth, Sir Harold. "The Human Right to Life: its Nature and Origin." In *Ethical Issues in Human Genetics Counseling & the Use of Genetic Knowledge*, edited by Bruce Hilton, Daniel Callahan, Maureen Harris, Peter Condliffe, and Burton Berkley, 169–72. New York: Plenum Press, 1973.

Holbrook, David. "Medical Ethics and the Potentialities of the Living Being." *British Medical Journal* 291 (17 August 1985): 459–62.

Holland, Alan J. "On Behalf of Moderate Speciesism." *Journal of Applied Philosophy* 1 (October 1984): 281–91.

Holtzman, Irving. "Patenting Certain Forms of Life: A Moral Justification." *Hastings Center Report* 9 (June 1979): 9–11.

Hostler, John. "The Right to Life," *Journal of Medical Ethics* 3 (September 1977): 143–45.

Humber, James M. "The Case Against Abortion." *Thomist* 39 (January 1975): 65–84.

———. "Abortion: The Avoidable Moral Dilemma." *Journal of Value Inquiry* 9 (Winter 1975): 282–302.

Hunt, W. Murray. "Are *Mere Things* Morally Considerable?" *Environmental Ethics* 2 (Spring 1980): 59–66.

Hurley, Mark J. "The Value of Human Life: Challenge to a Brave New World." *Hospital Progress* 58 (February 1977): 70–73.

Jackson, Douglas MacG. *Human Life and Human Worth.* London: CMF, 1958.

Jaggar, Alison. "The Sanctity of Life as a Human Ideal." *Journal of Social Philosophy* 5 (April 1974): 8–11.

James, William. "Is Life Worth Living?" In *Essays on Faith and Morals,* 1–31. London: Longmans, Green & Co., 1943. (Reprinted from *International Journal of Ethics* 6 [October 1895].)

Johnson, Edward. "Life, Death and Animals." In *Ethics and Animals,* edited by Harlan B. Miller and William H. Williams, 23–33. Clifton, N.J.: Humana Press, 1983.

Johnson, Paul R. "Selective Nontreatment of Defective Newborns: An Ethical Analysis." *Linacre Quarterly* 47 (February 1980): 39–53.

Jonas, Hans. *The Phenomenon of Life: Toward a Philosophical Biology.* New York: Harper & Row, 1966. Reissued by Chicago: University of Chicago Press, 1982.

———. "The Right to Die: In Twilight Zones with Anxious Choices." *Hastings Center Report* 8 (August 1978): 31–36.

Jones, Gary. "Euthanasia and the Insentient Patient." *Journal of Medicine and Philosophy* 5 (November 1980): 333–39.

———. "A Response to Preus." *Journal of Medicine and Philosophy* 9 (November 1984): 417–18.

Jones, Gerald E. "Reverence for Life in Religion: Eastern and Western Views." In *Deity and Death,* edited by Spencer J. Palmer, 107–20. Salt Lake City: Brigham Young University Press, 1978.

Jones-Lee, M. W. *The Value of Life: An Economic Analysis.* Chicago: Chicago University Press, 1976.

———, ed. *The Value of Life and Safety.* Proceedings of a conference held by the Geneva Association. Amsterdam: North-Holland Publishing Company, 1981.

Kadish, Sanford H. "Respect for Life and Regard for Rights in the Criminal Law." In *Respect for Life in Medicine, Philosophy and the Law,* edited by Stephen F. Barker, 63–101. Baltimore: Johns Hopkins University Press, 1976.

Kaplan, A. "Social Ethics and the Sanctity of Life." In *Life or Death: Ethics and Options*, edited by Edward Shils et al., 152–67. Seattle: University of Washington Press, 1968.

Kaplan, Morton A. "What is Life Worth?" *Ethics* 89 (October 1978): 58–65.

Kelly, Gerald. "The Duty to Preserve Life." *Theological Studies* 12 (December 1951): 550–56.

Kenny, Anthony. "Abortion and the Taking of Human Life." In *Medicine in Contemporary Society: Kings College Studies 1986–7*, edited by Peter Byrne, 84–98. London: King Edwards Hospital Fund for London, 1987.

Keyserlingk, Edward W. *Sanctity of Life or Quality of Life in the Context of Ethics, Medicine and Law*. Ottawa: Law Reform Commission of Canada, 1979.

Khatchadourian, Haig. "Medical Ethics and the Value of Human Life." *Philosophy in Context* 14 (1984): 42–50.

Kleinig, John. "The Value of Life." *Interchange* 28 (1980): 3–20.

Klinefelter, Donald S. "Aging, Autonomy and the Value of Life." In *Respect and Care in Medical Ethics*, edited by David H. Smith, 301–22. Lanham, Md.: University Press of America, 1984. Reprinted from *Journal of Applied Gerontology* 3, 1 (1984).

Kluge, E.-H. W. *The Practice of Death*. New Haven: Yale University Press, 1975.

———. "The Right to Life of Potential Persons." *Dalhousie Law Journal* 3 (January 1977): 837–48.

———. *The Ethics of Deliberate Death*. Pp. 57, 82–86, 90, 95–101. Port Washington, N.Y.: Kennikat Press, 1981.

Kohl, Marvin. *The Morality of Killing*. Chap. 1. London: Peter Owen, 1973.

———. "Euthanasia and the Right to Life." In *Philosophical Medical Ethics: Its Nature and Significance*, edited by Stuart F. Spicker and H. Tristram Engelhardt, 73–84. Dordrecht: Reidel, 1977.

———. "Is Human Life Itself a Value?" In *Philosophy of Democracy and Humanism*, edited by Paul Kurtz, 189–92. Buffalo: Prometheus, 1983.

———, ed. *Infanticide & the Value of Life*. Buffalo: Prometheus, 1978.

Koop, C. Everett. *The Right to Live; the Right to Die*. Wheaton, Ill.: Tyndale, 1976.

———. "The Slide to Auschwitz." *Human Life Review* 3 (Spring 1977): 101–14.

Kruger, Kobus. "The Value of the Unborn Child: Abortion and Christian Ethics." *Journal of Theology for Southern Africa* 2 (March 1973): 7–14.

Kuhse, Helga. "Debate: Extraordinary Means and the Sanctity of Life." *Journal of Medical Ethics* 7 (June 1981): 74–82.

———. "The Sanctity-of-Life Doctrine in Medicine: A Critique." Ph.D. thesis, Monash University, 1983.

———. *The Sanctity-of-Life Doctrine in Medicine: A Critique*. Oxford: Clarendon Press, 1987.

Kuhse, Helga, and Singer, Peter. *Should the Baby Live? The Problem of Handicapped Infants*. Oxford: Oxford University Press, 1985.

Kushner, Thomasine. "Interpretations of *Life* and Prohibitions Against Killing." *Environmental Ethics* 3 (Summer 1981): 147–54.

Lecky, W.E.H, *History of European Morals from Augustus to Charlemagne.* Eleventh ed., vol. 2, 17ff. London: Longmans, Green & Co., 1894.

Leibowitz, Constance. *The Value of Human Life.* Ph.D. thesis, New York University, 1973. (Ann Arbor, Mich.: University Microfilms International, 1986. Publication no. 74–13353.)

Lindsay, James. "The Ethical Value of Individuality." *International Journal of Ethics* 30 (1919–20): 423.

Linnerooth, Joanne. "The Value of Human Life: A Review of the Models." *Economic Inquiry* 17 (January 1979): 52–74.

Linzey, Andrew. *Animal Rights: A Christian Assessment of Man's Treatment of Animals.* Chap. 4. London: SCM Press, 1976.

Lockwood, Michael. "Singer on Killing and the Preference for Life." *Inquiry* 22 (Summer 1979): 157–70.

Lombardi, Louis G. "Inherent Worth, Respect, and Rights." *Environmental Ethics* 5 (Fall 1983): 257–70.

Long, Perrin H. "On the Quantity and Quality of Life." *Medical Times* 88 (May 1960): 613–19.

Mabe, Alan R. "Euthanasia, Rights, and the Duty to Live." In *Ethics: Foundations, Problems and Applications,* edited by Edgar Morscher and Rudolf Stranzinger, 300–304. Distributed in U.S. by D. Reidel, 1981.

McCloskey, H. J. "The Right to Life." *Mind* 84 (July 1975): 403–25.

McCormick, Richard A. "The Quality of Life, The Sanctity of Life." *Hastings Center Report* 8 (February 1978): 30–36. Also in *In libertatem vocati estis (Gal. 5:13): miscellanea Bernhard Häring,* edited by H. Boelaars, 625–41. Rome: Academia Alfonsiana, 1977.

———. "Dignity of the Human Person." In *Notes on Moral Theology 1965 through 1980,* 27–38. Washington: University Press of America, 1981.

———. *How Brave a New World: Dilemmas in Bioethics.* Revised edition. Washington: Georgetown University Press, 1985.

McFadden, Charles Joseph. *The Dignity of Life: Moral Values in a Changing Society.* Huntingdon: Our Sunday Visitor, 1976.

McGraw, J. R. (Editorial) "Reverence for Life." *Renewal* 7 (February 1967): 2–3.

Mackinnon, Barbara. "Pricing Human Life." *Science, Technology and Human Values* 11 (Spring 1986): 29–39.

Maclaren, Elizabeth A. "Dignity." *Journal of Medical Ethics* 3 (1977): 40–41.

McMahon, Jeff. "Death and the Value of Life." *Ethics* 99 (October 1988): 32–61.

Margolis, Joseph. "The Rights of Man." *Social Theory & Practice* 4 (Spring 1978): 423–44.

———. "Human Life: Its Worth and Bringing It to an End." In *Infanticide and the Value of Life,* edited by Marvin Kohl, 180–91. Buffalo, N.Y.: Prometheus Books, 1978.

Maurita, Mary. "Sanctity of Life." *Hospital Progress* 54 (November 1973): 56–59.

May, William E. "Ethics and Human Identity: The Challenge of the New Biology." *Horizons* 3 (Spring 1976): 17–37.

Mead, Margaret. "Rights to Life." In *Abortion: The Moral Issues*, edited by E. Batchelor. New York: Pilgrim Press, 1982.

Menzel, Paul T. "Pricing Life: Reflections on the Cost of Health Care." *Hospital Progress* 63 (January 1982): 46–49, 56, 58.

Meye, R. P. s.v. "Life, Sacredness of." In *Baker's Dictionary of Christian Ethics*, edited by C.F.H. Henry, 390–92. Canon Press, 1973.

Miles, John A. "Jain and Judaeo-Christian Respect for Life." *Journal of the American Academy of Religion* 44 (September 1976): 453–57.

Mishan, E. J. "Evaluation of Life and Limb: A Theoretical Approach." *Journal of Political Economy* 79 (July/August 1971): 687–705.

―――. "Consistency in the Valuation of Life: A Wild Goose Chase?" *Social Philosophy & Policy* 2 (Spring 1985): 152–67.

Mitchell, Basil. "The Value of Life." In *Medicine, Medical Ethics and the Value of Life*, edited by Peter Byrne, 34–46. Chichester: John Wiley, 1990.

Mix, C. Rex, and Quinn, Catherine. *Life and Death Issues: A Report of a Four Year Exploration into the Value of Human Life*. Austin, Tex.: Hogg Foundation for Mental Health, University of Texas, 1977.

Molinski, Waldemar. s.v. "Life, II: Moral Theology," In *Sacramentum Mundi*, edited by Karl Rahner, 3:312–15. London: Burns & Oates, 1968.

Mooney, Gavin H. *The Valuation of Human Life*. London: Macmillan, 1977.

Morison, Robert S. "The Dignity of the Inevitable and Necessary." In *Death Inside Out*, edited by Peter Steinfels and Robert Veatch, 97–100. New York: Harper & Row, 1974.

Morris, Bertram. "The Dignity of Man." *Ethics* 57 (October 1946): 57–64.

Murphy, Jeffrie G. "The Killing of the Innocent." *The Monist* 57 (October 1973): 527–50.

Murray, John. *Principles of Conduct*, 107–22. London: Tyndale, 1957.

Narveson, Jan. "Animal Rights." *Canadian Journal of Philosophy* 7 (March 1977): 161–78.

Nathanson, Stephen. "Nihilism, Reason, and the Value of Life." In *Infanticide and the Value of Life*, edited by Marvin Kohl, 192–205. Buffalo: Prometheus Books, 1978.

―――. *An Eye for an Eye?: The Morality of Punishing by Death*. Chap. 1. Totowa, N.J.: Rowman & Littlefield, 1987.

Needleman, L. "Valuing Other People's Lives." *Manchester School* 44 (December 1976): 309–42.

Nelson, J. Robert. "What Does Theology Say about Abortion?" *Christian Century* 90 (31 January 1973): 124–28.

―――. "On Life and Living: The Semitic Insight." *Journal of Medicine & Philosophy* 3 (June 1978): 129–43.

―――. "Life, the Undefined Presupposition." In *Orthodox Theology and Diakonia: Trends and Prospects*, edited by D. Constantelos, 355–72. Brookline, Mass.: Hellenic College Press, 1981.

———. *Human Life: A Biblical Perspective for Bioethics*. Philadelphia, Pa: Fortress Press, 1983.

Newman, Jay. "An Empirical Argument against Abortion." *New Scholasticism* 51 (Summer 1977): 384–94.

Nolan-Haley, Jacqueline M. "Amniocentesis and the Apotheosis of Human Quality Control." *Journal of Legal Medicine* 2 (September 1981): 347–63.

Noonan, John T., Jr. "An Almost Absolute Value in History." In *The Morality of Abortion*, 1–59. Cambridge, Mass.: Harvard University Press, 1970.

Norton, Bryan G., ed. *The Preservation of Species: The Value of Biological Diversity*. Princeton: Princeton University Press, 1986.

Oden, Thomas C. "Beyond an Ethic of Immediate Sympathy." *Hastings Center Report* 6 (February 1976): 12–14.

Order of Christian Unity, Medical Committee. *Light in the Darkness: Disabled Lives? Papers on Some Contemporary Medical Problems*. Oxford: Unity Press, 1981.

O'Rourke, "Ethical Norms for Respect for Human Life." In *Human Life and Health Care Ethics*, edited by James Bopp, Jr., 52–66. Frederick, Md.: University Press of America, 1985.

Paske, Gerald H. "Why Animals Have No Right to Life: A Response to Regan." *Australasian Journal of Philosophy* 66 (December 1988): 498–511.

———. "The Life Principle: A (Metaethical) Rejection." *Journal of Applied Philosophy* 6 (1989): 219–25.

Passmore, John. *Man's Responsibility for Nature: Ecological Problems and Western Traditions*. London: Duckworth, 1974.

Peden, Creighton. "The 'Sacred Natural Process' Interpretation." *Journal of Social Philosophy* 5 (April 1974): 6–8.

Pepper, S. C. "Survival Value." *Zygon* 4 (March 1969): 4–11.

Perkins, Thomas C. "Medical Termination of the Irreversibly Comatose: A Moral Analysis from a Christian Perspective." Ph.D. dissertation. Ann Arbor, Mich.: University Microfilms, 1975.

Peters, Karl E. "The Development of Earth and the Quality of Life." *Religious Humanism* 10 (Summer 1976): 134–38.

Phillips, Anthony C. J. "Respect for Life in the Old Testament." *King's Theological Review* 6 (Autumn 1983): 32–35.

Phillips, Melanie, and Dawson, John. *Doctors' Dilemmas*, 23–27. New York: Methuen, 1985.

Preus, Anthony. "Respect for the Dead and Dying." *Journal of Medicine and Philosophy* 9 (November 1984): 409–15.

Przetacznik, F. "The Right to Life as a Basic Human Right." *Human Rights Journal* 9 (1976): 585–609.

Pucetti, Roland. "The Life of a Person." In *Abortion and the Status of a Person*, edited by W. B. Bondesman et al., 169–82. Dordrecht: Reidel, 1983.

Punke, H. "Technology and Ethical Reverence for Life." *Modern Churchman* 24 (Summer 1981): 87–92.

Quinn, Warren. "Abortion: Identity and Loss." *Philosophy & Public Affairs* 13 (Winter 1984): 24–54.

Rachels, James. "Medical Ethics and the Rule against Killing: Comments on Professor Hare's Paper." In *Philosophical Medical Ethics: Its Nature and Significance*, edited by Stuart F. Spicker and H. Tristram Engelhardt, Jr., 63–69. Dordrecht: Reidel, 1977.

———. "The Sanctity of Life." In *Biomedical Ethics Reviews 1983*, edited by James M. Humber and Robert F. Almeder, 29–42. Clifton, N.J.: Humana Press, 1983.

———. "Do Animals Have a Right to Life?" In *Ethics and Animals*, edited by Harlan B. Miller and William H. Williams, 275–84. Clifton, N.J.: Humana Press, 1983.

———. *The End of Life*. Oxford: Oxford University Press, 1985.

Rackman, Emanuel. "Violence and the Value of Life: The Halakhic View." In *Violence and Defense in the Jewish Experience*, edited by Salo W. Baron and George S. Wise, 113–41. Philadelphia: Jewish Publication Society of America, 1977.

Ramcharan, B.G. "The Right to Life." *Netherlands International Law Review* 30, 3 (1983): 297–329.

———, ed. *The Right to Life in International Law*. The Hague: Martinus Nijhoff, 1985.

Ramsey, Paul. "The Sanctity of Life: In the First of It." *Dublin Review* 241 (Spring 1967): 3–23.

———. "The Morality of Abortion." In *Moral Problems*, edited by James Rachels, 3–27. New York: Harper & Row, 1971.

———. "Moral Issues in Fetal Research." In *Appendix: Research on the Fetus*, National Commission for the Protection of Human Subjects of Biomedical and Behavioral Research, DHEW (OS) 1976, 128.

———. "Prolonged Dying: Not Medically Indicated." *Hastings Center Report* 6 (February 1976): 14–17.

Rand, Ayn. "The Objectivist Ethics" (1961). Chap. 1, in *The Virtue of Selfishness*. New York: New American Library, n.d.

Ranly, Ernest W. "Albert Schweitzer's Philosophy of Civilization." *Thought* 38 (June 1963): 237–54.

Regan, Tom. "The Moral Basis of Vegetarianism." *Canadian Journal of Philosophy* 5 (October 1975): 181–214.

———. *The Case for Animal Rights*. Berkeley, Calif.: University of California Press, 1983.

Reich, Walter. "The 'Duty' to Preserve Life." *Hastings Center Report* 5 (April 1975): 14–15.

Reich, Warren T. s.v. "Life: Quality of Life." In *Encyclopedia of Bioethics*, edited by Warren T. Reich, 829–40. New York: The Free Press, 1978.

Rescher, Nicholas. "The Social Value of a Life." Chap. 14 in *Risk: A Philosophical Introduction to the Theory of Risk, Evaluation and Management*, Lanham, Md.: University Press of America, 1983.

Rhoads, Steven E. *Valuing Life: Public Policy Dilemmas*. Westview Special

Studies in Science, Technology and Public Policy, Boulder, Colo.: Westview Press, 1980.

Ricaud, M. A. *La vie est sacrée.* N.p.: Desilee de Brouwer, 1948.

Rice, Charles E. *The Vanishing Right to Live: An Appeal for a Renewed Reverence for Life.* Garden City, N.Y.: Doubleday, 1969.

Richards, B. A. "Inalienable Rights: Recent Criticism and Old Doctrine." *Philosophy & Phenomenological Research* 29 (March 1969): 391–404.

Richards, Stewart. "Forethoughts for Carnivores." *Philosophy* 56 (January 1981): 73–88.

Richardson, Herbert W. "What is the Value of Life?" In *Updating Life and Death: Essays in Ethics and Medicine,* edited by Donald R. Cutler, 169–80. Boston: Beacon Press, 1968.

Rist, John M. "Aristotle: The Value of Man and the Origin of Morality." *Canadian Journal of Philosophy* 4 (September 1974): 1–21.

―――. *Human Value: A Study in Ancient Philosophical Ethics.* Leiden: E. J. Brill, 1982.

Ritchie, D. G. *Natural Rights.* Pp. 127–34. London: Allen & Unwin, 1894.

Robbins, W. W. "Theological Values of Life and Nonbeing." *Zygon* 5 (December 1970): 339–52.

Rolston, Holmes, III. "The Irreversibly Comatose: Respect for the Subhuman in Human Life." *Journal of Medicine & Philosophy* 7 (November 1982): 337–54.

Rose, Michael. "Genetics and the Quality of Life." *Social Indicators Research* 7 (January 1980): 419–41.

Roupas, T. G. "The Value of Life." *Philosophy & Public Affairs* 7 (Winter 1978): 154–83.

St.John-Stevas, N. *The Right to Life.* London: Hodder & Stoughton, 1963.

―――. "Law and the Sanctity of Life." *Dublin Review* 508 (Summer 1966): 99. Reprinted in *Life or Death: Ethics and Options,* edited by E. Shils et al. Seattle: University of Washington Press, 1968.

Sapontzis, Steve F. "Must We Value Life to Have a Right to It?" *Ethics and Animals* 3 (March 1982): 2–11.

―――. "On Being Morally Expendable." *Ethics and Animals* 3 (September 1982): 58–72.

Schacter, Oscar. "Human Dignity as a Normative Concept." *American Journal of International Law* 77 (October 1983): 848–54.

Schelling, Thomas C. "The Life You Save May Be Your Own." In *Problems in Public Expenditure Analysis,* edited by Samuel B. Chase. Washington: Brookings Institution, 1968.

―――. "The Value of Preventing Death." In *Health Economics,* edited by M. H. Cooper and A. J. Culyer, 295–321. Harmondsworth: Penguin, 1973.

Schiller, M. "Are There Any Inalienable Rights?" *Ethics* 79 (July 1969): 309–15.

Schrödinger, E. *What is Life? The Physical Aspects of the Living Cell.* Cambridge: Cambridge University Press, 1962.

Schuyler, Joseph B., S.J. "Life Evaluations in Developing Countries." In *Human Life: Problems of Birth, of Living, and of Dying*, edited by William C. Bier, S.J., 14–28. New York: Fordham University Press, 1977.

Schweitzer, Albert. *The Philosophy of Civilization*. Third ed. Trans. by C. T. Campion. London: A & C Black; New York: Macmillan, 1949.

———. *The Teaching of Reverence for Life*. New York: Holt, Rinehart & Winston, 1965.

Sendaydiego, Henry B. "Indefinite Prolongation of Terminal Human Life." *Journal of the West Virginia Philosophical Society* 9 (Fall 1975): 24–27.

Shea, M. C. "Embryonic Life and Human Life." *Journal of Medical Ethics* 11 (1985): 205–9.

Shepard, P. S. "Reverence for Life at Lambarene." *Landscape* 8 (1959): 26–29.

Sherlock, Richard. "Public Policy and the Life Not Worth Living: The Case Against Euthanasia." *Linacre Quarterly* 47 (May 1980): 121–32.

———. *Preserving Life: Public Policy and the Life Not Worth Living*. Chicago: Loyola University Press, 1987.

Shils, Edward. "The Sanctity of Life." Chap. 1 in *Life or Death: Ethics and Options*, edited by E. Shils et al. Seattle: University of Washington Press, 1968.

Shinn, Roger L. "Ethical Issues." In *New Options, New Dilemmas*, edited by Anne S. Allen, 23–30. Lexington, Mass.: Lexington Heath, 1986.

Siegel, Seymour. "A Jewish View." *Human Life Review* 2 (Fall 1976): 140–43.

Singer, Peter. s.v. "Life: Value of Life." In *Encyclopedia of Bioethics*, edited by Warren T. Reich, 2:822–29. New York: The Free Press, 1978.

———. *Practical Ethics*. Cambridge: Cambridge University Press, 1979.

———. "Unsanctifying Human Life." In *Ethical Issues Relating to Life and Death*, edited by John Ladd, 41–61. New York: Oxford University Press, 1979.

———. "Can We Avoid Assigning Greater Value to some Human Lives than Others?" In *Moral Issues in Mental Retardation*, edited by R. S. Laura and A. F. Ashman, 91–100. Beckenham: Croom Helm, 1984.

———. "Animals and the Value of Life." In *Matters of Life and Death: New Introductory Essays in Moral Philosophy*. Second ed., edited by Tom Regan, 338–80. New York: Random House, 1986.

———. "Animal Liberation or Animal Rights." In *New Options, New Dilemmas*, edited by Anne S. Allen, 3–14. Lexington, Mass.: Lexington Heath, 1986.

Shibata, Shingo. "The Right to Life vs. Nuclear Weapons." *Journal of Social Philosophy* 8 (September 1977): 9–14.

Smith, A. Delafield. *The Right to Life*. Durham: University of N. Carolina Press, 1965.

Smith, Harmon L. "Abortion and the Right to Life." In *Ethics and the New Medicine*, 17–54. Nashville: Abingdon, 1970.

———. "Abortion, Death, and the Sanctity of Life." *Social Science and Medicine* 5 (June 1971): 211–18.

Smith, Holly M., and Strong, Carson. "What Makes a Life Worth Saving?" *Hastings Center Report* 14 (February 1984): 48.

Sneed, Marcy C., ed. *Human Life: Our Legacy and Our Challenge.* New York: McGraw-Hill, Webster Division, 1976.

Sommers, Christina Hoff. (Book Review) "Tooley's Immodest Proposal: *Abortion and Infanticide*" *Hastings Center Report* 15 (June 1985): 39–42.

Spitler, Gene. "Justifying a Respect for Nature." *Environmental Ethics* 4 (Fall 1982): 55–60.

Steinfels, Margaret O'Brien. "In Vitro Fertilization: 'Ethically Acceptable' Research?" *Hastings Center Report* 9 (June 1979): 5–8.

Stell, Lance K. "Dueling and the Right to Life." *Ethics* 90 (October 1979): 7–26.

Stevens, Edward. "The Quality of Life." In *The Morals Game*, 109–26. New York: Paulist Press, 1974.

Stevens, John C. "Must the Bearer of a Right Have the Concept of That to Which He Has a Right?" *Ethics* 95 (October 1984): 68–74.

Stith, Richard. "Toward Freedom from Value." *The Jurist* 38 (1978): 48–81.

Stott, John W. R. "Reverence for Human Life." *Christianity Today* 16 (9 June 1972): 8–12.

Suckiel, Ellen Kappy. "Death and Benefit in the Permanently Unconscious Patient." *Journal of Medicine & Philosophy* 3 (March 1978): 38–52.

Sullivan, Leonor K. "The Right to Life—When does Human Life Begin?" *Congressional Record* (Daily ed.) 121 (30 September 1975): H9337-H9338.

Sullivan, Thomas D. "The Right to Life and Self-Consciousness." *America* 139 (7 October 1978): 222–24.

Sumner, L. Wayne. *Abortion and Moral Theory.* Princeton: Princeton University Press, 1981.

Suter, R. "Moore's Defence of the Rule 'Do No Murder.'" *The Personalist* 54 (1973): 361–75.

Swyter, Jai. "When is Life Without Value? A Study of Life-Death Decisions on a Hemodialysis Unit." *Omega* 9, 4 (1978–79): 369–80.

Szalai, Alexander. "Changes in the Valuation of Human Life." In *The Search for Absolute Values*, edited by ICF. 2 vols. New York: ICF Press, 1977.

Szawarski, Z. "The Value of Life" (in Polish). *Etyka* 21 (1985): 41–70.

Szent-Gyorgyi, A. *The Living State: With Observations on Cancer.* New York: Academic Press, 1972.

Tammelo, Ilmar. "The Entitlement to Life." *Anales de la Catedra Francisco Suarez* 12, 2 (1972): 97–113.

Taylor, Paul W. "The Ethics of Respect for Nature." *Environmental Ethics* 3 (Fall 1981): 197–218.

———. *Respect for Nature: A Theory of Environmental Ethics.* Princeton: Princeton University Press, 1986.

———. "Inherent Value and Moral Rights." In *New Options, New Dilemmas*, edited by Anne S. Allen, 15–30. Lexington, Mass.: Lexington Heath, 1986.

Temkin, Owsei. "The Idea of Respect for Life in the History of Medicine."

In *Respect for Life in Medicine, Philosophy & the Law*, edited by Owsei Temkin, William Frankena, and Sanford H. Kadish, 1–23. Baltimore: Johns Hopkins University Press, 1976.

Thaler, R., and Rosen, S. "The Value of Saving a Life: Evidence from the Labor Market." In *Household Production and Consumption*, edited by Nestor E. Terlechyi. New York: Columbia University Press, 1976.

Thomas, Larry. "Human Potentiality: Its Moral Relevance." *Personalist* 59 (July 1978): 266–72.

Thomasma, David C. "An Apology for the Value of Human Life: A Response to Paul T. Menzel's 'Pricing Life.'" *Hospital Progress* 63 (April 1982): 49–52, 68.

———. *An Apology for the Value of Human Life*. St. Louis, Mo.: Catholic Health Association of the United States, 1983.

Thomson, J. Arthur. "Professor James on 'Nature.'" *International Journal of Ethics* 6:235.

Tiefel, Hans O. "The Unborn: Human Values and Responsibilities." *Journal of the American Medical Association* 239 (26 May 1978): 2263–67.

Tillich, Paul. "Dimensions, Levels and the Unity of Life." In *Buddhism and Culture: Dedicated to Daisetz T. Susuki*, edited by Susumu Yamaguchi, 181–90. Kyoto: Nakano Press, 1960.

———. "The Inviolability of Life." In *Systematic Theology*. Chicago: University of Chicago Press, 1967.

Tomlin, E.W.F. "The Concept of Life." *Heythrop Journal* 18 (July 1977): 289–304.

Tooley, Michael. *Abortion and Infanticide*. Oxford: Clarendon Press, 1983.

Train, R. "Reverence for Life." *Frontiers* 42 (1978): 38–39.

Trammell, R. L. "The Presumption against Taking Life." *Journal of Medicine and Philosophy* 3 (March 1978): 53–67.

Treub, H. *The Right to Life and the Unborn Child*. New York: Wagner, 1903.

Troyer, John. "Euthanasia, the Right to Life, and Moral Structures: A Reply to Professor Kohl." In *Philosophical Medical Ethics: Its Nature and Significance*, edited by Stuart F. Spicker and H. Tristram Engelhardt, Jr., 85–95. Dordrecht: Reidel, 1977.

Tuck, W. P. "Schweitzer's Reverence for Life." *Theology Today* 30 (January 1974): 339–45.

Usher, Dan. "The Value of Life for Decision Making in the Public Sector." *Social Philosophy and Policy* 2 (Spring 1985): 168–91.

VanDeVeer, Donald. "Interspecific Justice and Animal Slaughter." In *Ethics and Animals*, edited by Harlan B. Miller and William H. Williams, 147–62. Clifton, N.J.: Humana Press, 1983.

Varner, G. E. "Do Species Have Standing?" *Environmental Ethics* 9 (Spring 1987): 57–72.

Veatch, Robert M. "Justice and Valuing Lives." In *Life Span: Values and Life-Expanding Technologies*, edited by Robert M. Veatch, 197–224. San Francisco: Harper & Row, 1979.

Viscusi, W. L. "Labor Market Valuations of Life and Limb: Empirical Evidence and Policy Implications." *Public Policy* 26 (Summer 1978): 359–86.

Visscher, Maurice B. "A Humanist View of Reverence for all Life." *Religious Humanism* 7 (Autumn 1973): 152–55.

Von Wahlert, Gerd. "The Unity of Creation: A Biologist's Point of View." In *Unity in Today's World: The Faith and Order Studies on "Unity of the Church—Unity of Humankind,"* edited by Geiko Mueller-Fahrenholz, 125–36. Geneva: World Council of Churches, 1978.

Walker, Vern R. "Presumptive Personhood." *Linacre Quarterly* 45 (May 1978): 179–86.

Warnock, Mary. "Do Human Cells Have Rights?" *Bioethics* 1 (January 1987): 1–14.

Wasserstrom, Richard. "Ethical Issues Involved in Experimentation on the Nonviable Human Fetus." In *Biomedical Ethics,* edited by T. A. Mappes and Jane S. Zembaty, 438–44. New York: McGraw-Hill, 1981.

Wennberg, Robert. *Life in the Balance.* Grand Rapids, Mich.: Eerdmans, 1985.

West, D. "On Goodrich's 'The Morality of Killing.'" *Philosophy* 45 (1970): 233–36.

Williams, Alan. "Response: 'QALYfying the Value of Life.'" *Journal of Medical Ethics* 13 (September 1987): 117–23.

Williams, Glanville. *The Sanctity of Life and the Criminal Law.* London: Faber, 1958.

Wollheim, Richard. *The Thread of Life.* Cambridge, Mass.: Harvard University Press, 1984.

Wood, T. s.v. "Life, Sacredness of." In *Dictionary of Christian Ethics,* edited by J. Macquarrie, 195–96. London: S.C.M., 1967.

Woods, Eleanor. "The Furtherance of All Life." *Humanist* 24 (May–June, 1964): 70–72.

Young, Robert. "Some Criteria for Making Decisions Concerning the Distribution of Scarce Medical Resources." *Theory and Decision* 6 (1975): 439–55.

Zeckhauser, Richard. "Procedures for Valuing Lives." *Public Policy* 23 (Fall 1975): 419–64.

Zeckhauser, Richard, and Shepard, Donald S. "Where NOW for Saving Lives?" *Law and Contemporary Problems* 40 (Autumn 1976): 5–45.

———. "Principles for Saving and Valuing Lives." In *The Benefits of Health and Safety Regulation,* edited by Allen R. Ferguson and E. Phillip LeVeen, 91–130. Cambridge, Mass.: Ballinger, 1981.

Zygon. (Special Issue) "Genetic Engineering, Persons, and the Sacred." *Zygon* 19 (September 1984).

INDEX OF NAMES

INDEX OF SUBJECTS

The Princeton University Press series "Studies in Moral, Political, and Legal Philosophy" is under the general editorship of Marshall Cohen, Professor of Philosophy and Law and Dean of Humanities at the University of Southern California. The series includes the following titles, in chronological order of publication:

Understanding Rawls: A Reconstruction and Critique of A Theory of Justice by R. P. Wolff (1977). Out of print

Immortality by R. D. Milo (1984)

Politics & Remembrance: Republican Themes in Machiavelli, Burke, and Tocqueville by J. J. Smith (1985)

Understanding Marx: A Reconstruction and Critique of Capital Hobbesian Moral and Political Theory by R. P. Wolff (1985)

Hobbesian Moral and Political Theory by G. S. Kavka (1986)

The General Will before Rousseau: The Transformation of the Divine into the Civic by P. Riley (1986)

Respect for Nature: A Theory of Environmental Ethics by P. W. Taylor (1986). Available in paperback

Paternalistic Intervention: The Moral Bounds on Benevolence by D. VanDeVeer (1986)

The Longing for Total Revolution: Philosophic Sources of Social Discontent from Rousseau to Marx and Nietzsche by B. Yack (1986)

Meeting Needs by D. Braybrooke (1987)

Reasons for Welfare: The Political Theory of the Welfare State by R. E. Goodin (1988)

Why Preserve Natural Variety? by B. G. Norton (1988). Available in paperback

Coercion by A. Wertheimer (1988). Available in paperback

Merleau-Ponty and the Foundation of an Existential Politics by K. H. Whiteside (1988)

On War and Morality by R. L. Holmes (1989). Available in paperback

The Rhetoric of Leviathan: Thomas Hobbes and the Politics of Cultural Transformation by D. Johnston (1989). Available in paperback

Desert by G. Sher (1989). Available in paperback

Critical Legal Studies: A Liberal Critique by A. Altman (1989)

Finding the Mean: Theory and Practice in Aristotelian Political Philosophy by S. G. Salkever (1990)

Marxism, Morality, and Social Justice by R. G. Peffer (1990)

Speaking of Equality: An Analysis of the Rhetorical Force of 'Equality' in Moral and Legal Discourse by P. Westen (1990)

Friedrich Nietzsche and the Politics of the Soul: A Study of Heroic Individualism by L. P. Thiele (1990)

Valuing Life by J. Kleinig (1991)